Images of Gramsci

A comprehensive reassessment of the relevance of Gramsci's theory and practice at the beginning of the twenty-first century.

Whilst commentaries on Antonio Gramsci and arguments surrounding his political and intellectual legacy have proliferated, little attention has been hitherto directed to linking the connections and contentions between Political Theory and International Relations. This volume brings together leading authorities engaged in common debates to produce, for the first time, a major collection that clarifies, addresses, and lays bare the manifest connections and contentions within political and international theory surrounding the legacy of Antonio Gramsci.

In Part I, scholars examine various approaches to Gramsci's thought, including his methodological principles, the specific conception of civil society he offers, his writings on war and cultural struggle, the spatial dimension of his thinking, and his philosophy of history. Part II focuses on very new developments in Gramsci scholarship concerning the questioning of contemporary world order. This includes reflections on his relevancy to issues of globalising capitalism, transformations in the state, revolutionary praxis, orientalism and empire, as well as European regionalism.

This book was previously published as a special issue of the leading *Critical Review of International Social and Political Philosophy. (CRISPP).*

Andreas Bieler is Senior Lecturer in the School of Politics and International Relations at the University of Nottingham, UK. He is author of Globalisation and Enlargement of the European Union (Routledge, 2000) and The Struggle for a Social Europe: Trade Unions and EMU in Times of Global Restructuring (Manchester University Press, 2006).

Adam David Morton is Senior Lecturer in the School of Politics and International Relations at the University of Nottingham, UK. His research focuses on issues of state formation, resistance, and economic restructuring in Mexico and Latin America. He is author of Unravelling Gramsci: Hegemony and Passive Revolution in the Global Political Economy (Pluto Press, 2007).

RIPE SERIES IN GLOBAL POLITICAL ECONOMY

Series Editors: Louise Amoore (*University of Durham, UK*), Randall Germain (*Carleton University, Canada*) and Rorden Wilkinson (*University of Manchester, UK*)

Formerly edited by Otto Holman (*University of Amsterdam*), Marianne Marchand (*Universidad de las Américas-Puebla*), Henk Overbeek (*Free University, Amsterdam*) and Marianne Franklin (*University of Amsterdam*)

The RIPE series editorial board are:

Mathias Albert (*Bielefeld University, Germany*), Mark Beeson (*University of Queensland, Australia*), A. Claire Cutler (*University of Victoria, Canada*), Marianne Franklin (*University of Amsterdam, the Netherlands*), Stephen Gill (*York University, Canada*), Jeffrey Hart (*Indiana University, USA*), Eric Helleiner (*Trent University, Canada*), Otto Holman (*University of Amsterdam, the Netherlands*), Marianne H. Marchand (*Universidad le las Américas-Puebla, Mexico*), Craig N. Murphy (*Wellesly College, USA*), Robert O'Brien (*McMaster University, Canada*), Henk Overbeek (*Vrije Universiteit, the Netherlands*), Anthony Payne (*University of Sheffield, UK*) and V. Spike Peterson (*University of Arizona, USA*)

This series, published in association with the *Review of International Political Economy*, provides a forum for current debates in international political economy. The series aims to cover all the central topics in IPE and to present innovative analyses of emerging topics. The titles in the series seek to transcend a state-centred discourse and focus on three broad themes:

- the nature of the forces driving globalisation forward
- resistance to globalisation
- the transformation of the world order.

The series comprises two strands:

The *RIPE Series in Global Political Economy* aims to address the needs of students and teachers, and the titles will be published in hardback and paperback. Titles include

Transnational Classes and International Relations
Kees van der Pijl

Gender and Global Restructuring:
Sightings, Sites and Resistances
Edited by Marianne H Marchand and Anne Sisson Runyan

Routledge/RIPE Studies in Global Political Economy is a forum for innovative new research intended for a high-level specialist readership, and the titles will be available in hardback only. Titles include:

Images of Gramsci

Connections and Contentions in Political
Theory and International Relations

Edited by
Andreas Bieler and Adam David Morton

 Routledge
Taylor & Francis Group

LONDON AND NEW YORK

First published 2006 by Routledge

2 Park Square, Milton Park, Abingdon. Oxon, OX14 4RN

Simultaneously published in the USA and Canada
by Routledge
270 Madison Ave, New York, NY 10016

Routledge is an imprint of the Taylor & Francis Group, an informa business

© 2006 Taylor & Francis Group Ltd

Reprinted 2006
Transferred to Digital Printing 2008

Typeset in Times by Genesis Typesetting Ltd, Rochester, Kent

British Library Cataloguing in Publication Data
A catalogue record for this book is available from the British Library

Library of Congress Cataloging in Publication Data
A catalog record for this book has been requested

Publisher's Note
The publisher has gone to great lengths to ensure the quality of this
reprint but points out that some imperfections in the original may be apparent

ISBN 10: 0-415-36670-4 (hbk)
ISBN 10: 0-415-46365-3 (pbk)

ISBN 13: 978-0-415-36670-0 (hbk)
ISBN 13: 978-0-415-46365-2 (pbk)

Contents

Notes on Contributors

Andreas Bieler is Senior Lecturer in the School of Politics and International Relations at the University of Nottingham, UK. He is author of Globalisation and Enlargement of the European Union (Routledge, 2000) and The Struggle for a Social Europe: Trade Unions and EMU in Times of Global Restructuring (Manchester University Press, 2006).

A. Claire Cutler is a Professor of International Law and International Relations in the Political Science Department at the University of Victoria, Victoria, British Columbia, Canada. Her current research concern is developing a radical political economy of international law in the context of the material, institutional, and ideological foundations of the emerging global business civilisation. Her recent publications include *Private Power and Global Authority: Transnational Merchant Law in the Global Political Economy* (Cambridge University Press, 2003) and *Private Authority and International Affairs* (State University of New York Press, 1999).

Maurice Finocchiaro is Distinguished Professor of Philosophy Emeritus at the University of Nevada, Las Vegas, graduate of MIT and UC Berkeley; author of *Gramsci and the History of Dialectical Thought* (Cambridge University Press, 1988) and *Beyond Right and Left: Democratic Elitism in Mosca and Gramsci* (Yale University Press, 1999), and recipient of grants and fellowships from the Guggenheim Foundation, National Endowment for the Humanities, American Council of Learned Societies, and the National Science Foundation.

Peter Ives is an Assistant Professor in the Politics Department at the University of Winnipeg, Canada. He is author of *Gramsci's Politics of Language: Engaging the Bakhtin Circle and the Frankfurt School* (University of Toronto Press, 2004) and *Language and Hegemony in Gramsci* (Pluto Press, 2004). He is beginning research on the 'new language question' facing the European Union in light of the advent of so-called 'global English'.

Bob Jessop is Professor of Sociology and Director of the Institute for Advanced Studies at Lancaster University. He is best known for his contributions to state theory, critical political economy, the political economy of postwar Britain, and his critique of welfare regimes. His books include *The Capitalist State: Marxist Theories and Methods* (Martin Robertson, 1982), *Nicos Poulantzas: Marxist Theory and Political Strategy* (Macmillan 1985), *Thatcherism: A Tale of Two Nations* (Polity, 1988), *State Theory: Putting the Capitalist State in Its Place* (Polity, 1990), and *The Future of the Capitalist State* (Polity, 2002). Two new books will appear in 2005: *Beyond the Regulation Approach* (Edward Elgar, co-authored with Ngai-Ling Sum) and *State Power* (Polity). He is currently researching the contradictions of the knowledge-based economy.

Adam David Morton is Senior Lecturer in the School of Politics and International Relations at the University of Nottingham, UK. His research focuses on issues of state formation, resistance and economic restructuring in Mexico and Latin America. He is author of Unravelling Gramsci: Hegemony and Passive Revolution in the Global Political Economy (Pluto Press, 2007).

Mustapha Kamal Pasha specialises in global and comparative political economy, Social Theory and Islamic and South Asian Studies at the School of International Service, American University in Washington, DC. He has been an Advanced Research Fellow of the Japan Society for the Promotion of Science (JSPS), during 2004–2005, based at the International Peace Research Institute, Meijigakuin University (PRIME) in Tokyo, Japan.

Kees van der Pijl taught at the University of Amsterdam for many years. Since 2000 he is a Professor of International Relations at the University of Sussex. His writings deal with transnational classes and the history of International Relations theory. Recent publications include *Global Regulation – Managing Crises After the Imperial Turn* (co-editor, Palgrave, 2004). He is currently finishing *Global Rivalries from the Cold War to Iraq* which will appear with Pluto Press in 2005.

Andrew Robinson recently received his PhD in Politics and is a part-time tutor at the School of Politics, University of Nottingham. His thesis is on the role of oppressive discourse in the work of John Rawls and he has written on issues ranging from the political theories of Slavoj Žižek and Ernesto Laclau, to the role of everyday resistance in the construction of revolutionary movements, and the structure of militarist discourse in the 'war on terror'. He has articles published in several journals, including *Utopian Studies*; *Historical Materialism* (co-authored with Simon Tormey); and *Theory and Event*. He is currently researching structures of oppressive discourse and attempting to reconfigure postcolonial theory along Deleuzian lines, with the issue of oppression and resistance and the struggle against oppressive social relations standing as the leitmotif of his research.

William I. Robinson is Professor of Sociology, Global and International Studies, and Latin American and Iberian Studies at the University of California at Santa Barbara. He has lectured broadly in recent years at universities and in public forums in North and Latin America, Africa, East Asia, and Europe on globalisation, international affairs, development, the global crisis and social change. His most recent books are: *A Theory of Global Capitalism: Production, Class, and State in a Transnational World* (John Hopkins University Press, 2004); *Transnational*

Conflicts: Central America, Social Change, and Globalisation (Verso, 2003); and *Promoting Polyarchy: Globalisation, U.S. Intervention, and Hegemony* (Cambridge University Press, 1996).

Mark Rupert is Professor of Political Science at Syracuse University's Maxwell School of Citizenship and Public Affairs, and teaches in the areas of international relations and political economy. Mark's research focuses on the intersection of the US political economy with global structures and processes. He is the author of *Producing Hegemony: The Politics of Mass Production and American Global Power* (Cambridge, 1995); and *Ideologies of Globalisation: Contending Visions of a New World Order* (Routledge, 2000); and he is co-editor (with Hazel Smith) of *Historical Materialism and Globalisation* (Routledge, 2002). Along with Scott Solomon, he is currently finishing work on *Globalisation and International Political Economy* to be published in 2005 by Rowman and Littlefield.

Anne Showstack Sassoon was Professor of Politics, Kingston University and is Visiting Professor, School of Politics and Sociology, Birkbeck College, University of London. She studied at the University of California, Berkeley, the University of Padua, and the London School of Economics and has taught in Canada, Denmark, Italy and elsewhere. She is the author of *Gramsci's Politics* (University of Minnesota Press, 1987 2d. ed.) and her most recent book is *Gramsci and Contemporary Politics: Beyond Pessimism of the Intellect* (Routledge, 2000).

Introduction: International Relations as Political Theory

ANDREAS BIELER & ADAM DAVID MORTON

The historian Gwyn A. Williams (1975: 306) once wrote that 'one braces oneself for the oncoming explosion' in studies on Antonio Gramsci, 'a cultural shock of the first order and', subsequently, 'the possible collapse of the Gramsci market'. Thirty years on, commentaries on Gramsci and debates surrounding his political and intellectual legacy still abound and show no sign of abating. The continued vitality of Gramsci studies is particularly evidenced in discussions of his legacy in Political Theory and International Relations (IR). Yet, these have gone on largely in isolation from each other, with little attention directed to linking them. This collection aims to address this lacuna by bringing together leading Gramsci experts from both fields. In part, there is sympathy with the view that IR has committed a negation of political theory, seeing the latter as in some sense unnecessary, leading to a neglect of alternative readings, debates and contentions (Walker 1993). In our view, theories of IR must engage with readings of modern social and political theory, indeed we should view 'international relations as political theory'. In the case of this volume, such an engagement means treating Gramsci seriously, entering into the debates surrounding his legacy, and bringing his questions to bear on our own era but without becoming obsessed with the limits of the answers.

Recent discussions of Gramsci within political theory range from Joseph Buttigieg's immensely important English translation of the complete critical edition of the *Prison Notebooks* (Gramsci 1992,1996); to Richard Bellamy's work on Gramsci, Italian social theory and Benedetto Croce that argues that themes in Gramsci's social and political thought addressed a particular set of issues arising out of a given time and space (Bellamy 1987, 1990, 2001); Joseph Femia's positioning of Gramsci within wider currents of Italian political realism which serves as a connecting link between Marxist historicism and a Machiavellian heritage (Femia 1998); Ernesto Laclau and Chantal Mouffe's post-Marxist rendering of the political as emerging from within articulatory practices of discursive production so that hegemony becomes a social space of relational identities joined within a discursive formation (Laclau & Mouffe 2001; also see Martin 1998); and Anne Showstack Sassoon's relating of Gramsci to contemporary politics (Sassoon 2000, 2001). These studies are merely the latest manifestation of a large body of work that has traced Gramsci's political theory. The significance of these and other debates is that different 'images' of Gramsci have indeed been authorised from readings of his texts. This has also been evident in classical debates expressed inter alia in Perry Anderson's analysis of the precise forms and functions of Gramsci's concept of hegemony (Anderson 1976/1977); in Renate Holub's comparative analysis of Gramsci and broader critical theorists on Marxist aesthetics (Holub 1992); or in Wolfgang Fritz Haug's focus on the notion of 'philosophy of praxis' as a renewal of Marxian theory (Haug 2000).

Over a similar period, there has also been a ferment of activity surrounding the use of Gramsci in International Relations (IR) and International Political Economy (IPE). In the 1980s, Robert Cox developed a seminal analysis of world order by highlighting aspects of the global political economy and the rise of neoliberalism that drew to a large extent on the thinking of Gramsci (Cox 1981, 1983, 1987). The work of Stephen Gill has similarly traced the construction of legal or constitutional devices that serve to remove or insulate economic institutions from democratic accountability. These techniques form a 'new constitutionalism' based on the market civilisation of neoliberalism (Gill 1990, 1995). Building on these contributions, a series of similar, yet diverse, neo-Gramscian perspectives have emerged in IPE (Morton 2001). This work involves an array of associated studies on hegemony in the global political economy ranging from, inter alia, the institutionalisation of mass production in the United States (Rupert 1995); to the promotion of low-intensity democracy or 'polyarchy' as an adjunct of US hegemony (Robinson 1996); to processes of transnational capital and labour formation in the dissemination and resistance of global capitalism (Bieler 2000; van der Pijl 1998).

Most recently, there has been a strident critique of these neo-Gramscian perspectives, which have been reproached for a lack of engagement with the historical contextual theory and practice of Gramsci's writings (Germain & Kenny 1998). In contradistinction, and through a detailed discussion of the philosophical meaning, interpretation and appropriation of Gramsci's writings, a renewed case has also been made for the relevance of his work to alternative historical and contemporary circumstances (Morton 2003). What these latest interventions have made clear is the intersection of many debates within and between Political Theory and International Relations. To date, however, these literatures have remained largely separate and confined to disciplinary quarters (e.g. Mouffe 1979; Sassoon 1982; Gill 1993; Overbeek 1993). Hence the imperative of bringing together, for the first time, connections and contentions in Political Theory and International Relations in order to overcome customarily sacrosanct disciplinary boundaries.

Karl Marx famously remarked in the *Eighteenth Brumaire* that:

the tradition of all the dead generations weighs like a nightmare on the brain of
the living. And just when they seem engaged in revolutionising themselves and
things, in creating something that has never yet existed, precisely in such
epochs of revolutionary crisis they anxiously conjure up the spirits of the past
to their service and borrow from them names, battle-cries, and costumes in
order to present the new scene of world history in this time-honoured disguise
and this borrowed language. (Marx 1869/1984: 10)

Gramsci was similarly attuned to both the practical uses and abuses of history for
political ends *and* the philosophical import of appreciating the dialogical relationship between past and present relevant to the history of ideas. The first contribution in this volume, by Sassoon, opens up the section on different 'Approaches to
Gramsci' by refocusing attention on the methodological lessons one can draw from
Gramsci as a useful point of departure for engaging in contemporary debates about
social science. She notes that Gramsci offers a series of vignettes linking the
general and the particular, past and present, to contest the socially and historically
constructed methodological hierarchies and divisions of labour embedded across
the social sciences. Most perceptively, Sassoon reveals how Gramsci appreciated
contending epistemological and methodological approaches to social action
inscribed, on one hand, within an explanatory account of positivist science based
on truth as correspondence and eschewing normative questions and, on the other
hand, in an understanding account of social action based on hermeneutics and
intersubjective meanings or the ways ideas are instantiated through institutions and
practices. 'To understand is to reproduce the order in the minds of actors; to
explain is to find causes in the scientific manner' (Hollis & Smith 1990: 87). This
opening essay therefore strikes at the heart of the philosophy of social action
relevant to the explaining and understanding divide of social science that shapes
political and international theory (see Smith 2001).

Methodological considerations are carried forward into Finocchiaro's analysis
of Gramsci's immediate reflections on the First World War and what significance
one can draw from them in relation to current geopolitical conditions. Three
approaches are outlined that prove useful in any exegetical exercise: the deductive
nomological approach, involving the application of Gramsci's general concepts
and principles; the straight methodological approach, consisting of identifying and
importantly internalising Gramsci's method of thinking; and the inductive or
analogical approach, deriving from reflecting on a situation faced by Gramsci that
has some similarity to current situations and drawing relevant conclusions.
Finocchiaro adopts the latter approach to examine Gramsci's attitude towards the
First World War with the background aim of pondering how his arguments could
be extrapolated from and applied to the current 'war on terror' against elements
of radical Islam. Significantly, Gramsci's 'Germanophilia' across a range of journalistic writings, prison letters and prison writings is noted alongside his refusal
to collapse analysis into caricatured assumptions or base politics on religious
affiliation.

Jessop's contribution asserts that Gramsci's philosophy of praxis involves both the historicisation *and* spatialisation of analytical categories so that many of his key concepts can be interpreted according to issues of place, space and scale. This spatial sensibility is evident not simply in terms of metaphors used to convey ideas but in the actual spatiality of the social relations and practices themselves that confronted Gramsci. For example, it can be seen in his analysis of the spatial division of labour between town and countryside, between north and south, and among the different regional, national and international economies that all inscribed the fragmented process of Italian state formation within the dynamics of uneven and combined development (also see Morton 2005). The conclusion drawn is therefore the imperative to acknowledge the spatiality as well as the historicity of the state as a social relation. As a warning to general scholarly debate, Jessop counsels against indulging in a simplified re-scaling of concepts such as passive revolution, historical bloc or hegemony from the national to the transnational; for Gramsci explored complex issues of interscalar articulation and reciprocal influence within which the national level was taken as *nodal* rather than *dominant*. Whether today's scholars internalise this mode of interscalar articulation in an appreciation of the dynamics of global capitalism – rather than maintaining *either* the national *or* the transnational as dominant – becomes a central contention about contemporary world order, which is addressed in the next section of the volume.

One of the insights in the *New Science* offered by Giambattista Vico is a critique of philologists and philosophers as social classes and what they see in texts through a purely discursive perspective, as if that perspective *was* the world (Vico 1984: 63§138–40). Morton implicitly tackles the discourse-theoretical claims of Ernesto Laclau and Chantal Mouffe in this vein by embarking on a 'double reading' of Gramsci. He first delineates a dominant discourse-theoretical reading to demonstrate how certain stable assumptions are rendered and articulated about Gramsci's historical materialism which silence alternative readings. Then he produces a second reading that reveals elements of internal tension that assimilate, anticipate and ultimately fend off certain discourse-theoretical positions on the history of ideas. Thus, Morton provides insight into both the questionable stabilising effects of viewing history as a metapolitical concern that is unknowable other than through the discourse of philosophers and the equally problematic assembly of an extrinsic historical account based on objective economic forces. The result is an elaboration of historical materialism as the *philosophy of praxis* that transcends the established poles of both traditional idealism and materialism. He thereby offers a reading of Gramsci that can contribute to new elements of contemporary historical materialist state theorising, approaches to understanding the international dimension of the capitalist states-system, and thinking on transnational class-agency within the contemporary global political economy.

Within his trilogy on the making of the modern states-system, the historian Eric Hobsbawm (1962: 256) remarks in *The Age of Revolution* that 'it is plainly no accident that the revival or birth of national literate cultures in Germany, Russia, Poland, Hungary, the Scandinavian countries and elsewhere should coincide with – and

indeed should often be the first manifestation of – the assertion of cultural supremacy of the vernacular language and of the native people, against a cosmopolitan aristocratic culture often employing a foreign language'. His thought here is of the
importance of the standardisation of language to projects of state formation. The
very shaping of identities through language (transforming peasant, proletariat, bourgeois), is intrinsic to wider social processes of conflict over property relations.
These issues have long been overlooked within the burgeoning exegesis of
Gramsci's thought in and beyond the *Prison Notebooks*. Ives's approach to Gramsci
not only appreciates Gramsci's reflections on the function of language within social
power relations and historical processes of state formation; it also embeds his
discussion within contemporary controversies of social theory by revealing deeply
troubling aspects about Laclau and Mouffe's post-Marxist dismissal of Gramsci's
approach to language. For Gramsci rejected the notion that language could be
understood as nomenclature, as a collection of words representing a non-linguistic
'reality'. Once this is acknowledged, Ives contends, the trajectory from a non-
linguistic economically based Marxism to linguistic social theory – posited as
central to discourse-theoretic arguments within post-Marxism – becomes untenable.
The result is a combination of powerful exegetical analysis and contemporary
critique to demonstrate that an historical materialist understanding of political
economy is entirely compatible with a theory of linguistics. In contrast, dominant
post-Marxists such as Laclau and Mouffe come to deracinate the very enterprise of
political economy, denying altogether the social function of economic analysis and
any systematic critique of capitalism. Taken together, the approaches to Gramsci
provided by Morton and Ives stand as a staunch response to, and rejection of, the
verities of discourse theory associated with Laclau and Mouffe. They therefore
rearticulate the value of a historical materialist reading of Gramsci and his legacy to
contemporary political theory.

   The task of reflecting on a more fundamental challenge to capitalism is then taken
up by Andrew Robinson's contribution, which embarks on an exegesis of Gramsci's
thought on issues of common sense, ideology and the manufacturing of consent to
theorise the potential for transformative politics in a contemporary context. The
image of Gramsci here is a forgotten one: one that critiqued common sense – or the
taken for granted – in everyday life in order to deepen an understanding of hegemony
as well as mount effective and substantial social transformation. A novel reading of
Gramsci's distinction between organic and arbitrary or willed ideologies is produced
to note that those ideologies described as 'organic' – lived directly within actual
social relations – contain a strong libidinal investment, a mobilisation of desire,
whereas more arbitrary or willed ideologies are superficial, lacking social actuality
and reflecting a mediated or weak relation to desire. Transformative practice has to
therefore consider constructing new ways of thinking and acting which can circumvent bourgeois politics on a psychological, cognitive and social level to produce lasting changes capable of overcoming capitalist exploitation. As Gramsci forewarned,
political action has to take place on the terrain of 'effective reality' rather than idle
fancy, yearning or daydreaming. But at the same time, the endeavour to give shape

and coherence to particular social forces within 'effective reality' necessarily involves concern about issues of 'concrete fantasy' within the extant equilibrium of forces. 'What "ought to be" is therefore concrete; indeed it is the only realistic and historicist interpretation of reality; it alone is history in the making and philosophy in the making, it alone is politics' (Gramsci 1971: 126, Q13§1; 171–172, Q13§16).[1] The challenge, then, is to ground a normative conception of radical subjectivity in existing struggles, movements and tendencies beyond the normalisations associated with the reproduction of capitalist societies.

This way of understanding globalising capitalism, its relations of power and reified structures of governance, as well as the political resistance of situated social agents against such processes, is taken up in the first contribution linking Gramsci to different 'Approaches to World Order'. Rupert articulates clearly and with authority a Gramscian-inflected historical materialism that assists in appreciating the plural transformative politics of anti-capitalist resistance movements within globalising capitalist conditions (also see Morton 2002; Bieler & Morton 2004). Linking with Andrew Robinson's focus on popular 'common sense' as the terrain of struggle to enable critical social analysis and transformative political practice, Rupert then explores the relational social ontology at the nub of Gramsci's thinking on the forging of emancipatory collective action and social self-determination. In Rupert's view, the basis for collective action and 'transformative politics from within a capitalist context must necessarily entail shared anti-capitalist commitments in order to open up future possible worlds which are obscured by the social identities of abstract individualism and disabling ideologies of fetishism and reification produced by capitalism'. The supercession of the historical circumstances of capitalist modernity will therefore require an infinite variety of anti-capitalist commitments in order to effectuate a transformative politics, call into question capitalist social power, and transform the identities and interests underpinning it.

A more cautionary note is struck in van der Pijl's contribution that resonates with the sub-theme of the volume, namely the connections *and* contestations linked to different images of Gramsci. For van der Pijl, Gramsci's concerns are organically related to the tasks of the managerial-technical cadre of contemporary capitalism. The effect of changes in the structure of globalising capitalism on economy and society has led to the rise of this managerial–technical cadre that acts as a renewed context of socialisation and identity formation. Tracing links between Gramsci and the neo-Machiavellians of Mosca, Michels, Pareto and Sorel, it is this new cadre that is today employed in management consultancies, academia, international organisations and other relays of neo-liberal discipline that has subordinated its outlook to those of the ruling class. The Gramscian legacy, in van der Pijl's view, is the ability to recognise the reproductive apparatus of national and transnational hegemony within such opinion-moulding institutions and agencies, which regulates and mitigates the impact of globalising capitalism on society. Dialectically, though, it is also possible to visualise how this thinking about the core modern cadre role might become increasingly engaged in processes of epochal transformation capable of transcending the historical specificities of capitalist modernity. Yet as Marx (1987:

263) remarked, 'no social formation is ever destroyed before all the productive forces for which it is sufficient have been developed, and new superior relations of production never replace older ones before the material conditions for their existence have matured within the framework of the old society'. We are therefore very much in the 'anarchic turbulence' of the interregnum within which there are likely to be 'a great variety of morbid symptoms' before such transformation (Gramsci 1971: 94, Q19§26; 276, Q3§34).

Bieler critically engages with Open Marxist approaches to understanding capitalism within the European Union (EU) and affirms the potential advantages offered by drawing from a Gramscian frame of reference. His claim is that Gramsci's thinking and practice offers the opportunity to reject economism in all forms to realise the open-ended nature of historical development within the EU. Gramsci's dialectical understanding of the relationship between structure and agency allows one to trace the contours and grids of different relational power interests across the regional and global landscape. Indeed, Gramsci's appreciation of the role of ideas as the representation of specific material interests makes it possible to focus on the social purpose underlying the activities of various social forces within and beyond the EU. At the same time, though, Bieler also offers some pointers for the next wave of debate on transnational class formation within a European setting. Among them is his appeal for more work on the impact of national as well as European institutional set-ups on European integration that could draw on relational state theory. Likewise, there continues to be an over-concentration on processes of corporate governance at the expense of a concrete consideration of resistance.

Discussion then turns to issues of international law and world order. In her contribution, Cutler makes a compelling case for a Gramscian conception of the commodity form of law as the specific form of law under capitalism. Linking with Rupert's earlier discussion of the fetishism of commodities, Cutler extends the debate to analyse the homology between the legal form and the commodity form to transcend the 'constitutionalistic fetishism' that Gramsci disparaged (Gramsci 1995: 16–17, Q3§56). The result is a *praxis conception of law* that provides a way of understanding the centrality of the commodity form of law to processes of juridification. As she states 'law operates to simultaneously materialise and mystify the social relations of production and exchange as it reproduces the fetishised commodity form in a fetishised legal form'. At the root of an ostensibly rational and legal framework is therefore coercion, oppression and inequality. Gramsci is central here for he stated that 'the so-called unitary state is just that – "so-called" – because in reality, right at its heart, there is a very serious split', between legislation applied in a de jure fashion and how laws are recognised de facto within individual consciences. If laws do not therefore affect specific interests, legislators become 'engaged in a sordid attempt to empty them of their ethical content' (Gramsci 1995: 63, Q16§11). This insight has clear resonance at a time – March 2005 – when the British government is under scrutiny to publish the full documentation behind the legal advice to go to war in Iraq, due to the impression that the attorney-general, Lord Goldsmith, provided a false prospectus about the legality of war and that the government therefore relied on fluctuating advice from its senior lawyer. Legality here stands as one further sordid attempt to empty the process of juridification of any ethical content.

The final two contributions conclude the collection in a manner that encapsulates the premise of analysing the connections and contentions of different images of Gramsci relevant to contemporary conditions of world order. Pasha rightly disapproves of the manner of inclusion of the non-West within accounts of the world-historical expansion of uneven development due to the predominant reproduction of binary constructions reflected in core–periphery, strong–weak capacities. What this results in is the idea of homogenised cultural space on a global scale within which transnational hegemony is dispensed. The neo-Gramscian theorisation, albeit with some notable exceptions, lacks an appreciation of cultural reception in the non-West. Yet, at the same time, these regions are smuggled back into analysis as the principal site of counter-hegemonic struggles in the era of globalisation. The major oversight, in Pasha's view, in explanations of the global march of transnational hegemony is the neglect of national processes. 'Without securing the spatial confines of national space, transnational or "global" hegemony is unimaginable.' Culture becomes regarded as fungible, an empty container of shallow signifiers, that oversimplifies the spatial terrain of hegemony. His conclusion is that there is a latent or 'soft Orientalism' to most formulations of transnational hegemony. William Robinson's conception of globalisation is seen as paradigmatic in employing a deterministic and *thin* notion of culture in relaying the latest phase of capitalist modernity. The offence is compounded when employing a notion of *thick* culture to bestow counter-hegemonic substance to political resistance.

The robust response from William Robinson is the need to expunge a putative 'state-centrism' from the discussion of transnational hegemony. In his view, globalisation represents a new stage in the history of world capitalism involving the integration of national and regional economies into a new global production and financial system and related processes of transnational class formation. Whether Robert Cox's early attention to the partial transnationalisation of national production and financial systems amounts to 'state-centrism' remains a point of contestation. After all, Cox clearly indicated that 'it becomes increasingly pertinent to think in terms of a global class structure alongside or superimposed upon national class structures' (Cox 1981: 147). Robinson also seems to share commonalities with other analyses that have traced the class fractionology extant in global capitalist structures to suggest transnational class formation (Bieler 2000; Apeldoorn 2004; Overbeek 2004). Yet Robinson's exclusive contribution here is to assert vigorously how national and regional accumulation patterns reflect certain spatial distinctions specific to an integrated global capitalist configuration of power and production. It is precisely this configuration that he sees as bringing together a transnational capitalist class that transcends state-centrism and the territorially bounded politics of space, place and scale. One is perhaps reminded at this juncture, though, of Jessop's earlier contention in the volume that Gramsci explored complex issues of interscalar articulation and reciprocal influence within which the national level was taken as *nodal* rather than *dominant*. Whether we have transcended this mode of interscalar articulation within the contemporary dynamics of global capitalism remains an open question for future debate. At this stage, we would concur with Susanne Soederberg (2001: 184) that the architecture of the governance of global capitalism is 'an annex of the US state', whilst nevertheless serving the interests of the 'transnational bourgeoisie as a whole'.

Finally, this volume on different images of Gramsci across political and international theory offers three major lines of enquiry that can be pursued in future debate. First, the extent to which an internalisation of Gramsci's reflections on the interscalar articulation of the dynamics of global capitalism is relevant to the present. In a sense, it has to be asked how his contribution can be understood in relation to the lack of homogeneity of the global political economy stemming from the combined and uneven development of capital accumulation. Second, the role that Gramsci might play in addressing themes of critical state theory in relation to both the prehistory of the modern capitalist states-system *and* contemporary manifestations of imperialism. Third, the degree to which Gramsci offers the means of relating the accumulation of capital and the international history of the state to a historical materialist value-theoretical approach, which locates the problematic of capital within the vertical relation between appropriators and producers. As Gramsci (1971: 402, Q10II§10) indicated, 'in economics the unitary centre is value, alias the relationship between the worker and the industrial productive forces'. Pursuing these and other lines of enquiry will ensure the continued significance of sustaining an engagement with, across, and beyond political and international theory on Gramsci's legacy.

Acknowledgements

This volume stems from a major interdisciplinary international workshop hosted at the University of Nottingham (24–25 October 2003). The event was co-funded by both the Department of Politics and International Relations at Lancaster University and the School of Politics at the University of Nottingham as well as the British International Studies Association (BISA), the International Political Economy Group (IPEG) of the same organisation, and the Political Studies Association (PSA). We remain thoroughly grateful to the participants of the workshop, to those colleagues who have shown unstinting support in the project, namely Richard Bellamy, Terrell Carver, Randall Germain, Caroline Kennedy-Pipe, Donna Lee, Nicola Phillips, Rorden Wilkinson, and all the anonymous peer reviewers that commented on each piece.

Notes

1. The attentive reader will note here a specific convention associated with citing the *Prison Notebooks*. Because the complete translation of the critical edition is still underway, in addition to giving the reference to the Gramsci selected anthologies, the notebook number (Q) and section (§) accompanies all citations. This convention has been adopted across the whole volume for all such citations in each

contributor's piece. The concordance table used is that compiled by Marcus Green and can be found at the website of the International Gramsci Society, http://www.italnet.nd.edu/gramsci. We would like to thank Peter Ives for his prompt to adopt this convention.

References

Anderson, P. (1976/1977) The antinomies of Antonio Gramsci, *New Left Review* I, 100, pp. 5–78.

van Apeldoorn, B. (2004) Theorising the transnational: a historical materialist approach, *Journal of International Relations and Development*, 7(2), pp. 142–176.

Bellamy, R. (1987) *Modern Italian Social Theory: Ideology and Politics from Pareto to the Present* (Cambridge: Polity Press).

Bellamy, R. (1990) Gramsci, Croce and the Italian political tradition, *History of Political Thought*, 11(2), pp. 313–337.

Bellamy, R. (2001) A Crocean critique of Gramsci on historicism, hegemony and intellectuals, *Journal of Modern Italian Studies*, 6(2), pp. 209–229.

Bieler, A. (2000) *Globalisation and Enlargement of the European Union: Austrian and Swedish Social Forces in the Struggle over Membership* (London: Routledge).

Bieler A. & Morton, A.D. (2004) 'Another Europe is possible'?: labour and social movements at the European Social Forum, *Globalizations*, 1(2), pp. 303–326.

Cox, R.W. (1981) Social forces, states and world orders: beyond International Relations theory, *Millennium: Journal of International Studies*, 10(2), pp. 126–155.

Cox, R.W. (1983) Gramsci, hegemony and International Relations: an essay in method,. *Millennium: Journal of International Studies*. 12(2), pp. 162–175.

Cox, R.W. (1987) *Production, Power and World Order: Social Forces in the Making of History* (New York: Columbia University Press).

Femia, J.V. (1998) *The Machiavellian Legacy: Essays in Italian Political Thought* (London: Macmillan).

Germain, R. D. & Kenny, M. (1998) Engaging Gramsci: International Relations theory and the new Gramscians, *Review of International Studies*, 24(1), pp. 3–21.

Gill, S. (1990) *American Hegemony and the Trilateral Commission* (Cambridge: Cambridge University Press).

Gill, S. (Ed.) (1993) *Gramsci, Historical Materialism and International Relations* (Cambridge: Cambridge University Press).

Gill, S. (1995) Globalisation, market civilisation and disciplinary neoliberalism, *Millennium: Journal of International Studies*, 24(3), pp. 399–423.

Gramsci, A. (1971) *Selections from the Prison Notebooks*, ed. & trans. Q. Hoare and G. Nowell-Smith (London: Lawrence and Wishart).

Gramsci, A. (1992) *Prison Notebooks*, vol.1, ed. J.A. Buttigieg, ed. & trans. J.A. Buttigieg & A. Callari (New York: Columbia University Press).

Gramsci, A. (1996) *Prison Notebooks*, vol.2, ed. and trans. J.A. Buttigieg (New York: Columbia University Press).

Haug, W.F. (2000) Gramsci's 'philosophy of praxis', *Socialism and Democracy*, 14(1), pp. 1–19.

Hobsbawm, E. (1962) *The Age of Revolution, 1789–1848* (London: Weidenfield & Nicolson).

Hollis, M. & Smith, S. (1990) *Explaining and Understanding International Relations* (Oxford: Clarendon Press).

Holub, R. (1992) *Antonio Gramsci: Beyond Marxism and Postmodernism* (London: Routledge).

Laclau, E. & Mouffe, C. (2001) *Hegemony and Socialist Strategy: Towards a Radical Democratic Politics* (London: Verso).

Marx, K. (1984 [1869]) *The Eighteenth Brumaire of Louis Bonaparte* (London: Lawrence and Wishart).

Marx, K. (1987 [1859]) Preface to *A Contribution to the Critique of Political Economy*, in: Marx, K. & Engels, F. *Collected Works*, vol.29 (London: Lawrence and Wishart).

Martin, J. (1998) *Gramsci's Political Analysis: A Critical Introduction* (London: Macmillan).

Morton, A.D. (2001) The Sociology of theorising and neo-gramscian perspectives: the problems of "school" formation in IPE', in Bieler, A. & Morton, A.D. (Eds), *Social Forces in the Making of the New Europe: The Restructuring of European Social Relations in the Global Political Economy*, pp. 25–43. (London: Palgrave).

Morton, A.D. (2002) 'La Resurrección del Maíz': globalisation, resistance and the Zapatistas, *Millennium: Journal of International Studies*, 31(1), pp. 27–54.

Morton, A.D. (2003) Historicising Gramsci: situating ideas in and beyond their context, *Review of International Political Economy*, 10(1), pp. 118–146.

Morton, A.D. (2005) The age of absolutism: capitalism, the modern states-system and international relations, *Review of International Studies*, 31(3), pp. 495–517.

Mouffe, C. (Ed.) (1979) *Gramsci & Marxist Theory* (London: Routledge).

Overbeek, H. (Ed.) (1993) *Restructuring Hegemony in the Global Political Economy: The Rise of Transnational Neoliberalism in the 1980s* (London: Routledge).

Overbeek, H. (2004) Transnational class formation and concepts of control: towards a genealogy of the Amsterdam project in International Political Economy, *Journal of International Relations and Development*, 7(2), pp. 113–141.

van der Pijl, K. (1998) *Transnational Classes and International Relations* (London: Routledge).

Robinson, W.I. (1996) *Promoting Polyarchy: Globalisation, US Intervention and Hegemony* (Cambridge: Cambridge University Press).

Rupert, M. (1995) *Producing Hegemony: The Politics of Mass Production and American Global Power* (Cambridge: Cambridge University Press).

Sassoon, A.S. (Ed.) (1982) *Approaches to Gramsci* (London: Readers and Writers).

Sassoon, A.S. (2000) *Gramsci and Contemporary Politics: Beyond Pessimism of the Intellect* (London: Routledge).

Sassoon, A.S. (2001) Globalisation, hegemony and passive revolution, *New Political Economy*, 6(1), pp. 5–17.

Smith, S. (2001) 'Many (dirty) hands make light work: Martin Hollis's account of social action, *Critical Review of International Social and Political Philosophy*, 4(4), pp. 123–148.

Soederberg, S. (2001) The new international financial architecture: imposed leadership and 'emerging markets', in: Panitch, L. & Leys, C. (Eds), *The Socialist Register: A World of Contradictions*, pp. 175–192. (London: Merlin Press).

Vico, G. (1984) *The New Science of Giambattista Vico*, trans. T.G. Bergin & M.H. Fisch from the Third Edition (1744) with the addition of 'Practic of the New Science' (Ithaca: Cornell University Press).

Walker, R.B.J. (1993) *Inside/Outside: International Relations as Political Theory* (Cambridge: Cambridge University Press).

Williams, G.A. (1975) *Proletarian Order: Antonio Gramsci, Factory Councils and the Origins of Italian Communism, 1911–1921* (London: Pluto Press).

Gramsci and the Secret of Father Brown

ANNE SHOWSTACK SASSOON

> Keep a journal...It...encourages you to capture 'fringe-thoughts': various ideas which may be by-products of everyday life, snatches of conversation overheard on the street, or, for that matter, dreams. Once noted, these may lead to more systematic thinking, as well as lend intellectual relevance to more directed experience. (Mills 1967)

Moving from the particular to the general is often viewed with great suspicion in the social sciences. To raise issues of authenticity, intuition or of the 'feel' and 'smell' of the matter under investigation runs the risk of scholarly ridicule. Reflecting on a narrow range of experiences, one's own or those of others, can, of course, not only be misleading but self-indulgent. Yet careful testing of general claims against particular phenomena also has a long theoretical lineage. Over-generalisation and theoretical abstraction can be equally misleading. Given the socially and historically constructed methodological hierarchies and divisions of labour embedded in the human sciences, in which philosophy and mathematics sit at the apex, the uneasy relationship between general and particular is unsurprising.

It can be argued that the content and form of Gramsci's work in prison largely override these hierarchies and divisions of labour. Severely constrained by being confined, but avoiding to a large extent political prohibitions and unhampered by academic straightjackets, Gramsci's creativity in going against the grain of so much taken-for-granted thinking on the left derives from combining rigour with an intellectual openness which allowed him to engage with the widest possible array of sources of knowledge (Buttigieg 1992: 15). That the backdrop was a cata-strophic defeat, at the very moment when the Russian Revolution was supposed to have initiated the triumph of progress, makes his contribution all the more precious.

This article summarises work in progress that is a result of many years of thinking about major methodological issues in Gramsci's writings that are relevant for re-thinking contemporary political relationships, in particular popular diffidence toward politics, politicians and policy-makers.[1] It investigates Gramsci's aim to go beyond the dichotomy between rationalism and irrationalism. It argues that this theme in his work has profound implications both for under-standing his writings and for their use in contemporary political analysis. It does this by drawing on some unusual material: his notes on Chesterton's Father Brown stories, his criticism of Conan Doyle, and his critique of positivism and populism, notably in his writings on the palaeontologist Cuvier and the criminolo-gist Cesare Lombroso. Consideration of Gramsci's way of working and how this contributes to making his approach so fertile is connected to a longstanding inter-est in intellectual practice and the possible usefulness of taking seriously details, small hints, serendipity, intuitions, the occasional to make new connections and to open up innovative questions which may lead to wider political and social under-standings – questions and understandings which could be missed if boxed into models or pre-conceived schema (Sassoon 2000e). It reflects a desire to reach out to different genres as potential sources of understanding that may supplement other modes of discourse.

It must be stressed that this line of research does not argue that the general derives from the particular. Indeed, it acknowledges the possibly 'conservative', indeed potentially 'reactionary' – meant in their historical sense – appropriation of the particular. Going from the particular to the general and back has, of course, a respectable philosophical pedigree – Marx himself could be mentioned – but one which is too often forgotten, certainly with the continued dominance of forms of positivism and scientism in the social sciences. It is certainly questionable whether contemporary debates about postmodernism adequately answer these concerns.

Gramsci and the Tension between the Particular and the General

Gramsci is one writer who offers help in finding ways to go beyond a number of theoretical and political dilemmas. What is striking in his approach is the way in which, at the same time as he poses general questions about philosophy, history and politics, he uses small pieces of information to lead to some profound and original approaches to social and historical analysis and, in contemporary terms, to go beyond the box of accepted political thinking, to make new connections. The pieces, some 'larger' than others, that do *not* fit pre-conceived schema are treated as seriously or even more seriously than those that *do*. For example, support from the popular classes for the fascist regime was regrettable, but it signified more than a 'mistake'. Far from simply betraying 'false consciousness' or tyrannical rule or a combination of these, such support indicates that sections of the population find that their needs are being answered when previously they were not. The pieces that do *not* fit, in this case the left's prognosis of who should 'reasonably' oppose fascism according to a particular socio-economic model, provide clues to wider patterns and possible insights and lead to new questions. Gramsci developed the concept of passive revolution in order, in part, precisely to explain how fascism was able to maintain support amongst wide sections of the population. Indeed, Gramsci's very way of working in prison reflected this use of the particular or small pieces of information. For example, a book review or a reference in an article often sparked off wider thinking and a denser web of connections;[2] connections that are increasingly apparent, as others have noted, in later, redrafted versions of notes that reflects a fundamental aspect of his ideas on philosophy, history and politics.[3]

At this point, what may appear a surprising connection can be made – between Gramsci's approach and the practice of psychoanalysis. Psychoanalytical practice takes seriously any material that is brought to an analytical session by the analysand. Everything is useful, although such 'accidental' or 'occasional' material does not in and of itself provide an explanation. The professional interpretive and generalising self-reflective capacity of the analyst (most important as the practice of psychoanalysis has developed) is essential to make full use of it.[4]

Alongside this order of concerns, an observation by Gramsci that draws on experience made a strong impression when working on his concept of the intellectuals (Sassoon 2000b,d). In this note, Gramsci attempts to explain why it is so difficult for 'those in the know', perhaps above all the left, to convince the population, say in a small village in the Italian south, without much or any formal education, that there was a better way to understand the world, to explain why they were subaltern, and to convince them that they should join a progressive political cause (Gramsci 1971: 339, Q11§12; 341, Q11§12). Gramsci argues that in fact popular resistance to enlightened ideas should not surprise us. Indeed this resistance was most 'rational'. It made 'good sense'.

If we were to put ourselves in the shoes of the person listening to the sophisticated analysis offered by a politician, or an intellectual, we might well think that today one set of intellectuals or politicians presents one analysis and sure enough tomorrow another lot will appear with other ideas, all argued articulately. What is the person with what Gramsci would consider fragmentary common sense to do? The 'person in the street' has, Gramsci would argue, the potential but not the tools or skills to engage with the more articulate and better educated (Sassoon 2000c,d). Better, we might well think, to hold onto what we 'know', what is 'obvious' and 'natural', that is, cling to the conservatism that stems from tradition and experience, while confronting the contest of ideas and flux of uncontrolled and uncontrollable events. Distrust of experts and politicians is anything but a new phenomenon.

At the same time, from a wider perspective, there are the many references in the *Prison Notebooks* to the limitations of Enlightenment thinking. In particular, Gramsci criticises the rationalistic models based on examples abstracted from the French Revolution and the succeeding period promoted by those Italian Risorgimento thinkers seeking to transform Italy, because these models did not take into account the specificities of Italian history and society (e.g. Gramsci 1971: 55–84, Q19§24). Gramsci's critique of the misuse of Enlightenment thought and of examples drawn from French history and of the inadequacy of the ensuing political strategies had a contemporary political objective. The Soviet example could not, he argued, serve as a model for socialist change in realities so different from that of 1917 Tsarist Russia (Gramsci 1971: 238, Q7§16). Of course, Gramsci himself draws extensively on historical examples, but he suggests that they must be *translated* from one time and place to another and firmly rooted in national specificities (Gramsci 1971: 84–85, Q19§28). The particular therefore must be used with great care.

Despite this critique, it can also be demonstrated that Gramsci is neither a populist nor an anti-rationalist. This leads to a long and complex discussion of the relationship between philosophy, common sense and good sense in Gramsci (Cirese 1981). In this context, Gramsci's attempt to put himself in the shoes of the person with whom he might disagree and who, in his judgement, is subordinate to the dominant hegemony, at least in part because of a lack of advanced intellectual skills and knowledge, reflects something profound in his thought. Gramsci criticises 'common sense' and nonetheless insists that popular culture is an essential starting point to be analysed in order to extract the 'good sense' within it. This 'good sense' is valued but anything but obvious, taken for granted, or in and of itself an adequate basis for an alternative hegemony (Gramsci 1971: 198–199, Q3§48; 223–233, Q3§42, Q3§119, Q7§80, Q1§133–134; 348, Q10II§44; 396–397 Q16§9; 419–425, Q11§13). Today it is easily forgotten how novel this appreciation of the significance of common sense and popular culture was in Gramsci's time and even more easily overlooked the extent to which Gramsci analysed and criticised its limitations. Yet the very paradoxes of popular culture allow for lessons to be learned from the elements of 'good sense' contained within it, for example, in Gramsci's terms from 'non-artistic' literature like detective novels (Gramsci 1985: 372, Q21§13).

Lessons from Father Brown

A conversation about some of these issues with a friend led me to Carlo Ginzburg, another writer concerned with the tension between the particular and general, and his essay 'Clues' (Ginzburg 1992a). In a rich and complex discussion, Ginzburg says his aim is to help to overcome what he considers the arid dichotomy between rationalism and irrationalism (Ginzburg 1992b: ix, 158). He offers no solution but makes some fascinating connections. He links *inter alia* the influential late nineteenth-century Italian art historian Morelli, who argued that it was the detail in a painting, for example the ear lobe in a portrait, where the copier or the follower, of, say Rembrandt, went wrong; Freud, who Ginzburg demonstrates, in a real piece of intellectual detective work, was familiar with Morelli; Conan Doyle and Sherlock Holmes; and the palaeontologist Cuvier. No mention of Gramsci – although in the preface to the Italian collection where the Italian version of this essay is found, Ginzburg's familiarity with Gramsci's work is made explicit (Ginzburg 1992b: ix.).[5]

Discussing this intriguing concatenation of characters with an Italian psychoanalyst friend, she explained that it was well known, at least in psychoanalytic circles, that Freud was indeed fascinated with Sherlock Holmes. Thus an interest in Gramsci's use of the particular and possible parallels with psychoanalytical methods arrived at detection and the use of clues, to Gramsci's references to G.K. Chesterton and Father Brown, and to Cuvier. To mirror his own way of working in prison, making use of hints and suggestions, an examination of his particular, rather brief comments, taking seriously Gramsci's fascination with detective novels (Gramsci 1985: 369–374, Q21§12–13), can shed light on much wider methodological and philosophical issues in Gramsci's work and far beyond.

Re-reading Gramsci's notes on Chesterton and Conan Doyle (Gramsci 1975: 19, Q1§24; 697–678, Q6§17; 1820–1822, Q15§58; 2126–2127, Q21§10; 2130, Q21§13; 2705, Q6§17n2; Gramsci 1985: 370–374, Q21§13) and a relevant letter from prison to his sister-in-law Tatiana (Gramsci 1994: 353–354), in which he vaunts the superiority of the writings of a politically reactionary Catholic writer in contrast to Conan Doyle, the enlightened physician, I found that I should not have been so surprised that a passage in a fictionalised preface which lends its name to a collection of stories, *The Secret of Father Brown* (Chesterton 1974: 7–14), encapsulated so well aspects of Gramsci's ideas.

In this introductory chapter, published in the same period as Gramsci's imprisonment, Chesterton sets up an encounter between the English detective Father Brown, visiting his friend, retired sleuth and – we eventually find out – former famous criminal, the hospitable Frenchman Flambeau, now living in a modest, dilapidated Spanish castle, and an affluent, refined, well-educated upper-class American traveller who has leased another castle nearby. The keen, curious but polite American asks Father Brown to explain the difference between his methods and those of other famous detectives such as Dupin or Sherlock Holmes. Expressing surprise that Father Brown always managed to arrive at the identity of the murderer, notwithstanding the fact that Father Brown's method, unlike that of other detectives, is never explained, the American surmises that, rather than make use of 'detective science', Father Brown can only have employed what the American considers its opposite – the occult. What was Father Brown's secret?

To the American's incredulity, Father Brown answers,

> 'I had murdered them all myself ... so, of course, I knew how it was done ... I had planned out each of the crimes very carefully ... I had thought out exactly how a thing like that could be done, and in what style or state of mind a man could really do it. And when I was quite sure that I felt exactly like the murderer myself, of course I knew who he was.' (Chesterton 1974: 11)

Calmed by what he considers a figure of speech, the American nonetheless provokes Father Brown to exclaim against this reduction of his method to metaphor.

> 'I mean that I really did see myself, and my real self, committing the murders. I didn't actually kill the men by material means ... I meant that I thought and thought about how a man might come to be like that, until I realised that I really *was* like that, in everything except actual final consent to the action.' (Chesterton 1974: 12; emphasis original).

When the American stares at him as if he were 'a wild animal' and declares that he simply cannot understand this account of 'the science of detection' (Chesterton 1974: 12), Father Brown replies with continued 'animated annoyance'.

> 'That's it', he cried, 'that's just where we part company. Science is a great thing when you can get it; in its real sense one of the grandest words in the world. But what do these men mean, nine times out of ten, when they use it nowadays? When they say detection is a science? They mean getting *outside* a man and studying him as if he were a gigantic insect; in what they would call a dry impartial light, in what I should call a dead and dehumanised light. They mean getting a long way off him, as if he were a distant prehistoric monster; staring at the shape of his 'criminal skull' as if it were a sort of eerie growth, like the horn on a rhinoceros's nose. When the scientist talks about a type, he never means himself, but always his neighbour; probably his poorer neighbour. I don't deny the dry light may sometimes do good; though in one sense it's the very reverse of science. So far from being knowledge, it's actually suppression of what we know. It's treating a friend as a stranger, and pretending that something familiar is really remote and mysterious. It's like saying that a man has a proboscis between the eyes, or that he falls down in a fit of insensibility once every twenty-four hours. Well, what you call 'the secret' is exactly the opposite. I don't try to get outside the man. I try to get inside the murderer ... Indeed, it's much more than that, don't you see? I *am* inside the murderer, thinking his thoughts, wrestling with his passions; till I have bent myself into the posture of his hunched and peering hatred; till I see the world with his bloodshot and

squinting eyes, looking up the short and sharp perspective of a straight road to a pool of blood. Till I really am the murderer'. (Chesterton 1974: 12–13; emphasis original)

In other words, Father Brown puts himself into the shoes, and the mind, of the murderer. He recognises what he and the murderer share. Father Brown reflects on himself in order to understand the other. Positivist criminology, studying human beings like insects, classifying them into types instead of aiding, in fact undermines understanding human psychology and hence determining who might have committed the crime and why.

Now, rather than assuming that in the absence of science Father Brown must perforce be depending on the occult, the American comes to understand that this method is in fact a *religious* exercise. Father Brown concurs.

'It's so real a religious exercise that I'd rather not have said anything about it … No man's really any good till he knows how bad he is, or might be; till he's realised exactly how much right he has to all this snobbery, and sneering, and talking about "criminals", as if they were apes in a forest ten thousand miles away; till he's got rid of all the dirty self-deception of talking about low types and deficient skills.' (Chesterton 1974: 13).[6]

Much more could be said, not only about these passages and not only with regard to Gramsci's ideas on the relation between science and religion but also about the American's moralistic concern that abandoning the 'scientific' method, and how empathising with the criminal leads to tolerance of crime (Chesterton 1974: 13). Indeed he is taken aback when at this point Flambeau, his host, confesses to his own criminal past and says that he was only redeemed by the fact that Father Brown, his friend, '"told me that he knew exactly why I stole, and I have never stolen since"' (Chesterton 1974: 15).[7] Going on to the stories themselves, Father Brown demonstrates the application of his psychological skills and the usefulness of the clues that do not fit as he notices in the everyday what others fail to recognise as significant.

The connection between Gramsci's approach to philosophy and politics and the secret of Father Brown, however brief Gramsci's comments, has a great deal to offer. We do not have to enter a discussion of criminology or to profess a religious belief to understand why Gramsci was so charmed by Chesterton's creation. In a letter to Tatiana, he describes Chesterton's subtle caricature of detective novels. Father Brown, he says, is a Catholic who mocks a mechanical, Protestant way of thinking and provides a defence of the Catholic Church against the Anglican. Sherlock Holmes is the 'Protestant', who reaches the outcome by starting from the outside, basing himself on science, on the experimental method, on induction. In contrast, Gramsci writes, as a Catholic priest, Father Brown has developed his psychological skills through hearing confession, and through his training in deciding cases of right and wrong (Gramsci 1985: 371, Q21§13; Gramsci 1994: 354). Without overlooking what science and experience might offer, Gramsci continues, he bases his work above all on deduction and introspection, and wins every time, in Gramsci's opinion, over Sherlock Holmes. To add insult to injury, Gramsci also claims that Chesterton is much the better writer despite Conan Doyle being given a knighthood! (Gramsci 1994: 353–354; see also Gramsci 1985: 371, 21§13).[8]

Putting oneself in the shoes of the 'criminal' is not so different from trying to understand why the person in the street harbours grave doubts about the prognosis offered by progressive intellectuals, experts and politicians. Imagining how one could come to support an alternative view, up to and including the most reprehensible, is not weakening opposition to it – quite the opposite. Trying to think how even advanced knowledge is connected to the 'good sense' contained within common sense, but also trying to understand the reasons, contemporary as well as historical, why large sections of the population hold on to what appears to them 'natural', however much this is in fact out of keeping with both their lived reality and a more advanced social, historical, and political understanding, is part and parcel of creating a strategy for a progressive, transformative politics based on a new hegemony which can never, according to Gramsci, succeed from on high if not rooted in the needs of the wider population. Making connections to such needs, however understood and expressed, even in the most reprehensible terms, does not mean accepting them as givens but rather as unavoidable starting points to be analysed and criticised for any effective political project which aims at going beyond the limitations of the present.

Words of Caution – Cuvier and Lombroso

But the relationship between particular and general is far from simple. A small piece of evidence might lead to greater understanding or to absurd conclusions. This brings us to Cuvier's little bone. Whereas the palaeontologist Cuvier might be able to reconstruct an extinct animal that once really existed from a tiny bone (Buttigieg 1992: 52–53), other, less skilled, 'scientists' could pick up a piece of a mouse's tail and reconstruct from it an absurdity, for example, a sea serpent (Gramsci 1975: 314, Q3§38; see also Gramsci cited in Buttigieg 1992: 42, and Gramsci 1992: 116, Q1§26). Worse was the misuse of natural science to analyse society (cited in Buttigieg 1992: 52–53). The critique of positivism and scientism could not be more explicit.

Just as Father Brown sees the limits of natural science as applied to criminology, without overlooking what a scientific method has to offer, Gramsci is well aware that a clue or small piece of information can either lead to a network of wider understandings or can result in nonsense and worse. Gramsci was quite clear in his critique of positivism, and of those, 'progressive' reformers, such as the criminologist Cesare Lombroso, who misused science (Buttigieg 1992: 398). However benevolent their reforms and however much attached to the socialist cause, they were in fact responsible for contributing to denigrating precisely those wider sections of the population who needed to become the basis for a progressive politics, Father Brown's 'poorer neighbours'. Biological determinism and positivist sociology was so criticised by Gramsci because it had serious deleterious political effects (Buttigieg 1992: 42ff).

Yet he was equally loath to exclude the significance of the smallest piece of information if used appropriately. We can find a parallel in Ginzburg's essay, 'Clues', which begins with an aphorism from Aby Warburg, 'God is in the detail', before explaining that its aim in examining the emergence of a new scientific paradigm was to help avoid getting stuck on the rocks of a presumed counter-position between rationalism and irrationalism (Ginzburg 1992a: 158). We might say that Gramsci was trying to avoid the Scylla and Charybdis of scientism and historicism or of dirigisme and populism.

Conclusion

It is, of course, in his notes on philosophy and history, in particular in his critique of Nikolai Bukharin and the misapplication of natural science to the philosophy of praxis, that Gramsci develops in much greater depth the insights expressed in such abbreviated form in his notes on Father Brown and Cuvier (on Gramsci's 'Anti-Bukharin' also see Morton in this volume). That such concerns are not only theoretically profound but politically pressing is the raison d'être of the *Prison Notebooks*. 'In the science and art of politics', Buttigieg (1992: 57–58) noted, 'one may end up with real catastrophes which cause irreparable harm', if political programmes are determined by reference to metaphysical, mechanistic formulas. Gramsci's goal of going beyond the dichotomy between rationalism and irrationalism must be set in the wider context of his writing in prison, in particular, his notes on the historical function of the intellectuals and how this contributes to the priority given to 'rationalism', the implications for the concept of the state and politics, and for occluding the social relations embedded in certain concepts of philosophy and the social sciences (Gramsci 1992: 229–331, Q1§150). Space does not permit a full discussion of the links between the 'fragments' examined here and Gramsci's overall project. Here we would simply argue that the very way that Gramsci worked is a useful point of reference for engaging in contemporary debates about social science methodology. Further, there are implications for political issues that are of wide concern. Taking the particular seriously and making use of insights from unexpected sources with care can add to, rather than distort, social and political analysis. Expanding the repertoire of epistemological tools might contribute to hearing messages from the wider society and re-building links between politics and policy-making and the population without falling into simplistic populism. Finally, we would endorse the suggestion that, as used in the notebooks, Gramsci's philological criticisms 'function simultaneously as a weapon and shield against all forms of dogmatism and mystification' (Buttigieg 1992: 64).

Acknowledgements

I would like to thank Mariella Ciambelli, Michael Donnelly, Donald Gillies, Grazia Ietto Gillies and Tanya Sassoon for leads and suggestions in pursuing this investigation and the two anonymous reviewers for their help with both form and content.

Notes

1. This piece is part of the early stage of a larger project: Clues to Modernity: Gramsci, Freud, Simmel, Benjamin.
2. An excellent example of how Gramsci develops wider points from very specific ones and connects them to ideas he was developing more generally can be found in his (second) note on 'The detective novel' (Gramsci 1985: 371–374, Q21§13). Following the convention established in this volume, reference to both critical edition and the Gramsci anthologies is accompanied by a citation of the notebook number (Q) and section (§).
3. See Joseph Buttigieg's discussion of the profound implications of Gramsci's critical philological method (Buttigieg 1992: 42–64).
4. This is related to the valorisation of the counter-transference in psychoanalytical writing and practice that goes beyond Freud.
5. It should be noted that this essay has appeared in slightly different forms at different times. An early version is 'Morelli, Freud, and Sherlock Holmes: clues and scientific method'; see Ginzburg 1983.
6. Yet, Father Brown notwithstanding, Mark Billingham writes that Chesterton's 'beliefs were at one time enshrined in the oath sworn on joining the British Detection Club. Members had to vow that their fictional sleuths would not be reliant on "divine revelation, feminine intuition, mumbo-jumbo, jiggery-pokery, coincidence or Act of God"' (Billingham 2004: 2). Gramsci, on the other hand, is in fact highly appreciative of what he considers the psychological insights imparted by the *practice* of being a priest, in particular hearing confessions and judging rights and wrong (Gramsci 1994: 354; see also Gramsci 1985: 371, Q21§13).
7. Without exaggerating the possible parallel or underestimating the difficulties of, in fact, achieving such rehabilitation, a link could be made with some aspects of psychoanalytical practice.
8. This is not to infer that Gramsci had no criticisms of Chesterton, see Gramsci 1985: 371, Q21§13.

References

Billingham, M. (2004) Murder most foul. Arts and Book Review. *The Independent*, 23 July, pp. 2–4.

Buttigieg, J.A. (1992) Introduction, in Gramsci, A., *Prison Notebooks*, Vol. 1, ed. J.A. Buttigieg, trans. J.A. Buttigieg and A. Callari (New York: Columbia University Press).

Chesterton, G.K. (1974 [1927]). *The Secret of Father Brown* (London: Penguin).

Cirese, A.M. (1987) Conception of the world, spontaneous philosophy, folklore, in Sassoon, A.S. (Ed.), *A Gramsci Reader*, 212–447 (London: Writers and Readers).

Ginzburg, C. (1983) Morelli, Freud and Sherlock Holmes: clues and scientific method, in Eco, U. and T.A. Sebeok (Eds), *The Sign of Three: Dupin, Holmes, Peirce*, pp. 81–118 (Bloomington, IN: Indiana University Press).

Ginzburg, C. (1992a [1986]) Spie, in Ginzburg, C., *Miti, emblemi, spie*, 158–209 (Turin: Einaudi).

Ginzburg, C. (1992b [1986]) *Miti, emblemi, spie* (Turin: Einaudi).

Gramsci, A. (1971) *Selections from the Prison Notebooks*, ed. and trans. Q. Hoare and G. Nowell-Smith (London: Lawrence and Wishart).

Gramsci, A. (1975) *Quaderni del carcere*, ed. V. Gerratana, 4 vols (Turin: Einaudi).

Gramsci, A. (1985) *Selections from Cultural Writings*, ed. D. Forgacs and G. Nowell-Smith (London: Lawrence and Wishart).

Gramsci, A. (1992) *Prison Notebooks*. Vol.1, ed. J.A. Buttigieg, trans. J.A. Buttigieg and A. Callari (New York: Columbia University Press).

Gramsci, A. (1994) *Letters from Prison*, Vol.1, ed. F. Rosengarten, trans. R. Rosenthal (New York: Columbia University Press).

Mills, C.W. 1967 [1959].On intellectual craftmanship, in Mills, C.W., *The Sociological Imagination*, pp. 195–226 (London: Oxford University Press).

Sassoon, A.S. (Ed.) (1981) *A Gramsci Reader* (London: Writers and Readers).

Sassoon, A.S. (2000a) Back to the future: the resurrection of civil society, in: Sassoon, A.S., *Gramsci and Contemporary Politics: Beyond Pessimism of the Intellect*, pp. 66–76 (London: Routledge).

Sassoon, A.S. (2000b) *Gramsci and Contemporary Politics: Beyond Pessimism of the Intellect* (London: Routledge).

Sassoon, A.S. (2000c) The challenge to traditional intellectuals: specialisation, organisation, leadership, in: Sassoon,A.S., *Gramsci and Contemporary Politics: Beyond Pessimism of the Intellect*, pp. 15–26 (London: Routledge).

Sassoon, A.S. (2000d) The politics of the organic intellectuals: passion, understanding, knowledge, in: Sassoon,A.S., *Gramsci and Contemporary Politics: Beyond Pessimism of the Intellect*, pp. 27–41 (London: Routledge).

Sassoon, A.S. (2000e) Subjective authenticity, cultural specificity, individual and collective projects, in: Sassoon,A.S., *Gramsci and Contemporary Politics: Beyond Pessimism of the Intellect*, pp. 124–136 (London: Routledge).

Gramsci, the First World War, and the Problem of Politics vs Religion vs Economics in War

MAURICE A. FINOCCHIARO

In this essay I plan to examine Gramsci's writings about the First World War, primarily his immediate reflections in 1914–1918, but also relevant reflections while in prison (1926–1937). Two general issues that will emerge are the questions of the relationship between politics and economics and between politics and religion in war. This latter question is also one that provided a semi-practical motivation for the present inquiry. For in the current geopolitical situation there is a war going on between the liberal democratic countries of the West and the 'terrorists' of radical Islam; and there is the risk that this war might become a religious war or war between civilisations. Many people are aware of this risk and are endeavoring to prevent this struggle from becoming a religious war. From the viewpoint of this risk, the First World War embodied this problem, and Gramsci was keenly aware of it, as may be seen from a passage in the *Prison Notebooks* in which he was commenting on Croce's attitude toward this problem:

> Croce reacts against the popular interpretation (with the resulting propaganda) of the war as a war of civilisations and hence a religious war, which (theoretically speaking) should lead to the annihilation of the enemy. Croce sees the category of war in that of peace and the category of peace in that of war, and he struggles to prevent the destruction of the possibility of mediation between the two categories. Peace will follow the war, and the peace may necessitate the formation of alliances that are very different from those of the war; but how would it be possible for states to collaborate after the unleashing of religious fanaticism during the war? It follows that no immediate political need can or should be elevated to a universal criterion. But these remarks do not describe precisely Croce's attitude. In fact, one cannot say that he is against the 'religious' interpretation of the war insofar as this is politically necessary in order for the great popular masses that are mobilised to be willing to sacrifice themselves in the trenches and to die; this is a technical political problem the solution of which is the task of political technicians. What Croce is concerned with is that intellectuals not lower themselves to the level of the masses, but rather understand that ideology is one thing (namely, a practical instrument of governing) and philosophy and religion are another thing (which must not be prostituted in the understanding of the priests themselves). (Gramsci 1975: 1212, Q10§1).[1]

Methodological Considerations

In examining Gramsci's views on this problem, one must steer clear of two opposite extremes and reach a judicious balance between them: one extreme would be the excessively historicist approach that interprets and evaluates Gramsci's ideas merely in the context of the particular situation in which he found himself (thereby making them irrelevant to the problems of other times and places); the other is the anachronistic and excessively abstract approach that interprets and evaluates his ideas without regard to the historical conditions from which they emerged.

The viability of this balanced approach has been theoretically elaborated and defended by Joseph Femia (1981) and practiced by the present author. Adam Morton (2003a; 2003b: 170–171) has also struggled with this issue and has aimed at such a balance, although the fact that he seems to reject my post-liberal and post-Marxist interpretation serves as a reminder that similarity of approach does not mean similarity of result. In their critique of the neo-Gramscian approach to international relations, Germain and Kenny (1998) may also be taken to be addressing the issue, but the response provided by Rupert (1998) suggests that the difficulties they envisage are not insurmountable.

Finally, the importance of the balanced approach has been unwittingly strengthened by Ghosh's (2001) reaffirmation of the historicist approach and criticism of the abstract-oriented approaches to Gramsci's concept of hegemony. For Ghosh goes to great lengths to demonstrate that Gramsci 'belongs to a now remote area of European thought' (2001: 14); that 'he was only ... a political activist and mobiliser ... not a "pure" or a "great intellectual" in the German sense' (2001: 29); and that

> to retain our attention today, he would have needed to display a more tangible grasp of the sensuous reality of 'human society, or social humanity' than in fact he did. But then this would be to attribute a passive, speculative and 'traditionally' intellectual stance which was simply alien to him. (2001: 43)

However, although such negative conclusions are supported by *some* evidence, this degree of support strikes me as inadequate, being merely sufficient to justify constructive interpretations, which require a lower standard of evidence. Moreover, the exercise is ultimately self-defeating; for if such conclusions were acceptable, they would show that hegemony is not a fruitful topic for which serious scholars would want to read Gramsci, and so they should search for different things in Gramsci's writings.

Another important distinction is worth making. It too involves three possible approaches. Here, the first approach, labeled deductive or nomological, involves trying to apply some of Gramsci's general concepts and principles, such as passive revolution, war of position, war of manoeuvre. A good example is Cox's (1983) articulation of the Gramscian concepts of hegemony, war of position, passive revolution and historical bloc and his application of these concepts to international relations and world order. Another noteworthy example is Augelli and Murphy's (1988) elaboration of Gramsci's concepts of ideology and supremacy and their application to understand the Ronald Reagan presidency and its success in the 1980s.

The second approach, labeled methodological, consists of identifying and internalising Gramsci's method of thinking and then applying it to the problem at hand. Of course, the Gramscian method must be characterised at a suitable level of generality, by means of principles that are not theoretical claims utilising concepts such as those mentioned under the first approach, but rather prescriptive rules that stipulate how one is to go about investigating a problem. One such rule might stipulate that one ought to follow a 'dialectical' manner of thinking, together with a suitable definition of 'dialectic' (cf. Finocchiaro 1988a). Gramsci himself (1975: 1841–1842) stressed the value of a methodological approach, when he remarked that 'the search for the leitmotif, the rhythm of thinking as it develops, must be more important than the casual single claims and separate aphorisms'. And this has been echoed in various ways by various authors (Gerratana 1975: xxxiv; Razeto Migliaro and Misuraca 1978: 13-14, 127-8; Finocchiaro 1988a: 1–2, 147–149, 1988b: 11–13; Morton 2003a: 134–137).

The third approach, labeled inductive or analogical, involves trying to find a situation faced by Gramsci that has some similarity to a current situation; determine what Gramsci said or did in that context; and then do or say something similar in the current situation. Sassoon's (2000: 93–104) essay on Gramsci, Blair, and us is an example of this approach.

These three approaches have advantages and disadvantages, but in this essay I shall follow the third, inductive or analogical one. So I shall examine Gramsci's attitude toward and reflections about the First World War, with an eye toward exploring how they could be extrapolated to the war against radical Islamic terrorism, although such an extrapolation will not be attempted here.

Gramsci's reflections can be found in two places, his newspaper writings during the war years (1914–1918) and his prison writings (letters and notebooks). The latter are of course more mature and theoretically deeper, but the former are invaluable for their immediacy and will be the main focus of this essay. The earlier writings during the war are the articles Gramsci wrote as a columnist for the Turinese socialist weekly *Il grido del popolo* and for the Turinese section of the Milanese socialist daily *L'Avanti!*.

Gramsci's newspaper articles covered many topics besides the cluster of the war and the interaction between politics and religion and between intellectuals and masses. All those discussions are perhaps related to each other as well as to the problem of politics versus religion in war stemming from Croce. However, for my present purposes, I shall leave all those topics in the background and focus on the themes directly related to this problem.

Before we proceed to examine some of these Gramscian reflections, some other introductory caveats are in order. These caveats are needed in order to address a problem of interpretation due to the complexity of Gramsci's journalistic writings. First, there is the fact that, to use Gramsci's own words, 'in ten years of journalism I have written so many lines as to be able to compile 15 or 20 volumes of 400 pages, but they were written on a daily basis and should, in my opinion, be allowed to perish in the same manner. I have always refused to compile such collections, even if selected' (Gramsci 1965: 480). The reply to this is that Gramsci may or may not have been right in saying this, and it is up to us to determine whether or not he was.

Second, for many reasons, not the least of which is Gramsci's literary talent as a great and inspired writer, these writings are full of satire, irony, sarcasm and wit, and so their interpretation requires that one be sensitive to the fact that Gramsci did not always mean what he said or say what he meant. There is no general hermeneutical rule here, but I trust no one will take Gramsci literally for what he said in the article published in *L'Avanti* on 15 October 1918, in which he proposed that in order to cope with the shortage of consumer goods caused by the war, one could either kill or place on suspended animation all superfluous persons, e.g., persons who were older than 60 and had no relatives (Gramsci 1984: 330–333).

Third, there is the fact that Gramsci was writing in official newspapers of the Italian Socialist Party and constantly described his point of view as that of 'us socialists'. The solution to this third difficulty involves a proper appreciation of the following observation made by Gramsci himself in a June 1918 article:

If I were a bourgeois journalist and wanted to guide my readers to help them find their way in the midst of the cobwebs of information and comments, to lead them to clarity in a *disinterested* manner, so that they could become persuaded that if one wants a certain end one must utilise certain means and follow a certain path; if I were a bourgeois journalist and I honestly wanted to act upon my readers so that they, once convinced of a truth, would in turn act upon their political parties, and the latter through their deputies and senators would act upon the government, the state, and the foreign executives; in essence I would not write differently from what I am writing. The tone would change, but not the arguments about the objective analysis of events. (Gramsci 1984: 91)

Moreover, when Gramsci speaks of 'us socialists', he is not parroting anybody, but rather expressing his own interpretation of socialism; and one should never forget that his so-called socialism may not correspond to other people's ideas. For example, on 12 February 1918 he commented on a campaign started in France and spread to Italy against luxury, not only to tax it heavily (which was already being done), but to suppress it altogether:

We are not democrats of the old school, according to whom democracy consisted and consists of being *habitués* of bars, untiring blasphemers, shabby in everything (from one's handbag and house to one's clothes and spirit), and sworn enemies of the refinements and the high enjoyments of material and spiritual life.

Not at all! We aspire not at the destruction of the superior goods of society but at their generalisation, and we fight not to suppress them (as if they were insulting) but to make them accessible to the masses (as elements of their intellectual and aesthetic improvement). (Gramsci 1982: 658)

Croce and the First World War

As my initial quotation indicates, an important context of Gramsci's reflections was Croce's thinking, and so it is useful to begin with the latter. Thus, for the topic at hand there is no need to rehearse the arguments about the relative weight of influence on Gramsci by the Italian milieu in general, and Croce in particular, on the one hand and by the communist international context in general, and Lenin in particular, on the other.

During the First World War, Croce had many occasions to comment on it, mostly from the pages of his own review *La Critica*, but also in newspaper articles and letters to the editor. No sooner had the war ended that one of his friends collected these essays and edited them as a book entitled *Pagine sulla guerra*. It first appeared in 1919, with a second edition in 1928. A third edition was published in 1950, at which time it became necessary to distinguish the First from the Second World War, and so Croce retitled the book *L'Italia dal 1914 al 1918* and added the phrase 'pagine sulla guerra' as a subtitle. In his prison writings, Gramsci (1965: 607–610; 1975: 1211, 1318) refers explicitly to this book several times.

Although Croce's reflections cover a wide variety of topics, four themes predominate. One is the defence of the common European patrimony in civil, intellectual and artistic matters (Croce 1965: 5). A second is the criticism of scholars who got into the habit of 'falsifying the truth under the pretext of serving the fatherland or a political party' (Croce 1965: 5). A third is the discussion of what Croce himself at one point labeled his 'Germanophilia' (Croce 1965: 70). And fourth, there is the conception of politics in terms of power (Croce 1965: 5–6).

In regard to the first theme of the common cultural heritage of the warring states, one of Croce's most striking points is that just as the achievements of ancient Greece in the fourth and fifth centuries BC belong to all humanity and not only to modern Greece; and just as the accomplishments of ancient Rome and of the Italian Renaissance have universal significance and not only specific relevance to the modern Italian state; so the Germany of Kant, Hegel, Goethe and Beethoven is no more a part of modern Germans than of Italians and Britons; as a matter of fact, the latter have understood and elaborated it better than the Germans themselves (Croce 1965: 22–23). Another example of European commonality is a principle of hierarchy of values that gives priority to truth over the Fatherland; although Croce held that patriotism was a positive and important value and was serious about practising, promoting and cultivating it, he also held that 'above the duty toward the fatherland is the duty toward the truth' (Croce 1965: 54). We will soon see how this principle was echoed by Gramsci, but for now let us see how it leads directly to Croce's second theme, which amounts to an exposure of violations of this principle.

For example, in May 1915 Croce objected to some German scholars who claimed that 'the true state of the future is not the nation-state, but the one that has transcended the natural element of nationality and is organised merely as a legal framework, such as Austria-Hungary' (Croce 1965: 54). In the same essay, Croce objected to Henri Bergson's application of his philosophical theories to attribute 'mechanicism to the German military high command and *élan vital* to the French military high command' (Croce 1965: 54). On many occasions Croce criticised Guglielmo Ferrero's attempts to show that 'German culture did not respect tradition, authority, and sound principles' (Croce 1965: 65) on such various topics as the interpretation of Homer and ancient Roman history. Elsewhere Croce inveighed against an Italian professor (whom he did not name) who had advanced an ethnographic theory that the Germans descended from the Huns (Croce 1965: 116–117).

Although these examples show that Croce did not spare German scholars, the *targets* of his criticism were primarily Italians (and secondarily scholars from allied countries), for he really believed that the exposure of such scholarly abuses was a contribution to the war effort, and it was clear that he wanted to help his own country (Croce 1965: 100–102). On the other hand, the *subject matter* of the criticism involved mostly German-related topics, such that much of it may also be seen in terms of the third theme of Germanophilia, an attitude which will be seen later to be shared by Gramsci.

For example, during the first year of hostilities (when Italy had not yet joined), Croce was one of those who advised caution. When in the autumn of 1914 many people were quick to accuse the Germans of barbarism for the damage to the Rheims cathedral, Croce agreed to sign an open letter asking that judgement be suspended until there was clear evidence available on which to base a sound judgement (Croce 1965: 15–19). In the autumn of 1916, he answered a number of anti-German criticisms in an interview by a Naples newspaper (Croce 1965: 70–76). To the objection that blamed the war on German culture, Croce replied that no scientific theory determines concrete action in an immediate and logical way. To the allegation of German cruelties, Croce answered that charges of cruelty are common in modern war, indeed have become part of war; and he cited Bertrand Russell's documentary refutation of the claim that some German soldiers cut off the nose of a Belgian girl. To the charge that the German political ideal was aristocratic, statist and militaristic, and thus antithetical to the democratic ideal of Italy and France, Croce replied that aristocracy and democracy are not chronological stages in the evolution of governments, but necessary aspects of all good government (cf. Finocchiaro 1999a: 114–143; 1999b).

Regarding the concept of politics as power, many people held that just as in a scientific dispute each side must believe that it has the truth and the opponent is in error, and just as in a moral controversy each side must think that it is right and the other wrong, so in a war each side must believe that it is right and the other wrong. Croce replied that this is true for scientific and moral disputes, but not for wars, which are political struggles; the difference is that in a war or political struggle, 'the only conceivable faith is faith in one's own power and ability; such faith ... supports and implies the respect and not the contempt of the enemy' (Croce 1965: 114).

Gramsci's 'Germanophilia' and Economics vs Politics

Let us now go on to examine the content of Gramsci's journalistic writings on the war. One of the most striking themes in his articles is the defence of Germany from misguided or ill-conceived attempts by supposed patriotic Italians to denigrate its culture, to free Italy from German influence, or to take other actions against Germany. For example, at one point the Catholic Church wanted prayers and other religious services on behalf of dead Italians to be extended on behalf of the dead of other nationalities, and nationalists criticised such alleged impartiality; on 27 November 1915, Gramsci objected to that criticism by calling it protectionism in regard to religious services, and he found it as undesirable as the idea that 'we should free ourselves from the Germans by boycotting the Leipzig edition of the Latin classics' (Gramsci 1980: 29–30). Another example involved one Ernesto Bertarelli giving a lecture in Turin in which he stressed that 'nature deprived Germans of beautiful women, therefore they do violence to beauty' (Gramsci 1980: 62) in general, such as damaging the Rheims cathedral; on 11 January 1916,

Gramsci criticised the lecture in part by paraphrasing Romain Rolland to the effect that 'a truly intelligent person is someone who does not make himself or his ideal the center of the universe' (Gramsci 1980: 63). Gramsci's point was, I suppose, that it was a sign of stupidity for Bertarelli to connect even the comparative beauty of women to the war. Similarly, consider Gramsci's response when one Professor Domenico Bulferetti gave a lecture in Turin arguing that Italy's alliance with Germany and Austria at the turn of the century had caused Italy nothing but harm; on 12 January 1916, Gramsci gave the following reductio ad absurdum:

> When I hear a history professor put forth these claims and proclaim that during thirty years of alliance Italy had received nothing but damage, humiliations, and insults, I can only conclude: '*Ergo*, all Italians (from the king to the government ministers, and from the deputies to the diplomats) were a big bunch of idiots and traitors'. And even I do not believe this, I who am not a nationalist. (Gramsci 1980: 66)

When the Faculty of Letters of the University of Turin adopted the motion that no foreigners should be hired as professors, Gramsci (1980: 81–82) satirised this motion in an article published on 18 January 1916. When Professor Vittorio Cian went so far as advocating that non-Italian professors should be dismissed, on 20 January Gramsci (1980: 85–86) wrote an article comparing him to Robert Michels, who was a German sociologist teaching at Turin; Gramsci claimed that if a referendum were held to determine whether to dismiss Cian or Michels, Cian would be selected for dismissal. On 19 February Gramsci noted that a new literary genre seemed to have arisen, the patriotic lecture, which stretched the truth against the enemy for the sake of the Italian Fatherland; in words reminiscent of Croce he added, 'the truth must always be respected, regardless of the consequences it may bring' (Gramsci 1980: 140). When Turin's artists' club proposed to replace the many German toys of Italian children with Italian-made ones that were supposedly better aesthetically, on 10 March 1916 Gramsci wrote, 'in reality, the artists' club has only wanted to prove that art can be transformed into a gun for the economic war' (Gramsci 1980: 183). When in the Turin municipal council one Dr Borini proposed the boycott of a medicine called preparation 606 (or salvarsan, or arsphenamine) that had been created by German Paul Ehrlich (Nobel prize for medicine) to cure syphilis, on 1 April 1916 Gramsci (1980: 232–233) ridiculed the idea.

Similarly, on 9 April in a nonsatirical article, while discussing the nationalist campaign to buy Italian products, Gramsci (1980: 246–247) argued that if the choice were among Italian, French or German aspirin, the German Bayer would be the best choice. With this article, if not before, the issue of economics versus politics in war became explicit in Gramsci's mind; this is a distinct problem from the Crocean one of religion versus politics, which was the only one Gramsci formulated in our initial quotation above.

On 13 May 1916, Gramsci criticised some stories spread by a conservative Milanese newspaper to the effect that Germany had just formed a trust to retain monopoly of the chemical industry, and was going to continue the policy of 'dumping' such products on international markets; the implication was that Italians should resist such dumping, thus favouring the Italian chemical industry. In his typical anti-protectionist manner, Gramsci (1980: 305–307) suggested that such stories were part of the attempt of Italian capitalists to profit at the expense of Italian consumers. Pursuing the discussion a week later, Gramsci (1980: 324–325) clarified that he did not deny that Germany engaged in some dumping before the war, but he denied that its economic success was due only or primarily to such dumping. For Gramsci this anti-German criticism was an example of consoling oneself by convincing oneself that one's competitor has used illegitimate means: 'however, in part because of its educational value, one must uphold the eternal and incontrovertible truth that only active and productive work emerges triumphant in the course of history, whereas half measures and petty cunning end up redounding against those who use them' (Gramsci 1980: 325). On the same (sub-)theme, on 5 August Gramsci praised an article by Luigi Einaudi in *Riforma sociale* that was critical of protectionism 'despite the war and the anti-German fashion' (Gramsci 1980: 471); Gramsci also endorsed Einaudi's criticism of extending the military war into an economic one, on the grounds that it was a trick for manufacturers to increase their profits without modernising their factories. And a week later, Gramsci summarised approvingly a memorandum of the Manchester Chamber of Commerce published by *Riforma sociale*, concluding that 'the hatred generated by political struggle and by the exasperation of the various nationalisms is a very bad counselor in economics, and they decry that such a disturbing element should become a part of the strong and healthy industrial organism of their country' (Gramsci 1980: 481).

And again, when one Agostino Faracovi promulgated stupidities regarding pharmaceutical drugs in general, and German ones in particular, on 20 October 1916 Gramsci more generally remarked:

> this is presumptuous, arrogant, and aggressively haughty and should make us cry like little lambs about the devastation brought upon Italian character by two years of polemics over Germany, Germans, German philosophy, German poetry, German cuisine, German women, and over the heap of Italian stupidities that reflect them and reflect on them. (Gramsci 1980: 586).

Other Themes

There are many other instances of Germanophile discussions in Gramsci's journalistic writings of those years, but it is beyond the scope of this essay to continue with descriptions, however brief.[2] Instead, it will be more useful to go on to the examination of other themes. It should be noted, however, that the previous discussion of Germanophilia has revealed another extremely important theme, namely the problem of whether the ongoing military war should be extended into the economic domain, and more generally what is the relationship between politics and economics in war.

On 22–26 August 1917, there was a popular insurrection in Turin against the war, and the army had to be called in to suppress it. It resulted in about 50 deaths, the arrest of all local socialist leaders, and the resignation of the chief of police. When the socialist leaders were put on trial, most of them were acquitted, but about half a dozen were condemned to prison terms of one to three years. The causes of these events were controversial: the nationalists attributed them to enemy agents working in association with anarchists and socialists; Gramsci tended to blame those events on a shortage of bread which led to workers' demonstrations that got out of hand due to the incompetence of the authorities. Gramsci wrote several times about these events, and this was his interpretation: 'the events of Turin reduce, as we have always claimed, to an episode of popular discontent which blew up without preparation and without anyone wanting it; which started for economic reasons; and which drew some sustenance from the undeniable and undenied political feelings of the working masses and much more from the lack of preparation, the incompetence, and the lack of foresight of civilian and military authorities' (Gramsci 1982: 807–808).

At the end of October and beginning of November 1917, the Italian Army lost an important battle at Caporetto, and this defeat forced it to retreat to the Piave river, thus losing almost all the territorial gains it had made in two and one-half years of war. This was a shock that led to much soul searching, as well as to specific measures such as the replacement of the military high command, an increase in censorship, and a witch-hunt for defeatists. But the country found the strength to resist and recover, and almost exactly a year later it was in the position of winning the decisive battle of Vittorio Veneto.

Although Caporetto became later a topic of more sustained reflections in prison, Gramsci could hardly fail to comment on it when it first happened. On 3 November 1917, he published an article in which he commented that the defeat had had the effect that those who earlier were merely talking about the war (as distinct from those who were actually doing the fighting) started feeling the bodily shivers which the soldiers had been experiencing all along. He pointed out that 'we socialists' (on account of our internationalism) had been feeling these shivers ever since Germany invaded Belgium; so for 'us' nothing has really changed with Caporetto (Gramsci 1982: 418–419).

One final related theme of Gramsci's articles was the problem of superprofits caused by the war. Gramsci favoured the supertaxation or confiscation of profits that were directly traceable to the war, arguing that 'if the Fatherland had the right to requisition my person and to send me to face death – and we complied – it should have equally requisitioned the work and property of the suppliers and should have made them work and produce gratis on behalf of the common cause' (Gramsci 1982: 590).

Conclusions

It is now time to draw some conclusions, however tentative. First, we can say that while the Great War was actually being fought, Gramsci did show an appreciation

for Croce's distinction between the political–military aspects of a war and its philosophical–religious aspect, and he did exhibit an ability to resist the temptation of
turning the political into a religious war. The motivation underlying this common
attitude was no doubt similar in part, that is respect for the truth. Moreover, such
an attitude expressed itself concretely in what I have called their common
Germanophilia

However, there were probably other, divergent reasons. For whereas Croce's
Germanophile attitude stemmed also from his long-standing knowledge of and
involvement with German philosophy and culture, this particular motive was absent
in Gramsci, for whom instead the main motive must have been proletarian internationalism. Now, from one point of view this contrast would seem to place Croce's
motivation in a more understandable and favourable light than Gramsci's motivation. For Croce regarded himself, with some justice, as the true heir of classical
German philosophy. On the other hand, insofar as Gramsci's Germanophilia was
motivated by proletarian internationalism, he was being blind to the fact that the
German Social Democratic Party had voted in favour of a declaration of war, and so
German proletarians seemed to care more about their fellow German capitalists than
their non-German proletarian brothers.

But this evaluation should be balanced by other considerations, especially the
following criticism made by Gramsci himself in the same note that begins with the
passage quoted at the beginning of this essay (Gramsci 1975: 1213, Q10§1). There
Gramsci criticises Croce's Germanophile attitude during the First World War as an
expression of what Gramsci labeled 'cosmopolitanism'. For Gramsci, cosmopolitanism was a kind of universalism that prescinded from the notion or reality of the
nation-state, and so was bound to disregard or unduly neglect differences and over-
estimate or magnify similarities among people; thus it was an inferior form of internationalism (cf. Gramsci 1975: 325–326, Q3§46; Morton 2003c: 44–45, 46, 48).

A second point to be raised about Gramsci's reflections is that he showed little
awareness or concern for Croce's problem of how political leaders can convince the
masses to fight and be willing to make sacrifices, including the ultimate one, without turning a political struggle into a religious one, without portraying the enemy as
evil. Gramsci's attitude should not surprise us, for he was critical of Croce's willingness to present the First World War to the popular masses as a religious war, even
though as an intellectual he knew better. In the same note quoted at length at the
beginning of this essay, Gramsci (1975: 1213) says that Croce's attitude is 'not
devoid of difficulties' and is a typical example of an approach exemplified in
several other cases. For example, although Croce believed that the key tenets of
organised religion were untenable, he was willing to let them be taught in public
schools; and although he regarded historical materialism as philosophically untenable, he was willing to admit that it performed a useful function among the masses of
industrial workers (cf. Finocchiaro 1988a: 11–17).

In this regard, Gramsci's problem was different: namely, how to convince the
masses to fight at all, how to convince them not to boycott or obstruct the war effort,
how to convince them to do anything against their proletarian brothers in Germany.

His answer to this, advanced later in the *Prison Notebooks*, was somewhat ad hoc: 'the last war has shown that it was not emotional feelings that kept the military masses in the trenches, but rather the fear of military tribunals or a sense of duty calmly and rationally considered' (Gramsci 1975: 1310, Q10§41v).

A key problem that Gramsci struggled with in the war years was that of how a war can be fought without turning it into an economic war, and this is my third point. Gramsci's thinking at that time was not that the economic war would have been counterproductive for the military one, but rather that an economic war would result in greater economic deprivations for the proletariat and in its greater exploitation by the capitalists. Later, in the *Prison Notebooks*, he qualified this position. He seemed to theorise that in modern war military operations and economic activity are inextricably tied. For modern warfare consists primarily of siege warfare or war of position, whereas war of movement or of manoeuvre has acquired a secondary role; that is, the roles of the war of position and the war of manoeuvre have been reversed in modern warfare as compared to what they were in traditional warfare. Now, the crucial point is that 'the war of position is ... made up of ... the whole organisational and industrial system in the territory behind the deployed army' (Gramsci 1975: 1615, Q13§24). And he reinforced this claim by arguing that during the Great War factory workers had performed as vital a role as soldiers at the front, and it was demagoguery to consider factory workers as draft dodgers (Gramsci 1975: 616–618, Q5§87).

Acknowledgements

The constructive comments and suggestions of the editors and two anonymous referees for this journal were gratefully received.

Notes

1. Following the convention established in this volume, reference to the Gramsci anthologies is accompanied by a citation of the notebook number (Q) and section (§).
2. Cf. Gramsci 1980: 705–707; Gramsci 1982: 84–86, 94–96, 143–146, 185–186, 217–219, 458–461, 524-6, 765–766; Gramsci 1984: 381–382. There are many other discussions of German themes in the *Prison Notebooks*, but I am not sure they are relevant here, even when it may *appear* that Gramsci is expressing a Germanophile attitude. For example, in prison Gramsci possessed, liked, and appreciated Erich Remarque's *All Quiet on the Western Front* (1928); cf. Gramsci 1975: 286–288, Q3§3; 712, Q6§38; 1123, Q9§43; 2212–2213, Q23§25; 2250–2253, Q23§57; 2710, Q6§38n3; and 3012, Q23§25n4. However, rather than appreciating the alleged pacifism of its content (1975: 2213, Q23§25) or the 'national-popular' character of the work (1975: 2252, Q23§57), Gramsci seemed primarily to want to stress that this was a *foreign* work popular *in Italy*, and hence to add further evidence for his criticism that 'in Italy literature has never been a phenomenon that could be characterised as national, but rather a "cosmopolitan" one' (1975: 2251, Q23§57).

References

Augelli, E. & Murphy, C. (1988) *America's Quest for Supremacy and the Third World: A Gramscian Analysis* (London: Pinter Publishers).

Cox, R.W. (1983) Gramsci, hegemony and international relations: an essay in method. *Millennium: Journal of International Studies,* 12(2), pp. 162–175.

Croce, B. (1965) *L'Italia dal 1914 al 1918: Pagine sulla guerra.* 4th ed. (Bari: Laterza).

Femia, J. (1981) An historicist critique of 'revisionist' methods for studying the history of ideas, *History and Theory,* 20(2), pp. 113–134.

Finocchiaro, M.A. (1988a) *Gramsci and the History of Dialectical Thought* (Cambridge: Cambridge University Press).

Finocchiaro, M.A. (1988b) *Gramsci critico e la critica* (Rome: Armando).

Finocchiaro, M.A. (1999a) *Beyond Right and Left: Democratic Elitism in Mosca and Gramsci* (New Haven, CT: Yale University Press).

Finocchiaro, M.A. (1999b) Croce and Mosca, in D'Amico, J., Trafton, D.A. & Verdicchio, M. (Eds), *The Legacy of Benedetto Croce,* pp. 117–144 (Toronto, ON: University of Toronto Press).

Germain, R.D. & Kenny, M. (1998) Engaging Gramsci: international relations theory and the new Gramscians, *Review of International Studies,* 24(1), pp. 3–21.

Gerratana, V. (1975) Preface, in: Gramsci, A., *Quaderni del carcere,* ed. V. Gerratana, 4 vols, pp. xi–xli (Turin: Einaudi).

Ghosh, P. (2001) Gramscian hegemony: an absolutely historicist approach, *History of European Ideas,* 27(1), pp. 1–41.

Gramsci, A. (1965) *Lettere dal carcere,* ed. E. Fubini (Turin: Einaudi).

Gramsci, A. (1975) *Quaderni del carcere,* ed. V. Gerratana, 4 vols (Turin: Einaudi).

Gramsci, A. (1980) *Cronache torinesi,* ed. S. Caprioglio (Turin: Einaudi).

Gramsci, A. (1982) *La città futura,* ed. S. Caprioglio (Turin: Einaudi).

Gramsci, A. (1984) *Il nostro Marx,* ed. S. Caprioglio (Turin: Einaudi).

Morton, A.D. (2003a) Historicising Gramsci: situating ideas in and beyond their context, *Review of International Political Economy,* 10(1), pp. 118–146.

Morton, A.D. (2003b) Social forces in the struggle over hegemony: neo-Gramscian perspectives in international political economy, *Rethinking Marxism,* 15(2), 153–179.

Morton, A.D. (2003c) The social function of Carlos Fuentes: a critical intellectual or in the 'shadow of the state', *Bulletin of Latin American Research,* 22(1), pp. 27–51.

Razeto Migliaro, L. & Misuraca, P. (1978) *Sociologia e marxismo nella critica di Gramsci* (Bari: De Donato).

Rupert, M. (1998) (Re-)engaging Gramsci: a response to Germain and Kenny, *Review of International Studies,* 24(3), pp. 427–434.

Sassoon, A.S. (2000) *Gramsci and Contemporary Politics: Beyond Pessimism of the Intellect* (London: Routledge).

Gramsci as a Spatial Theorist

BOB JESSOP

This essay argues that Gramsci's philosophy of praxis involves not only the *histori-cisation* but also the *spatialisation* of its analytical categories. These theoretical practices are deeply intertwined in his 'absolute historicism'. This argument is useful not only because Gramsci regularly explores geographical themes but also because 'bending the stick in the other direction' enriches our understanding of his overall approach. I do not claim that Gramsci was a geographer *manqué* or was more a geographer than historian. These are disciplinary questions inappropriate to the pre-disciplinary traditions of Italian philosophy and historical materialism and to the political agenda of Italian state formation. Conversely, while it is certainly appropriate to consider, like Said (2001),[1] the import of Gramsci's familiar spatial metaphors, it would be misleading to focus exclusively on these here. For this would divert attention from Gramsci's less obvious but more significant analyses of the inherent spatiality as well as temporality of social relations. This approach has

significant practical as well as theoretical implications and is my primary focus
here.

Spatialising the Philosophy of Praxis

Gramsci writes that, while everyone is an intellectual, not everyone is an intellectual
by social function (1971: 9, Q12§3).[2] One might add that, while everyone has a
practical sense of place, space and scale, not everyone is a geographer by social
function. This certainly holds for Gramsci himself. He was a deeply spatial thinker
but he did not explicitly prioritise spatial thinking. This may explain both why
Gramsci 'did not fully and explicitly develop his geographical insights' (Morera
1990: 89) and why the inherently spatial nature of his thought has been neglected.
But he did take geography seriously. He studied it alongside his major subject of
philology at Turin University (passing his geography exam in 1912). He called for
its teaching in primary schools together with reading, writing, sums and history; and
proposed that a potential party textbook contain a 'critical-historical-bibliographical
examination of the regional situations (meaning by region a differentiated
geo-economic organism)' (Gramsci 1985: 415, Q24§3). He continued to explore
geology, geography and geopolitics after leaving university and also taught history
and geography in prison following his arrest (Gramsci 1971: 30, Q12§1; Gramsci
1995: 195–217, Q2§*passim*, Q3§5*passim*, Q5§8, Q6§39, Q6§123, Q8§47; Hoare &
Nowell-Smith 1971: lxxxix). He noted the popularity of geographical novels
(Gramsci 1985: 360, Q21§6); and recommended that touring clubs promote national
culture by combining geography with sport (Gramsci 1995: 153, Q8§188). He
reflected on the geopolitical and geo-economic implications of the international
conferences in the 1920s for Italy, Europe, internationalism and future world politics (Gramsci 1995: 195–215, Q2§*passim*, Q3§5*passim*, Q5§8, Q6§39, Q8§47).
And he regularly approached political problems not only in terms of 'structural'
(economic and class) factors but also in regional terms (cf. Morera 1990: 149).

These interests reflect his experiences as a Sardinian in the most exploited and
oppressed part of the *Mezzogiorno* and his movement to Turin, the capital city of
Piedmont and the north's industrial centre. They also derive from his reflections on
more general influences in Italian economic, political and cultural development.
These include the Vatican's role as a cosmopolitan mini-state situated at the heart of
Italy supported by a traditional intellectual elite with a long-established supranational orientation serving the leaders of Europe; the long-running debate on the
Southern Question (especially from the 1870s); the spatiality of the *Risorgimento*
and the flawed Italian unification process dominated by the Piedmontese state; the
continuing economic and social problems posed by uneven development, dependent
development and, indeed, internal colonialism in Italy; the communists' political
problems in breaking the class alliance between northern capital and the southern
agricultural landowning class and in building an alliance between the northern
workers and southern peasants; the changing nature and forms of imperialism
(including the obstacles, challenges and opportunities involved in the diffusion of

Americanism and Fordism in Europe); and the problems for the wider communist movement posed by the Soviet Union's international isolation.

Gramsci's university training in philology under Umberto Bartoli also stimulated his spatial sensibilities. He followed the latter's new approach to linguistics as an historical science concerned with the social regularities of language (Gramsci 1985: 174, Q3§74). Bartoli developed a 'spatial' analysis of language that sought to trace 'how a dominant speech community exerted prestige over contiguous, subordinate communities: the city over the surrounding countryside, the "standard" language over the dialect, the dominant socio-cultural group over the subordinate one' (Forgacs & Nowell-Smith 1985: 164–167). He also charted the continuing flow of *innovations* from the prestigious *langue* to the receiving one, such that earlier linguistic forms would be found in a peripheral rather than central area, isolated rather than accessible areas, larger rather than smaller areas (Brandist 1996: 94–95). Gramsci inflected Bartoli's analysis in a strongly materialist direction and highlighted its practical implications. For he saw the problem of revolution as closely tied to the unification of the people – a task that had to pass through the medium of language if a coherent collective will was to emerge that could unify different classes, strata, and groups (Lo Piparo 1979; Helsloot 1989; Ives 2004). The resulting complexities are evident in his analyses of how language use is stratified. Among many examples is his comment on how country folk ape urban manners, how subaltern groups imitate the upper classes, how peasants speak when they move to the cities, etc. (Gramsci 1985: 180–181, Q29§2). In short, Gramsci's work on language as a medium of hegemony is not just historical but also highly sensitive spatially.

These influences suggest, as remarked earlier, that there is more to Gramsci as a spatial theorist than his famous use of several spatial metaphors (on which, see Figure 1). These have certainly been influential in the reception of his work but we should also consider his interest in the actual rather than metaphorical spatiality of

---

East/West Morphology of the State

North/South Popular Cosmology

War of Position

War of Manoeuvre

Base and Superstructure

Historical Bloc

Hegemonic Bloc

Molecular Transformation

Passive Revolution

United Front

Vanguard

Trenches, Fortifications, Bulwarks, Outer Perimeter

Figure 1.   Some spatial metaphors in Gramsci

social relations and practices, in their spatial conditioning and in the relevance of social relations and practices to spatial issues. For Gramsci was not only sensitive to the *historical specificity* of all social relations (Morera 1990: 85) but also to their *specific location in place, space and scale*. Indeed, these two are clearly interconnected in any ensemble of social relations. Thus I now consider how Gramsci integrates place, space and scale in his philosophy of praxis. However, because he does this in a largely 'pre-theoretical' manner, I will define these concepts before illustrating their significance for Gramsci's theory and practice.

Place (or locale) refers to a more or less bounded site of face-to-face relationships and/or other direct interactions among social forces. It is generally closely tied to everyday life, has temporal depth, and is bound up with collective memory and social identity. Its boundaries serve both to contain and to connect: they provide a strategically selective social and institutional setting for direct interactions that privileges some identities and interests over others and also structure possible connections to other places and spaces on a range of scales. For this and other reasons, the naming, delimitation and meaning of places are always contested and changeable and the coordinates of any given physical space can be connected to a multiplicity of places with different identities, spatio-temporal boundaries and social significance. Gramsci was sensitive to all of these aspects. He stresses the importance of place or locale in his comments on how common sense, popular culture and everyday practices are shaped by life in different types of cities and in the countryside, the design of locales (e.g., school architecture) or built forms (e.g., street lay-out and street names) (Gramsci 1971: 30–33, Q12§1; 40, Q12§2; 90–92, Q19§26; 282–283, Q22§2; Gramsci 1995: 155, Q3§49). He discusses the struggle for control over places (factories, public buildings, streets, neighbourhoods, etc.) (Gramsci 1977; 1978). He famously emphasised that hegemony in the United States is grounded in the factory (Gramsci 1971: 285, Q22§2). He contrasts the secure meeting places of the industrial and landowning bourgeoisie with the vulnerability of working-class premises and the problems of protecting the streets ('the natural place where the proletariat can assemble without cost') (Gramsci 1978: 35, 268–269). In addition to exploring the contestability of places and their intertwining with other places, he also comments on their links to memory, identity and temporality (Gramsci 1971: 93–95, Q19§26; 272–274, Q3§46; 324–325, Q11§12, 453 Q11§16; Gramsci 1978: 446). This is especially clear in his comments on the folklore of the subaltern and provincial classes and his discussion of the social origins of intellectuals in spatially specific rather than aspatial class terms and their implications for building different types of hegemony. And, of course, it pervades his analysis of the Southern Question with its emphasis on the rootedness (or otherwise) of social classes and political and intellectual forces in specific places, spaces and scales of economic and social life.

Space comprises the socially produced grids and horizons of social life. It offers a whole series of strategically selective possibilities to develop social relations that stretch over space and time. Gramsci considers space from several viewpoints: (a) the spatial division of labour between town and countryside, between north and south, between different regional, national, and even continental economies; (b) the territorialisation of political power, processes of state formation and the dialectic of domestic and external influences on political life; and (c) different spatial and scalar imaginaries and different representations of space. Gramsci did not believe that space exists in itself, independently of the specific social relations that construct it, reproduce it and occur within it. As a profoundly relational and practical thinker, he was never tempted by such spatial fetishism.[3] Nor did he accept the geographical determinism common in the nineteenth-century 'scientific' field and still reflected in folklore and common sense – a determinism that regards the physical and/or human environment as the most important determinant of social relations and their historical development. This would have been equally anathema to Gramsci's philosophy of praxis.[4] Instead he treated space like history, that is, in relational terms. For example, he regarded historical grammar (philology) comparatively, arguing that 'the linguistic fact, like any other historical fact, cannot have strictly defined national boundaries' (Gramsci 1985: 181, Q29§2). This is reflected in his exploration of local linguistic usages and particularisms, tendencies to territorial unity and fragmentation, and external influences on national languages. He concluded 'that history is always "world history" and that particular histories exist only within the frame of world history' (Gramsci 1985: 181, Q29§2; cf. Gramsci 1971: 182, Q13§17). This is directly comparable to his view that national states are not self-closed 'power containers' but should be studied in terms of their complex interconnections with states and political forces on other scales. Indeed he combines temporal and spatial perspectives in an early form of 'geographical historical materialism' (cf. Harvey 1982).

Scale comprises the nested (and sometimes not so nested) hierarchy of bounded spaces of differing size, e.g., local, regional, national, continental and global. Scale is typically the product of social struggles for power and control. Gramsci was extremely sensitive to issues of scale, scalar hierarchies of economic, political, intellectual and moral power, and their territorial and non-territorial expressions. He was not a 'methodological nationalist' who took the national scale for granted but typically analysed any particular scale in terms of its connection with other scales. Thus he examined relations of hegemony and domination at the local level (e.g., the Parisian urban bloc's domination of other French cities), regional level (e.g., Piedmontese domination of Italy's flawed and incomplete unification or the Giolittian strategy of passive revolution based on an alliance between a dominant northern urban bloc and a southern rural bloc), national level (e.g., the influence of the French bourgeoisie as the leading, dominant class throughout the continent), the transatlantic level (e.g., Americanism and Fordism), and the hemispheric level (e.g., the probable transfer of economic and political domination from America to Asia). The general methodological principles involved here are evident in his insistence on interpreting the organic connection of internal and international forces in Italian nation-formation as a problem of 'co-ordination and subordination' (Gramsci 1985: 199, Q21§1) and in his spatialised as well as historical analyses of the development, consolidation and crises of coherent historical blocs formed through reciprocal linkages between structure and superstructure. Finally, far from affirming that there is a simple 'nested hierarchy' of scales from the local to the global with distinct sets of economic, political and social relations on each scale, Gramsci was especially sensitive to the ways in which tangled hierarchies of scale acted as a source of economic, political and socio-economic instability. This can be seen, for example, in his comment that:

> In the period after 1870, with the colonial expansion of Europe, all these elements change: the internal and international organisational relations of the state become more complex and massive, and the Forty-Eightist formula of the 'Permanent Revolution' is expanded and transcended in political science by the formula of 'civil hegemony. (Gramsci 1971: 243, Q13§7)

A crucial issue in the analysis of scale is the relative dominance of different scales of economic, political, intellectual and moral life. Scale dominance is 'the power which organisations at certain spatial scales are able to exercise over organisations at other, higher or lower scales' (Collinge 1999: 568). It can derive from the general relationship among different scales considered as strategically selective terrains of power and domination and/or from the features, characteristics, capacities and activities of organisations located at different scales. One or more scales can gain special socio-political significance by playing the dominant role in the scale division of labour within and across different fields of social practice. In turn, nodal scales are non-dominant overall but nonetheless serve as the primary loci for delivering certain activities in a given spatio-temporal order or matrix (Collinge 1999: 569). Finally, subaltern scales are marginal or peripheral but may also become sites of resistance.

Gramsci operates implicitly with these distinctions in analysing historical and contemporary patterns of domination. For example, he can be interpreted as arguing that the national level was nodal rather than dominant in Italian state- and nation-building. For he lived in a conjuncture when, *Italia fatta, bisogna fare gli Italiani* (Italy being made, we must make the Italians) and could not have presumed the primacy of the national scale – especially politically – that appeared to characterise the dominant powers in continental Europe, namely, France and Germany. He argued that Italy was weakly integrated domestically, the national scale had not yet become dominant over local and regional scales, and that this posed problems both for the completion of the bourgeois revolution and for revolutionary communist strategy. Gramsci was also acutely aware of the international weakness of the Italian state and the influence of external factors on its development. On the other hand, he saw 'Italian Catholicism was felt not only as a surrogate for the spirit of the nation and the state but also as a worldwide hegemonic institution, an imperialistic spirit' (Gramsci 1985: 220–221, Q17§8). He also recognised the distinction between dominant and nodal scales on a continental as opposed to the world scale. Concerning European and World politics, for example, he wrote:

These two are not the same thing. In a duel between Berlin and Paris or between Paris and Rome, the winner is not master of the world. Europe has lost its importance and world politics depends more on London, Washington, Moscow, Tokyo than it does on the Continent. (Gramsci 1995: 195, Q2§24)

And, more generally, he remarked on the need to examine

the organic relations between the domestic and foreign policies of a state. Is it domestic policies which determine foreign policy, or vice versa? In this case too, it will be necessary to distinguish: between great powers, with relative international autonomy, and other powers; also, between different forms of government (a government like that of Napoleon III had two policies, apparently—reactionary internally, and liberal abroad). (Gramsci 1971: 264, Q8§141)

In short, for Gramsci, the international order should not be studied in terms of the mechanical interaction among formally sovereign nation-states but as a concrete, emergent international order, based on an informal hierarchy of states[5] and other international forces (such as Catholicism) that were characterised by complex and tangled internal and external relations. Thus his analyses of struggles for national hegemony were not confined to the national but closely examined the articulation and, indeed, interpenetration, of the local, regional, national and supranational scales. He commented on the opportunities and constraints involved for different social forces in the dissociation of scales across different institutional orders – notably the disjunction between the increasing formation of the world market and the continued survival of national states (Gramsci 1995: 220, Q15§5). He discussed the different scalar horizons of action and influence associated with such dissociations. The best-known example of this, of course, is the cosmopolitanism and external orientation of traditional intellectuals in Italy from Imperial Rome to the contemporary Catholic Church based in Rome and their impact on Italian and European politics. And, just as he remarked on the implications of dissociation and the possibilities of scale jumping available to some social forces but not others, he also identified and elaborated the need for new forms of interscalar articulation to mobilise multiple social forces behind specific projects and/or to form new historical blocs. This is especially clear in his comments on the Southern Question (see below) and on the appropriate political strategies to enable the Soviet Union to break out of the isolation produced by Stalin's policy of 'socialism in one country'.

Arguments about different scales of economic, political, intellectual and cultural organisation were also central to his analyses of individual identity formation and the creation of collective wills. For example, noting that Pirandello identified himself as local, national and European, Gramsci argued that he could only become an Italian and national writer because he had deprovincialised himself and become European (Gramsci 1985: 139, Q9§134; 141–142, Q14§15). This observation may reflect Gramsci's own thoughts regarding whether he himself was Albanian, Sardinian,

Italian or, perhaps, an internationalist starting out from a local, regional and national viewpoint (Gramsci 1994a: 267; 1994b: 86). More generally, Gramsci distinguished between the social functions of *northern* (industrial, technical) and *southern* (rural, organic) intellectuals in building different types of hegemony (Gramsci 1971: 11–12, Q12§1; 93–94, Q19§26). He also observed that the cosmopolitan role of traditional Italian intellectuals contributed to the continued territorial disintegration of the peninsular (Gramsci 1971: 18–19, Q12§1). And, in another example of scalar dissociation, he noted that intellectuals, because of their disembedding from national life, might fail to develop a specific national-popular project and draw instead on other national complexes or present abstract and cosmopolitan philosophies and world-views (Gramsci 1985: 118, Q15§20).

Gramsci and the Southern Question

The Southern Question was posed in many ways as a central problem in Italian state- and nation-building. Gramsci analysed these twin processes in terms of the 'passive revolution' that occurred as the Italian northern bourgeoisie sought to unify the peninsula in the face of a heterogeneous and divided population and vast regional disparities (Davis 1979). Italy's weak economic, political and social integration and the lack of dominance of the national scale inform Gramsci's early political writings, the 'Lyons Theses' (co-authored with Togliatti), and his incomplete essay on 'Some Aspects of the Southern Question' (1926). These discuss three issues: (a) the complex, multi-layered economic and political subordination of secondary centres of accumulation to the northern industrial and financial centre and its implications for class alliances; (b) the resulting complexities of class formation, regional disparities and fragmented forms of intellectual and moral life that block a Jacobin road to national unification; and (c) the problems this poses for the leading role of the proletariat, which is 'a minority of the working population and geographically distributed in such a manner, that it cannot presume to lead a victorious struggle for power unless it has previously resolved very precisely the problem of its relations with the peasant class' (Gramsci 1978: 316, cf. 233–234, 299). Thus, in their *Lyons Theses*, Gramsci and Togliatti write:

> Industrialism, which is the essential part of capitalism, is very weak in Italy. Its possibilities for development are limited, both because of the geographical situation and because of the lack of raw materials. It therefore does not succeed in absorbing the majority of the Italian population (4 million industrial workers exist side by side with $3^{1}/_{2}$ million agricultural workers and 4 million peasants). To industrialism, there is counterposed an agriculture which naturally presents itself as the basis of the country's economy. The extremely varied conditions of the terrain, and the resulting differences in cultivation and in systems of tenancy, however, cause a high degree of differentiation among the rural strata, with a prevalence of poor strata, nearer to the conditions of the proletariat and more liable to be influenced by it and accept its leadership.

Between the industrial and agrarian classes, there lies a fairly extensive urban petty bourgeoisie, which is of very great significance. It consists mainly of artisans, professional men and state employees. (Gramsci 1978: 343)

Gramsci takes this theme up again in his essay on the Southern Question. He claims that the capacity of the Italian proletariat, which is a minority class and geographically concentrated in the north, to become the leading (*dirigente*) and dominant class depends on its capacity to form class alliances, mobilising in particular the real consent and active support of the broad peasant masses (1978: 79–82, 129–131, 347, 449–450). But he adds the peasant question is historically determined in Italy; it is not the 'peasant and agrarian question in general'. In Italy the peasant question, through the specific Italian tradition, and the specific development of Italian history, has taken two typical and particular forms – the Vatican and Southern Questions (Gramsci 1978: 443).

This argument, his earlier analyses and his *Prison Notebooks* all involve a deeply spatialised rather than a-spatial analysis of classes, social categories and political forces. Gramsci identified five crucial forces in Italy based on the relation between city and countryside: '1. the Northern urban force; 2. the Southern rural force; 3. the Northern-Central rural force; 4. the rural force of Sicily; 5. that of Sardinia' (Gramsci 1971: 98, Q19§26). On this basis, he analysed the inter-urban and inter-regional relations on the analogy of a train whose locomotive would be the northern urban force. The key question then becomes which other forces should be mobilised by this locomotive to effect a rapid and successful path to communism. Accordingly he recommended that the communist party promote a hegemonic alliance of the proletariat with the peasantry and petty-bourgeois intellectuals and lead them in a war of position before the final military-political resolution of the conflict. This would dissolve the defensive alliance between northern industrialists and southern landowners, which also benefited from rural and urban petty-bourgeois support.

Gramsci on Economic Geography

Gramsci's analyses of economic relations are spatial as well as historical. Indeed, one could say that they are spatial because they are historical or, better still, that they are inherently spatio-temporal. Rejecting classical and vulgar political economy as well economic liberalism and economistic Marxism, he emphasised the broad historical location and specific spatio-temporal specificities of economic organisation and economic regularities. This is why he substituted the notion of *mercato determinato* (definite forms of organising and regulating market relations with their associated laws of tendency) for transhistorical economic analysis based on the actions of rational economic man. Thus he explored dependent development in the *Mezzogiorno* and the general tendency towards internal colonialism in Italy; the interrelations between different economic places and spaces, including geographical variations in relationships between town and country and how different parties aimed to remodel this relationship (Gramsci 1971: 90–102, Q19§26);

and the interconnection, articulation. and real or potential tensions between local, regional, national, international and transnational economies. He was well attuned to the spatial division of labour, issues of the differential integration of rural, urban and regional economies both within a national territory and in relation to foreign markets, the importance of scale in an emerging world market, and the conflict between place and space. And he paid special attention theoretically and practically to the class relations that follow from the placing, spacing and scaling of economic organisation. In short, as Morera, an acute interpreter of Gramsci's 'absolute historicism', argues 'Gramsci not only rejected sociology for abstracting from time conditions, but also from space. That is, from the geographical conditions of social processes' (Morera 1990: 89).

Turning to international economic relations, Gramsci attacked liberalism for taking the nation-state as its horizon of economic policy-making and assuming that the world economy could safely be left to market regulation (Vacca 1999: 160). In the same context, he argued that *laissez-faire, laissez-passer* could not be rooted in agriculture but only in commerce and strong industry – suggesting that different economic and political strategies and policies were grounded in specific relations to place and space. He also remarked upon the growing contradiction between cosmopolitanism in the world market and the nationalism of political life – which, he claimed, had to be the starting point for any move to internationalism in the revolutionary socialist movement (Gramsci 1995: 220, Q15§5). Gramsci was interested in the dynamics of uneven and combined development in an emerging global capitalism. His notes on Americanism and Fordism explored how the centre of economic dynamism was moving from old Europe to the United States and was prompting Europe to adapt. He did not adopt a narrowly economically-determinist view of American economic progress here – let alone a simplistic technological determinism. Instead he examined the specific historical and material conditions that had enabled a new techno-economic paradigm to develop there, including the establishment of an *economia programmatica* at the level of the enterprise. the factory town and the wider society. The originality and significance of Fordism as accumulation regime, mode of regulation and way of life hindered its diffusion to Europe because this required more than the export of technical means of production and a technical division of labour. Nonetheless, to the extent that it did spread to Europe, it also facilitated the hegemony of American imperialism.

In contrast to the Comintern, Gramsci emphasised the shift in the centre of economic gravity from Europe to the United States, which had developed a more rationally organised economy. If workers could take the lead in adopting this model, it could become the basis for the working class to guide world historical development (Vacca 1999: 9; Baratta 1997). But he also asked prophetically whether the centre of gravity might shift again, this time from the Atlantic to the Pacific.

The largest masses of the world's population are in the Pacific. If China and India were to become modern nations with great volumes of industrial production, their consequent detachment from a dependency on Europe would in fact rupture the current equilibrium: transformation of the American continent, shift in the axis of American life from the Atlantic to the Pacific seaboard, etc. (Gramsci 1995: 196, Q5§8)

Gramsci on Territoriality and State Power

Gramsci did not naturalise or fetishise national territory as the pre-given or pre-destined basis of state formation – and could not have done, indeed, given the historical problems of nation formation that he recognised and also struggled to overcome. The territorialisation of political power is a crucial first material step in national state formation and nation building.[6] It is unsurprising, then, that Gramsci studied the problems of the transition from medieval communes to absolutism and thence to a bourgeois liberal democratic state (e.g., Italy vs the Netherlands) and the need to break out of the economic-corporate phase of medieval urban relations with their political fragmentation. Thus he noted that the chief defect of previous Italian history was not class oppression but the absence of definite class formation, due to the fact that 'in Italy political, territorial and national unity enjoy a scanty tradition (or perhaps no tradition at all)' (Gramsci 1971: 274, Q3§46). Gramsci was also aware that territorial unity did not itself ensure political unity. This is apparent in his contrast between Bodin and Machiavelli:

> Bodin lays the foundations of political science in France on a terrain which is far more advanced and complex than that which Italy offered to Machiavelli. For Bodin the question is not that of founding the territorially united (national) state – i.e., of going back to the time of Louis XI –but of balancing the conflict-ing social forces within this already strong and well-implanted state. Bodin is interested in the moment of consent, not in the moment of force. (Gramsci 1971: 142, Q13§13)

Securing political unity also requires the institutional integration of the state through appropriate state forms, its embedding in the wider ensemble of social relations, and its capacity to engage in relatively unified action through appropriate state and national-popular projects. As symptoms of a failed national unification project in Italy, he regularly cited the Vatican and Southern Questions and the passive revolu-tion that occurred under the domination of Piedmont and the Moderate Party. And, in one of his most famous comparisons in state theory, he claims that:

> In the East the state was everything, civil society was primordial and gelati-nous; in the West, there was a proper relation between state and civil society, and when the state trembled a sturdy structure of civil society was at once revealed. (Gramsci 1971: 238, Q7§16)

This approach raised crucial issues concerning passive revolution, hegemony, and the historical bloc. Gramsci provides many other examples of problems in the mechanisms in and through which political unity is created and identifies enormous variability in its forms – ranging from sheer coercion through force–fraud–corruption and passive revolution to inclusive hegemony. Nor did he see this mainly as a technical question of public administration, political reform of the state apparatus, or constitutional design. Instead it was deeply related to the social bases of the state in class, religious–secular and territorial terms and to the concomitant articulation between political and civil society to form the state in its integral sense. This is reflected in the rich conceptual vocabulary he developed for analysing class relations and the different moments in the balance of forces in economic, political, military, intellectual and moral terms. And, for present purposes, it is especially important to note how much attention he paid to the local, regional and urban–rural origins and the cosmopolitan–national orientations of intellectuals, functionaries, bureaucrats, soldiers, the clergy and so forth (Gramsci 1971: 79, Q19§24; 203–204, Q13§29; 214–217, Q13§23; Gramsci 1995: 12, Q1§52). For, far from being a neutral instrument with wide-ranging capacities, the state had to be analysed theoretically and addressed politically in terms of its embedding in the wider ensemble of social relations in all their spatio-temporal specificity. This in turn implies the spatiality as well as the historicity of the state as a social relation.

> The chief defect of Italian intellectuals was not that they formed a powerful and resilient 'cultural hegemony', but that, because they were cosmopolitan rather than national, no authentic hegemony had ever been realised. Like the artificial or perverted state hegemony of Piedmont, the cultural tradition deriving from the Renaissance humanists could provide only a weak and eccentric form of hegemony, because it was not national. (Ghosh 2001: 36)

Gramsci and International Relations

Although Gramsci regrets the failure of the Italian nation-state compared with France's successful Jacobin state-building project, he recognises that even this took decades to accomplish and that contemporary nation-states were being forged in a much changed and deeply contested international context. For example, he suggests that, whereas Versailles re-established the prerogatives of nation-states, the Bolshevik world revolution project aimed at an eventual society of nations. After Versailles, the nation could no longer remain, if it ever had fully been, the dominant horizon of state life. Thus it was crucial to analyse how the internal balance of forces was overdetermined by international forces and a country's geopolitical position and to assess whether and how the latter balance modifies domestic forces, reinforcing or breaking progressive and revolutionary movements (Gramsci 1971: 116, Q10II§61). He therefore deemed it 'necessary to take into account the fact that international relations intertwine with these internal relations of nation-states, creating new, unique and historically concrete combinations' (Gramsci 1971: 182, Q13§17). He also noted that winning international hegemony was partly an educational relationship, affecting complexes of national and continental civilisations (Gramsci 1971: 350, Q10II§44;

cf. Gramsci 1995: 207–208, Q3§5). This applied not only to Americanism and Fordism but also to the role of the international communist movement and its involvement in united front activities.

When exploring the international dimensions of economic, political and sociocultural relations, Gramsci did not assume that the basic units of international relations were national economies, national states, or nationally-constituted civil societies. Instead, he explored the mutual implications of economic and political organisation, their social and cultural presuppositions, and the consequences of the dissociation of the dominant scales of economic, political, intellectual and moral life. This made him sensitive to the complexities of interscalar relations and he never assumed that they were ordered in a simple nested hierarchy.[7]

Gramsci's approach to international relations was never presented in systematic form. But it is nonetheless worth drawing out some of its implications because of the very widespread tendency to try to reconstruct it on the basis of a simple generalisation of his arguments from a presumed national scale to the transatlantic or wider transnational scale. But a simplified 're-scaling' of concepts such as passive revolution, historical bloc, hegemony, power bloc, etc., fails to capture the complexities of Gramsci's engagement with questions of place, space and scale. His philosophy of praxis and vernacular materialism (Ives 2004) made him very sensitive to the social construction of social relations, institutions and identities, including their international dimensions. Indeed he was careful to emphasise the social constitution of categories such as 'North–South' and 'East' and 'West', their reflection of the viewpoint of European cultured classes, their ideological representation of differences between civilisations, and their material significance in practical life (Gramsci 1971: 447, Q11§20). This also meant that he was interested in the material and intellectual struggles to reconstruct place, space and scale in response to the crisis of liberalism, dependent development and internal colonialism in Italy and to analogous crises in the international order with its imperialist rivalries and clash between capitalism and a fledgling socialism.

First, whereas Marx mainly developed an abstract-simple analysis of the capitalist mode of production, Gramsci took this for granted and focused on concrete conjunctures in emerging and developed capitalist social formations in a world shaped by imperialism and the Bolshevik Revolution. Second, Gramsci integrated his analysis of structure and superstructure with concrete political analyses. This was a key element in his concept of historical bloc and his systematic concern with the role of intellectuals in mediating these relations (see, for example, Portelli 1972). This analysis began beneath the national scale and extended beyond it (e.g., his analyses of Italian intellectuals, Americanism and Fordism, and failure of the Bolshevik Revolution to spread from the 'East' to the 'West'). Third, in opposing economism both theoretically and politically, Gramsci showed the role of political and civil society in constituting and reproducing economic relations on diverse scales up to and including the international. Fourth, in contrast to (neo-)realism in more recent International Relations theory, Gramsci did not fetishise the nation-state as the basic unit or scale of analysis. Indeed his work could be interpreted as a protracted reflection on 'the failure of the Italian state to constitute itself as a national state – a failure that reflects the laborious emergence of a modern Italian nation, impeded by a balance of internal and international forces' (Gramsci 1985: 199, Q21§1). Fifth, writing during and after the Great War with its inter-imperialist rivalries and open hostility between the capitalist bloc and the fledgling Soviet Union, Gramsci was especially concerned with two issues: (a) the international as well as national and regional context of the defeat of the working class movement and the rise of fascism; and (b) the spread of Americanism and Fordism as the basis for modernisation in Italy and Europe more generally. And, sixth, he was strongly interested in International Relations and studied work on geopolitics and demo-politics (which would now be called bio-politics) to better understand the political implications of the international balance of forces.

In this context, and in contrast to the methodological nationalism that still affects much thinking on International Relations, Gramsci did not draw a rigid distinction between the national and the international but explored issues of interscalar articulation and reciprocal influence in a more complex and dialectical manner.

> Do international relations precede or follow (logically) fundamental social relations? There can be no doubt that they follow. Any organic innovation in the social structure, through its technical-military expressions, modifies organically absolute and relative relations in the international field too. Even the geographical position of a national State does not precede but follows (logically) structural changes, although it also reacts back upon them to a certain extent (to the extent precisely to which superstructures react upon the structure, politics on economics, etc.). However, international relations react both passively and actively on political relations (of hegemony among the parties). (Gramsci 1971: 176, Q13§2)

Gramsci explores the links between economic, political and international strategy in his analysis of the inter-linkage between domestic class alliances and foreign economic policy. Italy's ruling class had to choose between rural democracy based on 'an alliance with the Southern peasants, a policy of free trade, universal suffrage, administrative decentralisation and low prices for industrial products'; or 'a capitalist/worker industrial bloc, without universal suffrage, with tariff barriers, with the maintenance of a highly centralised state (the expression of bourgeois dominion over the peasants, especially in the South and the Islands), and with a reformist policy on wages and trade-union freedoms' (Gramsci 1978: 449–450). As Gramsci then immediately added, it was no accident that the ruling class chose the latter solution.

Conclusions

Gramsci not only emphasised the *historical specificity* of all social relations but was also less explicitly attuned to their distinctive *location in place, space and scale*. Thus almost all of his crucial concepts are sensitive to issues of place, space and scale as well as to issues of periodisation, historical structures, specific conjunctures and social dynamics. Whether we consider the relations of production, the determined market (*mercato determinato*), the contrast between the dynamism of Americanism and Fordism and the relative stagnation of European and Soviet planned economies, the forms of class relations (economically, politically, intellectually), the territoriality of state formation and the relative strengths or weakness of specific states (considered both in terms of political and civil society), the spatial roots of intellectuals and their different functions in economic, political and moral organisation, the nature of political alliances, the appropriate forms of economic–corporate, political, and military strategy, etc., Gramsci emerges as a spatial thinker as much as he does as an historical thinker. This is rooted in his profoundly historicist concern with the spatio-temporality of all social relations. In addition, Gramsci's analysis of strategy was objectively as well as metaphorically sensitive to temporality and spatiality. Not only did Gramsci emphasise the interweaving of different temporalities into complex conjunctures and situations and search for the openings between a path-dependent present and possible futures. But he also regarded strategy as inherently spatial. He was always aware of the need to mobilise in and across specific places, spaces and scales, each with their own distinctive determinations and strategic selectivities. At stake in both cases is the transformation of spatio-temporal horizons of action and the interweaving of different temporalities and spatialities. It is only in this context that his notions of war of position and war of manoeuvre make sense. For Gramsci's interest in place, space and scale was not merely academic but had to do with his analysis of revolutionary conjunctures. Thus he argues that a collective will must be formed 'with the degree necessary and sufficient to achieve an action which is co-ordinated and simultaneous in the time and the geographical space in which the historical event takes place' (Gramsci 1971: 194, Q8§195). In short, his comments on the political failures of left strategy are also spatially as well as historically attuned.

Notes

1. For Said, Gramsci offered 'an essentially geographical, territorial apprehension of human history and society ... far more than Lukács he was political in the practical sense, conceiving of politics as a contest over territory, both actual and historical, to be won, fought over, controlled, held, lost, gained' (Said 2001: 464).

2. Following the convention established in this volume, reference to the Gramsci anthologies is accompanied by a citation of the notebook number (Q) and section (§).

3. Cf. Gramsci's argument that one can describe Italy's 'Jacobin' intellectuals as '"Italian" only because culture for many centuries was the only Italian "national" manifestation; this is simply a verbal illusion. Where was the basis for this Italian culture? It was not in Italy; this "Italian" culture is the continuation of the medieval cosmopolitanism linked to the tradition of the Empire and the Church. Universal concepts with "geographical" seats in Italy' (Gramsci 1971: 117, Q10II§61).

4. While Gramsci argues that natural resources and landscapes constrain as well as facilitate social practice, this does not involve monocausal determinism. Indeed, as Pandolfi notes, his 'vision of territory differed from the dangerous and arrogant categorisations of some proponents of the Southern Question, and he was careful to dissociate himself from their essentialism. Such geographical deter-

minisms ... only legitimated the authoritarian and imperialistic stances of the North. Rather, territoriality was a political perimeter; it referred to a peripheral place subject to imperial and strategic domination by the center' (Pandolfi 1998: 286).

5. Gramsci examined imperialism and imperialist rivalries within the context of a hierarchy of advanced capitalist, semi-advanced and peripheral capitalist states (e.g., England and Germany, France and Czechoslovakia, and Italy respectively) (Ghosh 2001: 3–4).

6. Gramsci notes how Rudolf Kjellén, a Swedish sociologist, sought to 'construct a science of the state and of politics on a new basis, taking as his starting point the territorial unit as organised politically (development of the geographical sciences – physical geography, anthropogeography, geopolitics) and the mass of human beings living in society on that territory (geo-politics and demopolitics)' (Gramsci 1995: 325, Q23§25).

7. Gramsci writes that 'a particular ideology, for instance, born in a highly developed country, is disseminated in less developed countries, impinging on the local interplay of combinations. This relation between international forces and national forces is further complicated by the existence within every state of several structurally diverse territorial sectors, with diverse relations of force at all levels (Gramsci 1971: 182, Q13§17).

Acknowledgements

The author would like to thank the two anonymous referees for their helpful comments and suggestions.

References

Baratta, G. (1997) Lotte di egemonia nell'epoca di 'Americanismo e postfordismo', *Critica Marxista,* 4, pp. 47–58.

Brandist, C. (1996) Gramsci, Bakhtin, and the semiotics of hegemony, *New Left Review* (I), 216, 94–110.

Collinge, C. (1999) Self-organisation of society by scale: a spatial reworking of regulation theory, *Environment and Planning D: Society and Space,* 17(5), pp. 557–574.

Davis, J.A. (Ed.) (1979) *Gramsci and Italy's Passive Revolution* (London: Croom Helm).

Forgacs, D. & Nowell-Smith, G. (1985)Introduction to language, linguistics, and folklore, in: Gramsci, A., *Selections from Cultural Writings,* ed. D. Forgacs & G. Nowell-Smith, trans. W. Boelhower, pp. 164–167 (London: Lawrence and Wishart).

Ghosh, P. (2001) Gramscian hegemony: an absolutely historicist approach, *History of European Ideas,* 27(1), pp. 1–43.

Gramsci, A. (1971) *Selections from Prison Notebooks,* ed. and trans. Q. Hoare & G. Nowell-Smith (London: Lawrence and Wishart).

Gramsci, A. (1977) *Selections from Political Writings 1910–1920,* ed. Q. Hoare, trans. J. Matthews (London: Lawrence and Wishart).

Gramsci, A. (1978) *Selections from Political Writings 1921–1926,* ed. Q. Hoare & G. Nowell-Smith (London: Lawrence and Wishart).

Gramsci, A. (1985) *Selections from Cultural Writings,* ed. D. Forgacs & G. Nowell-Smith, trans. W. Boelhower (London: Lawrence and Wishart).

Gramsci, A. (1994a) *Letters from Prison,* vol.1, ed. F. Rosengarten, trans. R. Rosenthal (New York: Columbia University Press).

Gramsci, A. (1994b) *Letters from Prison,* vol.2, ed. F. Rosengarten, trans. R. Rosenthal (New York: Columbia University Press).

Gramsci, A. (1995) *Further Selections from Prison Notebooks,* ed. and trans. D. Boothman (London: Lawrence and Wishart).

Harvey, D. (1982) *The Limits to Capital* (Oxford: Blackwell).

Helsloot, N. (1989) Linguists of all countries, unite! On Gramsci's premise of coherence, *Journal of Pragmatics*, 13(4), pp. 547–566.

Hoare, Q. & G. Nowell-Smith (1971) Introduction, in Gramsci, A *Selections from Prison Notebooks*, ed. and trans. Q. Hoare & G. Nowell-Smith, pp. xvii–xcvi (London: Lawrence and Wishart).

Ives, P. (2004) *Language and Hegemony in Gramsci* (London: Pluto).

Levy, C. (1999) *Gramsci and the Anarchists* (Oxford: Berg).

Lo Piparo, F. (1979) *Lingua, intelletuali, egemonia in Gramsci* (Bari: Laterza).

Morera, E. (1990) *Gramsci's Historicism: A Realist Interpretation* (London: Routledge)

Pandolfi, M. (1998) Two Italies: rhetorical figures of failed nationhood, in Schneider, J. (Ed.), *Italy's "Southern Question"*, pp. 385–289 (Oxford: Berg).

Portelli, H. (1973) *Gramsci y el bloque histórico* (Mexico: Siglo Veintiuno).

Said, E.W. (2001) History, literature, and geography, in Said, E.W., *Reflections on Exile and Other Literary and Cultural Essays*, pp. 453–473 (London: Granta).

Vacca, G. (1999) *Appuntamenti con Gramsci. Introduzione allo Studio dei Quaderni del Carcere* (Rome: Carocci).

A Double Reading of Gramsci: Beyond the Logic of Contingency

ADAM DAVID MORTON

The dialectical view of history developed by Antonio Gramsci was explicitly cast as a direct criticism of the speculative and idealist philosophy of Benedetto Croce (1866–1952), who spearheaded liberalism in Italy along with Giovanni Gentile (1874–1944), an official philosopher of Fascism. Gramsci regarded Croce as a philosopher that developed a subjective account of history based on the progression of philosophical thought rather than specific conditions of class struggle posed by problems of historical development (Gramsci 1995: 343–348, Q10I§7, §8; 369–370,

Q10II§1).[1] It is in this sense that Eric Hobsbawm provides an apt description of Croce as the first 'post-Marxist' (Hobsbawm 1987: 286). By contrast, the dialectical view of history advanced by Gramsci was developed as part of a practical struggle against the philosophy of Croce who was saturating the intellectual life of Italy with a liberal point of view. To this degree Gramsci explicitly presented his theory of history as 'Anti-Croce' in contesting liberal reformism in Italy to match the *Anti-Dühring* of Frederick Engels (Engels 1987; Gramsci 1995: 354–356, Q10I§11; 379–380, Q6§107). Put in Gramsci's own words, 'the philosophy of praxis is precisely the concrete historicisation of philosophy and its identification with history' (Gramsci 1971: 436, Q11§22).

The purpose of this essay is to embark on a 'double reading' of Gramsci's theory of history. The practice of a double reading entails embarking on a commentary of a first dominant reading to demonstrate how certain stable assumptions are rendered and articulated about a text which silence alternative readings. Then a second reading is produced that reveals elements of internal tension within the first reading to thereby expose and unsettle such assumptions and cast doubt on the reading (see Ashley 1988). This will proceed by, first, examining dominant contemporary post-Marxist claims that they develop a 'Gramscian matrix' which focuses on contingent hegemonic articulations within the plane of discursive practices. In the direct words of Ernesto Laclau and Chantal Mouffe (2001: xi) this 'means nothing other than retrieving an act of political institution that finds its source and motivation nowhere but in itself'. As Richard Bellamy (2001: 210) has noted, this 'recent post-Marxist reading of Gramsci can be regarded as an implicit return to his Crocean radical alternative'. On the basis of examining Laclau and Mouffe's dominant post-Marxist claims about Gramsci, a second reading is then offered that demonstrates how the latter's focus on changes in social relations, from which arise the problems that philosophers set themselves and elaborate on, threatens discourse-theoretical assumptions and thus both traditional idealism and materialism. This second reading is able to expose, unsettle and reveal problems with the stance that history is under the sway of ideas, which results in expunging social conflict over property relations from history and hypostatising capitalist exploitation. It is in this sense that such post-Marxists can be exposed, in the terms of Marx and Engels in *The German Ideology* (1976: 60), as 'conceptive ideologists', a point that will be affirmed in more detail in the conclusion.

Developing a double reading of Gramsci relates not to considering his texts as the product of interpretations elaborated from a point of view external to history, but of the formulation of political problems on the conception of political practice internal to history. Hence a double reading offers the potential to display 'alternate effects' of a text whilst functioning as an intervention in debate about political theory *and* practice that goes to the nub of understanding and acting within history (Althusser 1999: 32). Hence, following Gramsci's recommendation to embark on a first 'disinterested' reading, allowing an introduction to the issues at stake, and then a second 'critical' reading focusing more on the cracks, veilings, pentimenti or disguises between form and content (Gramsci 1994a: 359; Gramsci 1985 119–121, Q6§62;

370–374 Q21§13). It is through this technique of a double reading that insight is afforded into *both* the questionable stabilising effects of viewing history as an association of discourses *and* the equally problematic assembly of an extrinsic historical account based on objective economic forces. This leads to the realisation that a distinct philosophy of the internal relationship of ideas and material processes exists within historical materialism so that, 'it is not true that the philosophy of praxis "detaches" the structure from the superstructures when, instead, it conceives their development as intimately bound together and necessarily interrelated and reciprocal' (Gramsci 1995: 414, Q10II§41i).

The Logic of Contingency, Articulation and Discourse

It is taken as a given by Laclau and Mouffe that 'the era of normative epistemologies has come to an end' and that rereading Marxist theory itself deserves no more than deconstructing its central categories of analysis, abandoning the conception of subjectivity and social classes it offers, and its world-historical understanding of the consequences of combined and uneven development (Laclau & Mouffe 2001: 3, 4). On the basis of demolishing a self-identified 'orthodoxy' within Second International Marxism (Luxemburg, Kautsky, Plekhanov, Lenin, Trotsky) – that upholds a rationalist coincidence of 'interests' among pre-constituted classes – the concept of hegemony is nonetheless retained. It is argued that hegemony encompasses a field of political articulation within which identities are internally related so that hegemony is considered as a discursive 'nodal point' within a completely open system of articulatory practices. Hence 'both the hegemonic force and the ensemble of hegemonised elements would constitute themselves on the same plane – the general field of discursivity' (Laclau & Mouffe 2001: 135). A canon of Marxist theorising is thus deemed to uphold the structuring of social relations within which there is an essentialist conception of class agents linked to relations of production, endowed with objective historical interests. Within this reading of historical materialism, the social is sutured to such a degree that the very purpose of hegemony is eliminated. By contrast, the relational identities of social agents are viewed to emerge from within articulatory practices of discursive production. Hegemony therefore denotes a social space of relational identities joined within a discursive formation. It is 'not a determinable location within a topography of the social', but a dispersion, detotalisation and decentring of subject positions within an intertextuality that 'overflows it' due to the infinitude of discursivity (Laclau & Mouffe 2001: 113, 115, 139). What this signals is 'the impossibility of closure (i.e. the impossibility of society)', that is, 'presented as the precariousness of every identity, which manifests itself as a continuous movement of differences' (Laclau & Mouffe 2001: 122). Due to the total indeterminacy of the social, the discursive production of hegemony becomes a wholly contingent practice loosened from the moorings of past historical developments and present economic forms shaping human society. Contentiously, the unfolding of this logic of contingency, articulation and discourse is based on the view that 'there is no logical connection whatsoever between positions in the relations of production and the mentality of the producers' (Laclau & Mouffe 2001: 84–85).

This re-presentation of historical materialism, as the philosophical embodiment of the 'extra-mental character of the real' by Laclau and Mouffe (2001: 123), is itself based on a closed reading of Gramsci (also see Ives 2004b: 144–160). Rather than identifying and internalising Gramsci's method of thinking – by thinking in a Gramscian way about alternative historical and contemporary contexts – the opportunity to open up and engage with his complex historicist mode of thought (or philosophy of praxis) is prevented. This is, firstly, most meaningfully revealed in Laclau and Mouffe's (2001: 66) assertion that Gramscian categories should 'be situated at the level of the general theory of Marxism, and cannot be referred to specific geographical contexts'. Yet such a move obliterates the multiple concrete practical historical specificities that occupied Gramsci: in terms of Italian and European state formation embodied in 'the war between [capitalist] property rights and the feudal right of acquisition' (Gramsci 1975: 77); the failure of both liberalism and socialism in Italy; the study of the role of intellectuals, their origins and groupings within the enterprise of state and civil society relations; the 'class feeling' and 'pedagogic function' of the modern state linked to capitalism which 'begins the dissolution of traditional relations inherent in the institution of the family and in religious myth' to inculcate 'new, more complex and rigid norms and habits of order'; or the play of class struggle within *both* 'the development of international relations between states' and 'various groups that form a class within a nation' (Gramsci 1971: 298, Q22§9; Gramsci 1975: 62–64, 113). Additionally, such a move also obviates any understanding of the absolute historicism that occupied Gramsci, based on acknowledging the role of both past forms of thought and previous historical conditions in shaping subsequent ideas and existing social relations, through a dialogue between past and present (Morton 2003). The combined effect of this reading is that Laclau and Mouffe stop, indeed prevent, the texts of historical materialism (such as the *Prison Notebooks*) from generating new meanings in different contexts. It is then on this basis that they reject historical materialism and falsely assert a difference from the past. 'It is no longer possible to maintain the conception of subjectivity and classes elaborated by Marxism, nor its vision of the historical course of capitalist development' (Laclau & Mouffe 2001: 4). Within the history of ideas they succumb to the approach of particularism, which views the past as marked by an otherness that does not have purchase on the present to uphold 'a universal, non-contextual recommendation which claims to be true, but the possibility of whose truth is eliminated by virtue of its claim being non-contextual, both in space and time' (King 2000: 5, 301–302). It is this reading of Gramsci that permits a reduction of his concepts (e.g. hegemony and historical bloc) to undefined social and political spaces that are unified by discursive formations within an irreducible pluralism.

Beyond this closure, hegemony also becomes rendered as a constant interplay between autonomous and indeterminate discourses rather than linked to specific social interests and class identities in formation. This results in abstracting forms of collective agency from the prevailing social order and isolating and separating issues from social conditions and material interests. The problem here is that there is a failure to grasp the conditions of inequality and exploitation that constitute and confront social forces and shape processes of identity formation. The point that peoples' identities are constituted within the context of existing social relations, which are to some extent inherited from and shaped by past social conditions, is largely ignored. Questions attempting to ascertain what aspects of social experience enable the articulation of certain discourses, within the struggle over hegemony, are thus suppressed.

The result is an ideological hypostatisation of social conflict, formalised within the category of an antagonistic but totally contingent society, independent of relations immanent to the historical process itself. Rather than a conflict over property relations, history thus becomes a succession of articulatory practices discursively produced and formed. History has no basis in social conflicts so that 'contingency is held up as a standard of truth' (Adorno 1974: 154). One may then say with Adorno (1974: 245) that such a

negative philosophy, dissolving everything, dissolves even the dissolvent. But the new form in which it claims to suspend and preserve both, dissolved and dissolvent, can never emerge in a pure state from an antagonistic society. As long as domination reproduces itself, the old quality reappears unrefined in the dissolving of the dissolvent: in a radical sense no leap is made at all.

As witnessed earlier, the dissolvent of discursivity offers a wholly contingent and open view of the social, leading to the extreme stance of the 'impossibility of society'. One is reminded here of an invidious analogue with Margaret Thatcher's (1987: 8–10) aphorism that 'there is no such thing as society'. The characteristic conferred on the social by Laclau and Mouffe is one of extreme individuation that overlooks the processes of reification and alienation constitutive of such individuation. The dissolvent of the indeterminate – that is pushed into a form of determinacy itself – ends up failing to comprehend antagonistic political identities embedded in the enterprise of political economy. As Stuart Hall (1988: 53) noted in his critique of Thatcherism, 'the play of discursivity becomes nothing but a high-level, advanced game for academic deconstructionists, a matter of intellectual diversion, as the complexity of one discourse after another is perpetually unravelled'.

Whilst discourse theory might, perhaps, be adequate in questioning what Foucault (2003: 24) termed the '"how" of power', or the *effects* of hegemonic discourses, there is nevertheless abnegation in refraining from asking the 'who' of power. Who practices hegemony? What is lost in the complex game of discursivity is any point of condensation within social-power relations. Hegemony, as the message of capital, is no longer an articulation within specific social relations. It becomes, within discourse theory, merely a 'phagocytic essence', absorbing and engulfing everything within the dissolvent of discursivity (Poulantzas 1978: 151). The organic composition of capital and the relation of owners and producers to the social relations of production is thereby lost. Finally, if there is no logical connection between class identity and the realm of ideology, as proposed by discourse theorists such as Laclau and Mouffe, then one is left in the rather uncomfortable position that 'it is wholly coincidental that all capitalists are not also revolutionary socialists' (Eagleton 1991: 215 as cited by van Apeldoorn 2002: 19). The guidance of Adorno is therefore that, 'the more passionately thought denies its conditionality for the sake of the unconditional, the more unconsciously, and so calamitously, it is delivered up to the world' (1974: 247).

Rather than discourse creating identities and interests, it is my argument that social conditions compel action. Discourse does not simply act upon people; rather, people act through discourse. The suppression of agency linked to political economy means that the overriding economic significance of the promotion of certain discourses, in favour of particular interests and purposes, is missed. By extension, discourse-theoretic approaches lack the conceptual apparatus to account for the *strategic selectivity* involved in state practices as a condensate of class relations, or the differential impact on the balance of social forces, that shape the effectiveness of hegemonic strategies (Jessop 1990: 301). The fact that the 'effect of isolation', or the individuation of the social body, is itself an occlusion of class relations linked to techniques of power mediated through state practices is thus lost (Poulantzas 1973: 130–137). Hence the position that ideas are material, a process of articulation within which signs themselves become part of a socially created world, can be subsumed differently within an alternative reading of historical materialism. In the words of Raymond Williams (1977: 29, emphasis original), 'it is precisely the sense of language as an *indissoluble* element of human self-creation that gives any acceptable meaning to its description as "constitutive". To make it *precede* all other connected activities is to claim something quite different.' What is denied here is not that objects are signified through discourse. Instead, on the basis of unsettling some of the stable assumptions noted above in the first reading of historical materialism, the rather different assertion can be made that this is itself a material social practice: a practical activity developed through the political and social reproduction of relations of production in which exploitation occurs. To cite Stuart Hall (1997: 31), 'everything is within the discursive, but nothing is only discourse or only discursive'. It now remains to show how a second reading of Gramsci's theory of history can carry this emphasis forward.

Gramsci on Historical Materialism as the Philosophy of Praxis

Within a historical materialist frame of reference Gramsci speaks of a '"maieutic" mentality' – bringing latent ideas into consciousness – that is embodied in institutions whose development and activity informs human society. In an article of his in July 1919 he states:

> History is a continual process of becoming, and so it is essentially unforeseeable. But that does not mean that 'everything' is unpredictable in the process of historical becoming; that is that history is the domain of chance and

irresponsible whim. History is, at one and the same time, freedom and necessity. (Gramsci 1994c: 111)

This was a continuation of his position outlined in an earlier article of June 1918, where he declares 'history is an immanent necessity which finds its justification in the culture, the economic forms, and the ways of living of human society as determined by past developments' (Gramsci 1975: 56). This emergent theory of history was continually developed throughout the *Prison Notebooks* to emphasise ways in which the social domain was structured by previous historical circumstances, residues, or traces of the past that leave stratified deposits in popular philosophy (Gramsci 1971: 324, Q11§12; 409, Q7§24). Each individual is then 'the synthesis not only of existing relations, but of the history of these relations. He [*sic*] is a précis of all the past' (Gramsci 1971: 353, Q10II§54; also see Bieler & Morton 2001).

What is significant in this unfolding theory of historical materialism – as a philosophy of praxis – is its explicit articulation against the speculative philosophy of Croce.[2] In Notebook 10 Gramsci argues that 'one has to negate abstract or speculative "absolute philosophy" i.e. the philosophy born of the preceding philosophy', by analysing the practical tendencies and the social class sentiments philosophers represent. This includes asking what is 'social' in a philosopher's work, to address problems posed by historical development (Gramsci 1995: 387, Q10II§31i). Croce was emblematic here as he was regarded as 'a sort of lay pope ... a very effective instrument of hegemony even if from time to time he comes into conflict with this or that government' (Gramsci 1994b: 67). Croce was an intellectual 'standard bearer' or 'high priest' of the ideology of economic and political liberalism, presenting it as a 'normal way of life'. So that his teachings produced, 'the largest amount of "gastric juices" for the digestive process' of liberal social order (Gramsci 1994b: 173, 181–182; Gramsci 1995: 396, Q10II§41xii). In a prison letter dated 25 April 1932 addressed to his sister-in-law Tatiana Schucht, Gramsci continues that:

> To many people Croce's thought does not present itself as a philosophical system ... Croce's greatest quality has always been ... to spread without pedantry his conception of the world through a whole series of brief writings in which philosophy offers itself immediately and is absorbed as good sense or common sense ... so we have a great number of 'Croceans' who do not know that they are and perhaps do not even know that Croce exists (Gramsci 1994b: 167).

Crocean philosophy was thus representative of the world-wide movement of classical German philosophy, or Hegelianism, that upheld a solipsism of metaphysics within its concept of immanence and speculative history. The challenge, evoking Marx, was 'the problem of "putting man [*sic*] the right way up", of getting him to stand on his feet instead of his head' (Gramsci 1995: 356, Q10I§11; 369–370, Q10II§11). Most significantly in this respect, the Crocean concept of ethico-political history was signalled as an arbitrary and mechanical hypostatisation of the moment of hegemony within the philosophy of praxis (Gramsci 1995: 329, Q10I§Summary).

Ethico-political history encapsulated the reduction of hegemony to the notion of spirit moving in history. For Gramsci, Croce left out the moment of struggle within his historical account of the rise of the *Risorgimento* and its subsequent impact on the cultural and social landscape of Italian politics. 'One must not think of "ideology" or doctrine as something artificial and mechanically superimposed ... but rather as something historically produced, as a ceaseless struggle' (Gramsci 1996: 56, Q3§56). Hence ethico-political history was 'an arbitrary and mechanical hypostasis of the moment of hegemony, of political leadership, of consent in the life and development of the activity of the state and civil society' (Gramsci 1995: 343–344, Q10I§7). Yet, clearly, the philosophy of praxis does not exclude ethico-political history. Instead it asserts the moment of hegemony as essential to its conception of the state whilst attaching full weight to 'the economy of culture' meaning a political economy conception of historical development (Gramsci 1985: 183, Q29§3). Additionally, 'in history and the production of history the "individualised" presentation of states ... is merely metaphorical', due to vertical class divisions within, as well as horizontal stratifications between, states (Gramsci 1995: 344, Q10I§7). The contrasting formulation of Gramsci's 'state-hegemony-moral consciousness conception' of history was therefore itself wedded to the association of socio-economic content and political form (Gramsci 1995: 372–373, Q10II§41iii; 357, Q10I§12, 360, Q10I§13).

According to Gramsci, the conception of the state developed by dominant classes within capitalism itself derives from a separation of economics and politics. 'The state', as represented by the intellectual class supportive of dominant social forces, 'is conceived as a thing in itself, as a rational absolute.' Therefore,

> since the state is the concrete framework of a productive world and since intellectuals are the social element that identifies itself most clearly with governmental personnel, it is a characteristic of the function of the intellectuals to present the state as an absolute; thus the historical function of the intellectuals is conceived as absolute, and their existence is rationalised. (Gramsci 1992: 229, Q1§150; on this theory of the state, see Bieler & Morton 2003)

As a result of the separation of politics and economics, intellectuals thus come to represent the state as a rationalised, thing-like, or reified entity. Hence 'what is "politics" for the productive class becomes "rationality" for the intellectual class ... What is strange is that some ... believe "rationality" to be superior to "politics", ideological abstraction superior to economic concreteness' (Gramsci 1992: 231, Q1§151). The everyday conflict over politics is thus transformed into the enterprise of preserving order through rationality. Yet there is also a practical importance to all of this which is to highlight the *'material structure of ideology'* embedded in the social function performed by libraries, schools and architecture alongside street lay-outs, street names, prisons and prison regulations, publishing houses, newspapers and journals (Gramsci 1996: 52–53, Q3§49; Gramsci 1994a: 97; Bieler

2001). Overall awareness of these aspects of social power 'would inculcate the habit of assessing the forces of agency in society with greater caution and precision' (Gramsci 1996: 53, Q3§49). Therefore, rather than a formal history of concepts, attention is shifted to conditions of historical development and contestation over 'real historical facts which must be combated and their nature as instruments of domination exposed ... in order to destroy one hegemony and create another' (Gramsci 1995: 370, Q10II§1; 387, Q10II§31i; 395, Q10II§41xii). It is this more complex reading of Gramsci, understanding the state as a social relation or ensemble of socially embedded institutions and class forces, which offers an alternative focus to the contingent voluntarism of discourse theory. Textuality is dissolved back into terms of cultural struggle or specific and conflictive social relationships within the structurally-inscribed strategic selectivity of the state as a condition of emergence and existence.

This conception of the philosophy of praxis is also closely related to Gramsci's rejection of all kinds of economism, particularly those deemed to manifest within the writings of his contemporary Nikolai Bukharin.[3] The latter's *Historical Materialism: A Popular Manual of Marxist Sociology* was regarded as the epitome of inferior Marxist arguments due to its reliance on a 'theological' or transcendental world-view (Bukharin 1965; Gramsci 1995: 403–404, Q10II§41i). The 'Popular Manual' split Marxism in two: a doctrine of history and politics conceived as 'sociology' – constructed according to the methods of natural science – and 'philosophy proper' recognised as a variant of dialectical materialism. The problem, though, is the extraction of the dialectic – 'the marrow of historiography' – to a position separate from history and politics. Hence Gramsci's critique of materialism in the form of an 'Anti-Bukharin' to accompany his aforementioned contestation of liberal reformism in the form of an 'Anti-Croce'. Rather than developing a theory of integral history, which would go beyond both idealism and materialism within a new synthesis, Bukharin forwarded metaphysical extra-historical truths standing outside time and space that replaced the historical dialectic with a belief in extrinsic laws of causality. The variant of positivist science that resulted was erroneous because of assumptions about the predictability of historical events, the belief in mechanical causalism, and the exteriorised understanding of theory and history (Gramsci 1971: 435, Q11§22; 437, Q11§14; 438, Q11§15).

Hence Gramsci's associated criticism of the notion that economic crisis would result in an inevitable historical transformation of society.

> For the conception upon which the aversion is based can only be the iron conviction that there exist objective laws of historical development similar in kind to natural laws, together with a belief in a predetermined teleology like that of a religion: since favourable conditions are inevitably going to appear, and since these, in a rather mysterious way, will bring about palingenetic events, it is evident that any deliberate initiative tending to predispose and plan these conditions is not only useless but even harmful. (Gramsci 1971: 168, Q13§23)

In more detail, Gramsci argued that economic crisis would not automatically give rise to political crisis, or that ideas can be read off as mere epiphenomena of material forces. This was because '"civil society" has become a very complex structure and one which is resistant to the catastrophic "incursions" of the immediate economic element (crises, depressions, etc.)' (Gramsci 1971: 235, Q13§24). Instead, the cultural sphere of socio-political struggle, through which hegemony is constructed, tends to lag behind the thrust of economic events, slowing down the weight of economic crisis. 'It may be ruled out', Gramsci (1971: 184, Q13§17) proclaims, 'that immediate economic crises of themselves produce fundamental historical events; they can simply create the terrain more favourable to the dissemination of certain modes of thought'. Intellectual processes are more complex than this, to the extent that it was an Enlightenment error to believe that clear ideas could enter diverse consciousness with the same clarity and organising effects (Gramsci 1985: 417, Q24§3; Gramsci 1992: 128, Q1§43). Hence Gramsci's rejection of an outlook that 'sees as real and worthwhile only such movements of revolt as are one hundred per cent conscious' (Gramsci 1971: 200, Q3§48). Rather, political struggle and class formation itself are seen as historically produced within a process of becoming (Gramsci 1995: 369–370, Q10II§1).

The unsettling point, then, is that in elaborating his philosophy of praxis Gramsci attempted to transcend the established poles of both traditional idealism and materialism. It was his aim to adumbrate,

> an integral and original philosophy which opens up a new phase of history and a new phase in the development of world thought ... [that] goes beyond both traditional idealism and traditional materialism ... while retaining their vital elements. (Gramsci 1971: 435, Q11§22)

Not only was this philosophy of praxis aimed at absorbing the subjective conception of reality (idealism) it was also aspiring to circumvent the vulgar economism of Marxist orthodoxy (materialism). Hence the identification of a new moment of synthesis based on an historicisation of immanence linking classical German philosophy, French historical practice, and British political economy (Gramsci 1971: 399–400, Q10II§9). It is this historicist reformulation of the solipsism and transcendence of idealism, combined with a humanism that avoids the determinism and positivism of materialism, which is the substance of the philosophy of praxis (Kahn 2002: 133). A reformulation that is based on viewing history and politics as internally related, to realise the internal relations of ideology and philosophy in the conception, writing and practice of history as a *philosophy of praxis* (also see Rupert in this volume). Hence for, the philosophy of praxis, social being and social consciousness are not separated, humanity and nature are inextricably linked, and subject and object are indivisible. To commit any such separation would risk falling into a form of religion or into senseless abstraction (Gramsci 1995: 292, Q11§37). There is a return here, then, to the philosophical content of Marx's critique of political economy that set out to overcome the essential separation of philosophy, economics, and politics. After all, in accord with Herbert Marcuse, 'for Marx, essence and facticity, the situation of essential history and the situation of factual history, are no longer separate regions or levels independent of each other: the historical experience of man [*sic*] is *taken up into the definition of his essence*' (1972: 28, emphasis original).

This understanding of historical materialism as the philosophy of praxis can therefore be taken as a clear indication of what has been discerned by Peter Ives as the outflanking and 'double-pronged critique' of idealism and realism, which develops an epistemological position placing objectivity on a continuum with subjectivity.

> For Gramsci, starting from materiality does not posit two realms—material versus non-material, material versus ideal, extra-linguistic versus linguistic—between which there could be 'correspondence'. This does not rule out making pragmatic distinctions between ideas and objects or between words and thoughts. It does mean, however, that the philosophy of praxis cannot rest on divisions between subjectivity and objectivity, reality and thought, nor can it exacerbate them, nor can it equate them with the linguistic and non-linguistic. (Ives 2004a: 7, 9, 122, 167; also see Ives in this volume)

It is this realisation that is exposed by a second reading of Gramsci, which threatens and undoes the stable dismissal of historical materialism present in the first reading of discourse theory. This second reading, produced from within an emergent and ever changing historical materialism, assimilates, anticipates and fends off certain positions on the history of ideas. It does so by unsettling the account of history as a metapolitical concern that is unknowable other than through the discourse of intellectuals. At the same time, this alternative approach within historical materialism exposes certain internal tensions in reading Gramsci. These tensions render discourse-theoretical positions problematic in their dismissal of social classes in the making of history. As Gramsci, rather soberly, reminds us, 'that the objective possibilities exist for people not to die of hunger and that people do die of hunger, has its importance, or so one would have thought' whilst indicating at the same that 'the existence of objective conditions ... is not yet enough: it is necessary to "know" them, and know how to use them' (1971: 360, Q10II48ii).

Conclusion: Beyond Criticism in the Form of Parody

The method of a 'double reading' has been deployed in this article to unsettle some of the essential positions adopted within the discourse-theoretical approach of Laclau and Mouffe. Initially, this involved not only throwing into relief the rather denuded and-all-too-stable dismissal of Gramsci's concepts that they offer in relation to theory and practice within the history of ideas (first reading). It also involved elaborating the linkages between theory and history, philosophy and ideology, which Gramsci uniquely develops within his philosophy of praxis as historical materialism (second reading). The result is not a denial of positions articulated within discourse-theoretical arguments, as such, but a displacement of such arguments in the form of a positive counter-position (Althusser 1999: 41).

Returning to an idea cast-out earlier in the introduction, it is now time to elaborate Laclau and Mouffe as 'conceptive ideologists'. This refers to those 'who make the formation of the illusions of the class about itself their chief source of livelihood' by attempting to conjure the 'trick of proving the hegemony of the spirit in history' (Marx & Engels 1976: 60, 62). The political dimension of such writings can therefore be exposed as the removal of human beings from societal and thus historical change due to the reduction of history to the discursive realm. In the vocabulary of Gramsci:

> The history of philosophy as it is generally understood, that is as the history of philosophers' philosophies, is the history of attempts made and ideological initiatives undertaken by a specific class of people to change, correct or perfect the conceptions of the world that exist in any particular age and thus to change the norms of conduct that go with them; in other words to change practical activity as a whole. (Gramsci, 1971: 344, Q10II§17)

In this sense, the social function of Laclau and Mouffe can be cast in their own words as not 'to renounce liberal-democratic ideology, but on the contrary, to deepen and expand it' (Laclau & Mouffe 2001: 176), just as Croce's social function was to define, uphold and promote liberal values. Whether in relation to understanding history as an association of ideas, or the equally problematic reliance on an historical account of objective forces, Gramsci's (1996: 158, Q4§16) warning is that 'it is easy to impart the impression of having transcended a certain position by demeaning it, but this amounts to mere verbal sophistry: the transcendence has taken place only on paper, and the scholar will face the difficulty again in a frightening form'.

One of the main conclusions to draw, then, is the imperative to move beyond 'criticism in the form of parody': misrepresenting Marxist observations whether it be on the understanding of historical and contemporary processes of class-formation and identity, or in relation to wider theorising of the capitalist state (Fine & Saad-Filho 2004: 171). Whilst it would be amiss to regard the writings in and beyond the *Prison Notebooks* as some sort of *vade-mecum*, or handbook carried constantly for use, the viewpoint affirmed here is that much can be gained from internalising issues and questions inspired by a Gramscian way of thinking (Morton 2003, also see Finocchiaro in this volume). At the same time, the double reading offered here notes not only the protean nature of such writings but also the importance of sending people back to Gramsci himself in order to 'travel with Gramsci' in relation to the Marxist problematic (Crehan 2002: 175, 207). This is not to recommend a 'hotel gravy' approach, so that ideas, like hotel gravy, become indiscriminately poured over any historical/contemporary condition, or dish (Adorno 2000: 29). Rather, the stress is on a 'constant to-ing and fro-ing between past and present', linking general theories and concrete political problems and practices (Althusser 1999: 48). This could include, among other themes, a fuller appreciation of Gramsci's 'critique of capitalist civilisation' (Gramsci 1977: 13). For instance, by paying closer attention to such remarks that:

> Through the close interplay of the class struggle, as through the development of international relations between states, or through relations between various groups that form a class within a nation, *the spirit is taught to recognise that force (both mechanical as well as moral) is alone the supreme arbiter of strife.* (Gramsci 1975: 62 emphasis added)

After all, Gramsci indicated that 'in the international sphere, competition, the struggle to acquire private and national property, creates the same hierarchies and system of slavery as in the national sphere' (Gramsci 1977: 69; see also Morton 2005). Further appreciation of these and associated lines of thought would contribute towards opening new elements within contemporary historical materialist state theorising, approaches to understanding the international dimension of the capitalist states-system, or theorising on transnational class-agency within the contemporary global political economy; and it would also help to avoid any unwarrantable severance from Gramsci within such debate.

Acknowledgements

I would like to thank Andreas Bieler and Graham M. Smith for comments on earlier drafts of this essay as well as the two anonymous referees for extremely helpful and supportive suggestions.

Notes

1. Following the convention established in this volume, reference to the Gramsci anthologies is accompanied by a citation of the notebook number (Q) and section (§).
2. It is also worth adding that, clearly, Croce's writings had a substantial impact on Gramsci's early mode of thinking in the pre-prison years to the extent that he admitted to being 'tendentially somewhat Crocean' at this time, see Gramsci 1994b: 56; Gramsci 1995: 355, Q10I§11. Whilst Croce's writings are astoundingly voluminous, for representative texts embodying the characteristics criticised by Gramsci see *A History of Italy, 1871–1915* or *History of Europe in the Nineteenth Century* (Croce 1929, 1934).
3. Whilst it is well known that much invective within the *Prison Notebooks* was targeted towards Bukharin, it is less known that, at the same time, the latter was also one of the prominent Soviet officials, along with Maxim Litvinov, who made the first attempt to free Gramsci (between 1927 and 1928) when trying to organise an exchange of prisoners between the Soviet Union and Italy; see Gramsci (1994b: 312n2).

References

Adorno, T. (1974) *Minima Moralia: Reflections from Damaged Life*, trans. E.F.N. Jephcott (London: Verso).

Adorno, T. (2000) *Introduction to Sociology* (Cambridge: Polity Press).

Althusser, L. (1999) *Machiavelli and Us*, trans. & intro. G. Elliot (London: Verso).

van Apeldoorn, B. (2002) *Transnational Capitalism and the Struggle over European Integration* (London: Routledge).

Ashley, R.K. (1998) Untying the sovereign state: A double reading of the Anarchy Problematique, Millennium, *Journal of International Studies*, 17(2), pp. 227–262.

Bellamy, R. (2001) A Crocean Critique of Gramsci on historicism, hegemony and intellectuals, *Journal of Modern Italian Studies*, 6(2), pp. 209–229.

Bieler, A. (2001) Questioning cognitivism and constructivism in IR theory: reflections on the material structure of ideas, *Politics*, 21(2), pp. 93–100.

Bieler, A. & Morton, A.D. (2001) The Gordian knot of agency-structure in International Relations: a neo-Gramscian perspective, *European Journal of International Relations*, 7(1), pp. 5–35.

Bieler, A. & Morton, A.D. (2003) Globalisation, the state and class struggle: a 'critical economy' engagement with open Marxism', *British Journal of Politics and International Relations*, 5(4), pp. 467–499.

Bukharin, N. (1965 [1925]) *Historical Materialism: A System of Sociology* (New York: Russell & Russell).

Crehan, K. (2002) *Gramsci, Culture and Anthropology* (London: Pluto Press).

Croce, B. (1929) *A History of Italy, 1871–1915*, trans. C. Ady (Oxford: Clarendon).

Croce, B. (1934) *History of Europe in the Nineteenth Century*, trans. Henry Furst (London: Unwin).

Eagleton, T. (1991) *Ideology: An Introduction* (London: Verso).

Engels, F. (1987 [1878]) *Anti-Dühring*, in: Marx, K. & Engels, F., *Collected Works*, vol.25 (London: Lawrence and Wishart).

Fine, B. & Saad-Filho, A. (2004) *Marx's Capital*, 4th ed. (London: Pluto Press).

Foucault, M. (2003) *Society Must be Defended*, trans. D. Macey (London: Penguin).

Gramsci, A. (1971) *Selections from the Prison Notebooks*, ed. & trans. Q. Hoare & G. Nowell-Smith (London: Lawrence and Wishart).

Gramsci, A. (1975) *History, Philosophy and Culture in the Young Gramsci*, ed. P. Cavalcanti & P. Piccone (Saint Louis: Telos Press).

Gramsci, A. (1977) *Selections from Political Writings 1910–1920*, ed. Q. Hoare, trans. J. Matthews (London: Lawrence and Wishart).

Gramsci, A. (1985) *Selections from Cultural Writings*, ed. D. Forgacs & G. Nowell-Smith, trans. W. Boelhower (London: Lawrence and Wishart).

Gramsci, A. (1992) *Prison Notebooks*, vol.1, ed. & intro. J.A. Buttigieg, trans. J.A. Buttigieg & A. Callari (New York: Columbia University Press).

Gramsci, A. (1994a) *Letters from Prison*, vol.1, ed. F. Rosengarten, trans. R. Rosenthal (New York: Columbia University Press).

Gramsci, A. (1994b) *Letters from Prison*, vol.2, ed. F. Rosengarten, trans. R. Rosenthal (New York: Columbia University Press).

Gramsci, A. (1994c) *Pre-Prison Writings*, ed. R. Bellamy, trans. V. Cox (Cambridge: Cambridge University Press).

Gramsci, A. (1995) *Further Selections from the Prison Notebooks*, ed. & trans. D. Boothman (London: Lawrence and Wishart).

Gramsci, A. (1996) *Prison Notebooks*, vol.2, ed. & trans. J.A. Buttigieg (New York: Columbia University Press).

Hall, S. (1988) The toad in the garden: Thatcherism among the theorists, in Nelson, C. & Grossberg, L. (Eds), *Marxism and the Interpretation of Culture*, pp. 35–57 (Chicago, IL: University of Illinois Press).

Hall, S. (1997) Culture and power. Interview with P. Osborne and L. Segal [London, June 1997]. *Radical Philosophy*, 86, pp. 24–41.

Hobsbawm, E. (1987) *The Age of Empire, 1875–1914* (London: Weidenfield and Nicolson).

Ives, P. (2004a) *Gramsci's Politics of Language: Engaging the Bakhtin Circle and the Frankfurt School* (Toronto, ON: University of Toronto Press).

Ives, P. (2004b) *Language and Hegemony in Gramsci* (London: Pluto Press).

Jessop, B. (1990) *State Theory: Putting the Capitalist State in Its Place* (Oxford: Polity Press).

Kahn, B.L. (2002) Antonio Gramsci's reformulation of Benedetto Croce's speculative idealism, in: Martin, J. (Ed.), *Antonio Gramsci: Critical Assessments of Leading Political Philosophers,* vol. 2, pp. 117–138 (London: Routledge).

King, P. (2000) *Thinking Past a Problem: Essays on the History of Ideas* (London: Frank Cass).

Laclau, E. & Mouffe, C. (2001) *Hegemony and Socialist Strategy: Towards a Radical Democratic Politics,* 2d. ed. (London: Verso).

Marcuse, H. (1972 [1932]) The foundations of historical materialism, in: Marcuse, H., *Studies in Critical Philosophy,* trans. J. De Bres (London: New Left Books).

Marx, K. & Engels, F. (1976 [1845–46]) *The German Ideology,* in Marx, K. & Engels, F., *Collected Works,* vol.5 (London: Lawrence and Wishart).

Morton, A.D. (2003) Historicising Gramsci: situating ideas in and beyond their context, *Review of International Political Economy,* 10(1), pp. 118–146.

Morton, A.D. (2005) The age of absolutism: capitalism, the modern states-system and international relations, *Review of International Studies,* 31(3), pp. 495–517.

Poulantzas, N. (1973) *Political Power and Social Classes,* trans. T. O'Hagan (London: New Left Books).

Poulantzas, N. (1978) *State, Power, Socialism,* trans. P. Camiller (London: New Left Books).

Thatcher, M. (1987) Interview with *Woman's Own,* 31 October, pp. 8–10.

Williams, R. (1977) *Marxism and Literature* (Oxford: Oxford University Press).

Language, Agency and Hegemony: A Gramscian Response to Post-Marxism

PETER IVES

In 1979, Franco Lo Piparo provided a thorough account of Gramsci's university studies in linguistics and his concern with language. In the preface to that work, Tullio De Mauro, one of Italy's leading linguists, forecast a reopening and rethinking of Gramsci's legacy based on Lo Piparo's insights (De Mauro 1979: ix). This has not happened within the English scholarship, with a few exceptions (Salamini 1981; Boothman 1988; Helsloot 1989; Holub 1992; McNally 1995; San Juan 1995; Brandist 1996a,b). And while the Italian literature has shown much greater awareness of the *questione della lingua* and questions of language generally (Rosiello 1970, 1986;

Carrannante 1973; Gensini 1980; Passaponti 1981; Borghese 1981; Lichtner 1991; Tosel 1996), it has not compelled significant interaction between Gramscian scholarship and the prominent role that language has played in social and political theory since Gramsci's death. This is surprising given the various 'linguistic turns' such as Anglo-analytic language philosophy, structuralism, post-structuralism, discourse analysis, deconstruction, feminism, psychoanalysis and deliberative democracy.

Moreover, our age of so-called globalisation underscores the political importance of language, linguistic commodities and linguistic dimensions of labour. The entwining of capitalist commodity production with linguistic practices is evident in the growth of the Hollywood-based entertainment industry to the US economy and world cultural prestige. The economic power of transnational companies like Microsoft, Nike and Coca-Cola are rooted in linguistic products and symbolic (brand-name) status. These are the conditions that make a Gramscian response to post-Marxism more than just an intellectual exercise. It is part of a larger project of constructing a Gramscian approach to language that does not bifurcate language, communication or symbolic action from labour as do many theorists including Habermas and Bourdieu (see Ives 2004b). The whole issue of so-called 'English as a global language', the growing teaching English industry, and their role in the hegemony of a global capitalist elite are clearly well beyond the scope of this essay. But they are the pressing issues that should inform discussions of Gramsci and global political economy, which are explicitly taken up in the second section of the present volume. Yet these very issues are ruled out if we accept Ernesto Laclau and Chantal Mouffe's post-Marxist reading of Gramsci.

In 1985, Marxist critics were quick to attack Laclau & Mouffe's *Hegemony and Socialist Strategy* for being little more than liberal pluralism dressed in fancy words and postmodern jargon, for being relativist, idealist, anti-Marxist, or just confused. Laclau & Mouffe were criticised for presenting a 'descent into discourse' – a decay from well-grounded, material reality into the idealistic and problematic realm of language and discourse (Wood 1986; Palmer 1987; Geras 1987). On the other side, Laclau & Mouffe have been engaged by non-Marxist political theorists and activists, both liberals and radicals. They remain crucial theoretical points of reference for work on 'new social movements', identity politics (and their critiques of such politics) and multiculturalism. Both sides of the debate seem to agree on one thing: the line from Marxism to post-Marxism is the line from the economy to discourse or from 'reality' (conceived non-linguistically) to language. Recent Gramscian scholarship has attempted to shore up a Gramscian definition of hegemony in ways that actually reinforce this dichotomy of language versus materiality (Ghosh 2001; Joseph 2002).

With one notable exception (Golding 1992), there has been less focus on Laclau & Mouffe's specific reading of Gramsci – so pivotal to their project – especially their neglect of his writings on language. This omission is important since, as I will argue, they rely on a movement from economic analysis to linguistic concepts. Moreover, the term hegemony is increasingly being used in the manner that Laclau

& Mouffe have redefined it (e.g. Butler et al. 2000; and Torfing 1999). I argue that in order for them to 'use' Gramsci as they do they have to ignore his writings on language, since their contribution depends on surpassing Marxism by employing linguistic theory premised on the fundamental ideas of Ludwig Wittgenstein and Ferdinand de Saussure. I will begin by outlining the role of Gramsci within Laclau & Mouffe's trajectory from Marxism to post-Marxism and then turn to Gramsci's writings on language.

Laclau & Mouffe's use of Gramsci

For Laclau & Mouffe, 'hegemony' is the central concept that leads them from specific traditions within Marxism that pay great heed to questions of ideology and culture. Such lines within Marxism are critical of economic and class reductionism, and lead to Laclau & Mouffe's rejection of what they see as the fundamental tenets of Marxism: (1) the idea that history is 'inevitably' progressing towards the fall of capitalism and a communist revolution, (2) that the working-class will necessarily play the primary role in bringing about such a revolution and (3), that such historical movement is irreversible.

Gramsci plays a key role in Laclau & Mouffe's passage from the Marxism of Kautsky and Plekhanov through Luxemburg and Lenin into their 'post-Marxism' that incorporates ideas of Lacan, Foucault and Derrida. In their words, 'Our principal conclusion is that behind the concept of "hegemony" lies something more than a type of political relations *complementary* to the basic categories of Marxist theory. In fact, it introduces a *logic of the social* which is incompatible with those [Marxist] categories' (Laclau & Mouffe 1985: 3). My central point is that because their 'logic of the social' that propels them 'beyond' Gramsci depends heavily on linguistic concepts, they create a severe blind spot by neglecting Gramsci's own writings on language.

They argue that the concept hegemony developed within twentieth-century Marxism as a response to a crisis in the central ideas of Marxism. Put simply, they focus on the difficulties surrounding the relationships between class as an economic category (i.e. one's position within the economy) and class consciousness as a political category central to agency. According to Laclau & Mouffe, some Marxists, especially Gramsci, became increasingly concerned with the latter term, class consciousness, as a political impulse. However, Gramsci fails, according to them, to sever the agency of political consciousness from its connection to the former term, objective economic analysis. They credit Gramsci for his attention to non-economic issues such as culture and 'autonomous' politics but criticise him for not going far enough. The question is: what is at stake in going far enough? Does it mean denying economic analysis and critiques of capitalism altogether?

Many have criticised Laclau & Mouffe's position for abandoning economic analysis and the role of the capitalist economy in constructing counter-hegemonic movements. Some proponents of Laclau & Mouffe respond by arguing that there is still a place for economic analysis and fighting 'class struggles'. Anna Marie Smith, a former student of Laclau's, presents perhaps the best defence of Laclau & Mouffe's position arguing that it does not necessarily exclude economic analysis and class struggle. It just does not privilege economic location or class over other 'subject positions' and struggles. Her analysis of contemporary politics in the United States from a Laclau & Mouffe perspective attempts to illustrate this. However, Smith admits that Laclau & Mouffe overstate the inability of the left to theorise new social movements and progressive struggles aimed at non-class oppression (Smith 1998: 26, 36–40).

Laclau & Mouffe derive concepts from linguistics to describe this notion of political consciousness and oppose it to the economy as an objective, non-political realm.[1] This issue is usually engaged with on the terrain of debates around structuralism, post-structuralism, Althusser, Foucault and the like. Rather than retrace such debates, I will focus specifically on how language and linguistic concepts are understood in relation to politics since my contention is that both Laclau & Mouffe and their critics tend to theorise the economy and language as distinct and mutually exclusive. One of many reasons why Gramsci's writings are still very relevant for us now is that they help us rethink the often presumed opposition between language and the economy, or 'matter' more generally.

Thus, Gramsci plays a vital role in how Laclau & Mouffe understand agency and hegemony and frame them in opposition to determinism, economic analysis and class. They locate their basic criticisms of 'classical Marxist theory' in their argument that Rosa Luxemburg poses the central question about the complex relationship between the capitalist economy and political action. According to them, she never fully comprehends this question nor takes it to the logical conclusion. They argue that there may not be an 'overlap', as they call it, between class positions defined by capitalism and the political subjectivity (or consciousness) needed for revolution. In this way, Marx's critique of capitalism is framed as separable from the development of political agency. Likewise, they argue that Edward Bernstein's 'reformism' was not a mechanical economic determinism, but a different expression of a similar tension that they find in Luxemburg between the agency of the political realm that is 'autonomous' from determination by economic contradictions. They credit Bernstein for insisting that only the political sphere, specifically the political party and parliamentary democracy, can overcome the fragmentation of consciousness increased by the progress of capitalism.

Gramsci is pivotal for them because his notion of hegemony includes the *creation* of a 'collective will' – not merely an economic class coming into its own or becoming aware of itself – but the construction of a social-cultural unity. They applaud Gramsci's replacement of 'ideology' as a system of ideas, especially the suspect system of 'false consciousness' with the idea of 'an organic and relational whole, embodied in institutions and apparatuses, which welds together a historic bloc around a number of basic articulatory principles' (Laclau & Mouffe 1985: 67). The notion of 'articulation' is central for Laclau & Mouffe in replacing the idea of representation. Where representation suggests the presentation of class interests defined economically and then re-presented on the political or subjective terrain of consciousness, articulation suggests, as they write, 'unity between these agents is then not the expression of a common underlying essence but the result of political construction and struggle. If the working class, as a hegemonic agent, manages to articulate around itself a number of democratic demands and struggles, this is due not to any a priori structural privileges,' linked to its specific role within the capitalist economy (Laclau & Mouffe 1985: 65).[2]

However much Gramsci fits Laclau & Mouffe's requirements of freeing the political project of Marxism from its economic essentialism, he fails, according to them, to 'fully overcome the dualism of classical Marxism' because he retains the 'inner essentialist core' that privileges the working class due to its defining place within the capitalist economy. Another supporter of Laclau & Mouffe, Jacob Torfing, writes, 'the great attraction of Gramsci to many Marxists [analysing Thatcherism] hinged on the essentialist residue that prevented Gramsci from developing a completely non-economistic theory of hegemonic articulation. It is a great credit to Laclau & Mouffe that they succeeded in jettisoning this *essentialist remnant*, which was also present in their own earlier, Gramsci-inspired, critique of structural Marxism' (Torfing 1999: 36).

Thus, even though Gramsci himself criticises economic determinism and focuses on culture, politics and hegemony, he still, according to Laclau & Mouffe, *presupposes* that it is the working class that can form a hegemonic force not because what it *does* on the political level, but because what it *is* on the economic level. In their words, 'yet even for Gramsci, the ultimate core of the hegemonic subject's identity is constituted at a point external to the space it articulates: the logic of hegemony does not unfold all of its deconstructive effects on the theoretical terrain of classical Marxism' (Laclau & Mouffe 1985: 85). Its consciousness and role are then 'predetermined' by the objective economic conditions, not articulated autonomously in the political realm. So for Laclau & Mouffe, Gramsci is ambiguous and inconsistent in making a radical break with Marxism's reliance on the economy.

One may wonder what it means to say that for Gramsci the working-class is 'predetermined' as the unifying class within his counter-hegemony. For example, Gramsci's entire analysis of the Italian *Risorgimento* is precisely *an argument* (rather than a presupposition) about how the development of subaltern class consciousness in early twentieth-century Italy created the potential for the formation of a proletariat that could 'lead' a communist revolution. Moreover, Gramsci is famous for arguing that this proletariat would fail unless it included in its political consciousness the interests and struggles of other subaltern groups, especially the peasantry. This is why he formulated hegemony as more than just an alliance among subaltern social groups.

Perhaps it is too much to demand that in addition to providing a seminal post-structuralist theorisation of new social movements, *Hegemony and Socialist Strategy* must also include a convincing reading of all of Gramsci's incredibly wide-ranging concerns. However, Laclau & Mouffe's argument is premised on specific linguistic theories (namely those of Ferdinand de Saussure and Ludwig

Wittgenstein) that reject the idea that language is nomenclature – that it creates meaning by reference to something external to it such as ideas or physical objects. This is where they derived the criticism that Gramsci's hegemony remains tied to a Marxist dualism because the subject's identity is created external to the realm of politics. That Gramsci's own writings on language and politics share some similarities with such linguistic theories calls into question Laclau & Mouffe's entire argument. The large question at the centre of much of the debate concerns the effect of Laclau & Mouffe's charge that Marxism remains 'economically deterministic' (Smith 1998: 19–36, 103–15).

Laclau & Mouffe's introduction of linguistic analysis is at the centre of their rejection of Marxism, including Gramsci's Marxism. They utilise Saussure's synchronic approach to linguistics and his criticism of previous understandings of language as representation or nomenclature, that is, language as a mere instrument of communication. In linguistic terms, Laclau & Mouffe's criticism of Gramsci is that he retains Marx's primacy of the economic base and that his analyses of culture and politics are fundamentally defined by class positions as they are represented on the political terrain. They apply Saussure and Wittgenstein's understandings of language to political analysis in order to get 'beyond Gramsci' and finally overcome the persistence of economic determinism. Just as Saussure argues that meaning or linguistic value is produced solely within the differences of language (Saussure 1983: 110–120), Laclau & Mouffe argue that political subject positions and their potential alliances and conglomerations into political movements cannot be 'reduced' or traced back to pre-political (that is economic) determination. Rather, just as Saussure argues about language, subject positions are defined purely in terms of their relations with other subject positions. The implication is that Gramsci maintains a dualism akin to the pre-Saussurean division between 'the external' or economic world and its representation in language and politics. No matter how complex and sophisticated Gramsci's notion of 'hegemony', he retains, according to Laclau & Mouffe, some sense of a non-hegemonic 'level' (i.e. economic and non-political) that in the end 'determines' hegemonic formations.

Of course, Laclau & Mouffe are adopting *post*-structuralist concepts and not the structuralism of Saussure. They reject the notion of totality and the stability of such structures, accepting Derrida's critique of Saussure's insistence that language is a *stable* system of signs. Laclau & Mouffe also highlight the indeterminacy, lack of stability, and the contingency of political and social formation, including hegemonic 'articulations'. Nevertheless, their basic critique of Gramsci's supposed 'dualism' rests on Saussure's notion of language.

While I am not convinced of Leonardo Salamini's (1981: 31) contention that Gramsci was directly influenced by Saussure, it is clear Matteo Bartoli, his linguistics professor, was familiar with the linguistic circles from which Saussure developed his synchronic approach. Thus, one is compelled to ask about the adequacy of Laclau & Mouffe's reading of Gramsci. To support their argument about agency, hegemony, and Gramsci's supposed 'economistic core', they would have to at least engage Gramsci's writings on language.

Like Laclau & Mouffe, Gramsci also saw linguistics and language as fields rich with concepts and metaphors that are useful for political analysis. And what is most important, like them, Saussure, and Wittgenstein, Gramsci also rejected the notion that language could be understood as nomenclature, as a collection of words that represent non-linguistic things or 'reality'.

Gramsci, Linguistics and Politics

For Gramsci, language is not an abstract or overly philosophical topic. Unlike many other political and social theorists, Gramsci's interest in language grew from practical and everyday experiences as a Sardinian and then a student studying linguistics in Turin. Indeed, Matteo Bartoli took a keen interest in Gramsci precisely because he was one of the few Sardinian students (Fiori 1990: 73–4, 80–81). Linguistic differences and the 'standardisation' of Italian were concerns that resonated with political overtones. This distinguishes Gramsci from much current social and political theory influenced by linguistics that is quick to coin new terms, borrow specialist terminology and use them as jargon. Such theory tends to obfuscate many of the connections with 'common sense' and with those who have not been inculcated into the milieu of 'high' theory. As Anne Showstack Sassoon and others have explored, Gramsci's very method engages with previous concepts and ideas in such a manner that alters their significance or demands a more critical approach (Sassoon 1990; Buey 2001). The point that many have made about 'hegemony' not being Gramsci's own coinage, is true of many of the terms we now understand as 'Gramscian' including 'passive revolution', 'civil society', 'pessimism of the intellect, optimism of the will', 'everyone is an intellectual' and 'common sense'.

While this approach to the use of language separates Gramsci from Laclau & Mouffe who write dense texts overflowing with specialised terminology from psychoanalysis and linguistics, there are two important similarities between Gramsci and Laclau & Mouffe with respect to language. Many, such as Perry Anderson and Noam Chomsky, draw a distinction between politics and language specifically rejecting linguistic concepts and metaphors for political analysis (e.g. Anderson 1983: 44; Chomsky 1986). Gramsci, on the contrary, explicitly relates the study of language to that of politics, culture, philosophy and 'common sense'.

In elaborating his central argument that 'everyone is a philosopher' he notes that 'in "language", there is contained a specific conception of the world' and that philosophy or the spontaneous philosophy that everyone has and uses 'is contained in, 1) language itself, which is a totality of determined notions and concepts and not just of words grammatically devoid of content.' (Gramsci 1971: 323, Q11§12).[3] In Notebook 10, Gramsci writes:

> Language also means culture and philosophy (if only at the level of common sense) and therefore the fact of 'language' is in reality a multiplicity of facts more or less organically coherent and co-ordinated. (Gramsci 1971: 349, Q10§44)

Similarly he notes:

> I feel that if language is understood as an element of culture, and thus of general history, a key manifestation of the 'nationality' and 'popularity' of the intellectuals, this study [a history of the Italian language] is not pointless and merely erudite. (Gramsci 1985: 170, Q3§76)

This basic connection between an analysis of language and ideology, culture and operations of power is an important basis for Gramsci's discussions of Latin and vernaculars, his critique of Alessandro Manzoni's language policy and Esperanto, intellectual activity, 'common sense' and ultimately hegemony (see Ives 2004a).

The other basic point where Gramsci agrees with Laclau & Mouffe is that language cannot be understood as nomenclature or as a vehicle for communication – as a conduit for ideas – in the tradition of John Locke (see Ives 2004c: 28–30). Laclau & Mouffe do not really address the actual need to study language, but they use linguistics to argue against the notion of 'representation' and elaborate their notion of 'articulation'. They draw heavily on Saussure and Wittgenstein to make this point. For our purposes here, I will ignore their equally important reliance on more specific ideas of Foucault and Derrida.

To present what Gramsci clearly sees as a historical materialist approach to language (fully compatible with his Marxism), he insists that the process of language, the making of meaning with language, is based on metaphor. More specifically, it is based on the metaphorical relations of current language usage with previous uses of language (not some external non-linguistic realm that language 'represents' or refers to).

In Notebook 11, Gramsci writes: 'The whole of language is a continuous process of metaphor, and the history of semantics is an aspect of the history of culture; language is at the same time a living thing and a museum of fossils of life and civilisations' (Gramsci 1971: 450, Q11§28). What does Gramsci mean by stating that language is metaphorical? Of course, there is a distinction between language being used as a metaphor, as a method of describing more abstract workings of spontaneous philosophy, and whether or not language itself works through the process of metaphor – whereby words, phrases and idioms 'stand in for' or denote something else. What sort of things constitute this 'something else'? Are they material objects? Are they conceptual categories? Or even other words, phrases and idioms?

Using language as a metaphor for political analysis is about having it stand in for or represent how ideas and behaviours operate on a political terrain. Whether or not language itself operates using a process of metaphor – where words or linguistic structures stand in for objects, ideas or other words – is a different, if related, question. Gramsci's unambiguous position is that linguistic dynamics can be used as metaphors for political relations. But his response to the second question is more complex and qualified. In some important senses, he argues that all language operates metaphorically but we must be careful what metaphor means.

Gramsci engages in such questions in his critique of Nikolai Bukharin's, *The Theory of Historical Materialism: A Manual of Popular Sociology* (also see Morton in this volume). Bukharin takes up Marx and Engels' comment that they are developing an 'immanent' philosophy. Bukharin is concerned that it would be too easy to misinterpret this as an endorsement of the religious notion of 'immanence' meaning that God exists within the physical or temporal world. Bukharin argues that Marx and Engels should not accept such an idea even in the form presented by Kant or Hegel. Clearly, according to Bukharin, this literal notion of immanence is one of Marxism's key criticisms of Idealist and bourgeois philosophy that imports mystical, religious, or metaphysical notions of God into our understandings of the world. To explain Marx and Engel's use of 'immanence', Bukharin contends that it was *only* a metaphor (Bukharin 1969: 26).

Gramsci, not satisfied with the superficiality of Bukharin's position, asks why some terms remain in use 'metaphorically' while others are replaced with new words. Does not Bukharin's simple notion of metaphor forestall discussion of how Marx and Engels were using but modifying Hegel and Kant's concepts? Gramsci demands a more thorough understanding of this new *Marxist* conception of 'immanence'. He describes how this process of developing the concept of 'immanence' is a 'translation from the speculative form, as put forward by classical German philosophy, into a historicist form with the aid of French politics and English classical economics' (Gramsci 1971: 400, Q10§9; see also Gramsci 1995: 307–318, Q11§48–49, Q17§18iii, Q15§64, Q11§50). Crucial for us here is that in Gramsci's well-known criticisms of Bukharin's economistic Marxism, he uses both the linguistic concept of 'translation' and techniques that he was familiar with from studying linguistics to the realm of political analysis. He pays particular attention to how concepts and terms develop, where they were borrowed from and how they have been changed.

This is the context where Gramsci makes the above quoted point that language is a continual process of metaphor. Meaning is produced by having words 'stand in' or represent ideas that are usually expressed by different terms. Gramsci uses the example of the word *'disastro'* (disaster) to drive home this point (Gramsci 1971: 450, Q11§28). Etymologically, *dis-astro* referred to a misalignment of the stars. But if he described an earthquake as a disaster, no one would accuse him of believing in astrology. The misalignment of the stars then becomes a metaphor for a calamity or devastating event. The term disaster sheds its literal reference but retains a sense of its meaning. But to use the word *disastro* and have it understood neither the speaker nor listener requires any knowledge of this history. Rather, 'disaster' becomes almost synonymous with 'catastrophe' or 'calamity'. The nuanced difference in these terms bears no reference to any root in astrology. On this at least, Gramsci agrees with Saussure (and Laclau & Mouffe) that language is synchronic (at least as speakers use it) and its terms are defined in relation to one another, not some external referent. However, this agreement stops here, since Gramsci argues that while speakers may ignore the history of a language, that history retains some relevance.

Borrowing heavily from his linguistic studies with Bartoli, Gramsci argues that we should not totally ignore the roots of *disastro* in paganism, folklore and astrology. This would be analogous to what Bukharin is doing with Marx's use of 'immanence'. Rather, these traces are evidence of how modern civilisation developed from earlier and antithetical ideas. This is why Gramsci states, 'present language is metaphorical with respect to the meanings and ideological content which the words used had in preceding periods of civilisation' (Gramsci 1971: 450, Q11§28). However, he argues we should not think of language as metaphorical 'in respect of the thing or material and sensible object referred to (or the abstract concept'. That is, language is not metaphorical in the sense that a word takes the place of (or creates meaning by relating to) a given object or idea. Language is not a nomenclature for non-linguistic entities, either objects or ideas.[4] *Disastro* is not a metaphor for, or simple references to, the location of stars in non-linguistic 'reality'. In a manner remarkably similar to those of Wittgenstein and Saussure utilised by Laclau & Mouffe, Gramsci argues that language does not create meaning through a simple relationship between language and a non-linguistic world of objects or ideas. Gramsci rejects the notion that 'every proposition must correspond to the *true* and to *verisimilitude*' (Gramsci 1985: 180, Q9§1).

This development of 'metaphor' is fully consistent with Gramsci's general epistemology and his critique of the '"fearsome" question of the "objective reality of the external world"' that he describes as 'badly framed and conducted worse' (Gramsci 1971: 440–441, Q11§17). After arguing that the public belief in objectivity 'external' to humanity derives from religious notions that God created the world and then placed humans in it (Gramsci 1971: 441, Q11§17), Gramsci turns to Bertrand Russell's example that 'we can think of' the location of Edinburgh as North of the location of London regardless of whether humans exist on Earth. Gramsci responds, 'It could be objected that without the existence of man one cannot think of "thinking" … What would North-South or East-West mean without man? They are real relationships and yet would not exist without man and without the development of civilisation.' Gramsci understands North and South to be conventional, arbitrary and related to specific historical developments such as Californians accepting Japan as the 'Far East' (even though they travel West to arrive there). But they are also objectively real, 'they correspond to real facts, they allow one to travel by land and by sea, to arrive where one has decided to arrive' (Gramsci 1971: 447, Q11§20). This crucial argument shows that the dualism of which he is accused runs against his entire way of thinking. For him, 'Objective always means "humanly objective" which can be held to correspond exactly to "historically subjective"' (Gramsci 1971: 445, Q11§17).[5] If for Gramsci geographical locations and physical objects cannot be said to be explicable in abstraction from human consciousness, it would be absurd for him to consider economic 'reality' as separate from, and determining of, political and group consciousness. Yet this is exactly what Laclau & Mouffe's reading implies.

Where Gramsci differs from Saussure is the role of history and the development of language through this process of metaphor. Saussure's linguistics seemed to deny the importance of history, bracketing historical linguistics as merely a branch of the discipline that should be dominated by synchronic linguistics (see Ives 2004a: 16–20, 43–60). Foreshadowing post-structuralism and other critiques of structuralism, Gramsci argues that history and the historical residues within language are fundamental in operations of power, prestige and hegemony. Gramsci emphasises that meaning is created by language in its metaphorical development with respect to previous meanings. New meanings replace previous ones in a continual process of development. Gramsci concludes his discussion of 'language and metaphor' (Q11§24) noting that

> The new 'metaphorical' meaning spreads with the spread of new culture, which furthermore also coins brand-new words or absorbs them from other languages as loan-words giving them a precise meaning and therefore depriving them of the extensive halo they possessed in the original language. Thus it is probable that for many people the term 'immanence' is known, understood and used for the first time only in the new 'metaphorical' sense given to it by the philosophy of praxis. (Gramsci 1971: 452, Q11§24)

Through this discussion of 'immanence', Gramsci is describing the importance of his linguistic method to philosophy but especially hegemony. It is within this discussion that he writes:

> Language is transformed with the transformation of the whole of civilisation, through the acquisition of culture by new classes and through the *hegemony* exercised by one national language over others, etc..., and what it does is precisely to absorb in metaphorical form the words of previous civilisations and cultures. (Gramsci 1971: 452, Q11§24, emphasis added)

Contrary to Marxists including Wood, Geras and other critics of Laclau & Mouffe who dismiss Saussure, structuralism and post-structuralism for emphasising language at the expense of material objects or 'reality', Gramsci's Marxist notion of hegemony is fully compatible with such a conception of language (except his criticisms of Saussure's lack of historicism noted above).

Once the narrative of *Hegemony and Socialist Strategy* as a progressive movement away from the economy towards language and discourse as the site of the construction of political identities is questioned, it is untenable that Gramsci is positing the construction of identity on an entirely different plane from where hegemonic politics are played out. Rather he views the organisation of culture and social categories and identities as the terrain of hegemonic politics that includes (but is not reduced to) economic considerations. A more thorough reading of Gramsci's views on language would require Laclau & Mouffe to redraw their trajectory from Marxism to post-Marxism. They could no longer present a shift from non-linguistic economically based Marxism to social theory drawn heavily from (anti-nomenclature) linguistic theories rooted in Saussure and Wittgenstein. Instead, they would have to argue for a shift from Gramscian Marxism that also draws heavily on (anti-nomenclature) linguistic concepts in combination with economic analysis to a linguistically informed post-structuralism. This makes it clear that in order to expunge the 'essentialist remnant' from Gramsci, economic analysis has to be denied altogether as does the Marxist critique of capitalism (or any systematic critique of capitalism).

In addition to criticising Gramsci for 'presupposing' the working class as the agent of struggle due to his economic reductionism, Laclau & Mouffe also reject the notion that Gramsci's 'hegemony' is a singular or unitary formation, as opposed to a plural or un-centred formation:

> For Gramsci, even though the diverse social elements have a merely relational identity – achieved through articulatory practices – there must always be a *single* unifying principle in every hegemonic formation … a failure in the hegemony of the working class can only be followed by a reconstitution of bourgeois hegemony, so that in the end, political struggle is still a zero-sum game among classes. (Laclau & Mouffe 1985: 69)

Here they seem to admit that Gramsci's supposed 'essentialism' does not lie in his analysis of identity formation or class consciousness, but rather in his assessment of the kind of political formation that would be required to overthrow capitalism and the ideology, culture, and common sense that helps sustain it.

But here again, they do not engage with Gramsci's conception of 'unity' or his argument about its political role. As I have argued at length elsewhere, Gramsci's writings on language, including his concepts of spontaneous, immanent and normative grammar, address the central themes of much current debate on unity and diversity (Ives 2004b: ch. 2 and 40–51; see also Ives 2004a: 90–101; Ives 1997). Gramsci's complex picture of how agency is related to hegemony and Marx's critique of capitalism including its fragmentation of subaltern consciousness (so central to Laclau & Mouffe's resuscitation of Bernstein) can be rendered invisible only if Gramsci's attention to language is ignored, as Laclau & Mouffe do.

At stake in this argument is not so much the question of how Gramsci is interpreted or how 'hegemony' is used. More important is the lack of analysis and potential political activity that is prevented by the perpetuation of the dualism between economic analysis and linguistics, between 'material' and language. This dualism prevents us from grappling with many attributes of 'late' global capitalism because it conceals the importance of issues such as the relationship between information technology and global commodity production, the advent of 'global English' and, most importantly, it obscures the possibilities for new forms of political consciousness and agency.

Acknowledgements

This essay was first given at the 3rd International Conference on Gramscian Studies, co-hosted by La Fondazione Istituto Gramsci di Roma, Italia and the Benemérita Universidad Autónoma de Puebla, México (BUAP) held in Puebla, México (7-10

October 2003). Another version was presented at the 'Rethinking Marxism: Marxism and the World Stage' Conference, Amherst, Massachusetts (8 November, 2003). I would like to thank the organisers of both conferences and the many participants whose feedback contributed to this article. I would also like to thank the two anonymous reviewers.

Notes

1. Laclau (1990: 180–181) understands class struggle as the 'supplement' – in Derrida's sense – to Marxism's critique of capitalism as an economic system.
2. They define 'articulation' as 'any practice establishing a relation among elements such that their identity is modified as a result of the articulatory practice' (Laclau & Mouffe 1985: 105).
3. Because the complete translation of the critical edition is still underway, in addition to giving the reference to the Gramsci anthologies, I cite the notebook number (Q) and section (§), following the convention established in this volume.
4. This is why, Gramsci explains, we cannot think of translation as finding equivalents within language (see Gramsci 1985: 384–385, Q16§21 and Ives 2004b: 97–133).
5. This passage continues with a discussion of the historical unification of the cultural system through the disappearance of internal contradictions. While potentially ambiguous, this actually fits very well with Gramsci's discussion of spontaneous and normative grammars (see Ives 2004a: 90–101, 2004b: 40–51).

References

Anderson, P. (1983) *In the Tracks of Historical Materialism* (London: Verso).

Boothman, D. (1988) Translating signal and sign: the case of Gramsci's Quaderni, in: Loprieno, A. (Ed.) *Miscellanea fra linguistica e letteratura*, pp. 57–81 (Naples: Edizioni Scientifiche Italiane).

Borghese, L. (1981) Tia Alene in Bicicletta: Gramsci Traduttore dal Tedesco e Teorico della Traduzione, *Belfagor*, 36(6), pp. 635–665.

Brandist, C. (1996a) Gramsci, Bakhtin and the semiotics of hegemony, *New Left Review* (I),216, 94–109.

Brandist, C. (1996b) The official and the popular in Gramsci and Bakhtin, *Theory, Culture & Society*, 13(2), 59–74.

Brennan, T. (2001) Antonio Gramsci and postcolonial theory: 'Southernism', *Diaspora*, 10(2), 143–186.

Buey, F. (2001) Lingua, Linguaggio e Politica in Gramsci, in: Petronio, G. & Paladini Musitelli, M. (Eds), *Marx e Gramsci: Memoria e attualità* (Rome: Manifestolibri).

Bukharin, N. (1969) *Historical Materialism: A System of Sociology* (Ann Arbor, MI: University of Michigan Press).

Butler, J., Laclau, E. & Žižek, S. (2000) *Contingency, Hegemony, Universality* (London: Verso).

Carrannante, A. (1973) Antonio Gramsci e i problemi della lingua italiana, *Belfagor* 28, 544–556.

De Mauro, T. (1979) Preface, in: Lo Piparo, F. (Ed.), *Lingua Intellettuali Egemonia in Gramsci*, pp. v–xvi (Bari: Laterza).

Fiori, G. (1990) *Antonio Gramsci: Life of a Revolutionary*, trans T. Nairn (London: Verso).

Gensini, S. (1980) Linguistica e questione politica della lingua, *Critica Marxista*, 1, 151–165.

Geras, N. (1987) Post-Marxism?, *New Left Review* (I),163, 40–82.

Ghosh, P. (2001) Gramscian hegemony: an absolutely historicist approach, *History of European Ideas*, 27(1), pp. 1–43.

Golding, S. (1992) *Gramsci's Democratic Theory: Contributions to a Post-Liberal Democracy* (Toronto, ON: University of Toronto Press).

Gramsci, A. (1971) *Selections from the Prison Notebooks*, ed. and trans. Q. Hoare & G. Nowell-Smith (London: Lawrence and Wishart).

Gramsci, A. (1985) *Selections from Cultural Writings*, ed. D. Forgacs & G. Nowell-Smith, trans. W. Boelhower (London: Lawrence and Wishart).

Helsloot, N. (1989) Linguists of all countries...! On Gramsci's premise of coherence, *Journal of Pragmatics*, 13, 547–566.

Holub, R. (1992) *Antonio Gramsci: Beyond Marxism and Postmodernism* (New York: Routledge).

Ives, P. (1997) The grammar of hegemony, *Left History*, 5(1), pp. 85–104, reprinted in Martin, J.(Ed.), *Antonio Gramsci: Critical Assessments of Leading Political Philosophers*, vol. 2, pp, 319–336 (London: Routledge).

Ives, P. (2004a) *Language and Hegemony in Gramsci* (London: Pluto Press).

Ives, P. (2004b). *Gramsci's Politics of Language: Engaging the Bakhtin Circle and the Frankfurt School* (Toronto, ON: University of Toronto Press).

Ives, P. (2004c) Language, representation and suprastate democracy: questions facing the European Union, in: Laycock, D. (Ed.), *Representation and Democratic Theory*, pp. 23–47 (Vancouver, BC: University of British Columbia Press).

Joseph, J. (2002) *Hegemony: A Realist Analysis* (London: Routledge).

Laclau, E. (1990) *New Reflections on the Revolution of Our Time* (London: Verso).

Laclau, E. & Mouffe, C. (1985) *Hegemony and Socialist Strategy: Towards a Radical Democratic Politics* (London: Verso).

Lichtner, M. (1991) Traduzione e Metafore in Gramsci, *Critica Marxista*, 39(1), 107–131.

Lo Piparo, F. (1979) *Lingua Intellettuali Egemonia in Gramsci* (Bari: Laterza).

Lo Piparo, F. (1987) Studio del linguaggio e teoria gramsciana, *Critica Marxista*, 2(3), pp. 167–175.

McNally, D. (1995) Language, history, and class struggle, *Monthly Review*, 47(3), pp. 13–30.

Palmer, B.D. (1990) *Descent into Discourse: The Reification of Language and the Writing of Social History* (Philadelphia, PA: Temple University Press).

Passaponti, M.E. (1981) Gramsci e le questioni linguistiche, in: Gensini, S. & Vedovelli, M. (Eds), *Lingua, Linguaggi, e Società: Proposta per un aggiornamento*, 2nd ed., pp. 119–128 (Firenze: Tipolitografia F.lli Linari).

Rosiello, L. (1970) Problemi linguistici negli scritti di Gramsci, in: Rossi, P. (Ed.), *Gramsci e la cultura contemporanea*, vol. 2, pp. 347–367 (Rome: Editori Riuniti).

Rosiello, L. (1986) Linguistica e marxismo nel pensiero di Antonio Gramsci, in: Ramat, P., Niederehe, H.-J. & Koerner, K. (Eds), *The History of Linguistics in Italy*, pp. 237–258 (Amsterdam: John Benjamins).

Salamini, L. (1981) *The Sociology of Political Praxis: An Introduction to Gramsci's Theory* (London: Routledge).

San Juan, E. Jr (1995) *Hegemony and Strategies of Transgression* (Albany, NY: State University of New York Press).

Saussure, F. de (1983) *Course in General Linguistics*, ed. C. Bally & A. Sechehaye, trans. R. Harris (La Salle, IL: Open Court).

Sassoon, A.S. (1990) Gramsci's subversion of the language of politics, *Rethinking Marxism* 3(1), 14–25, reprinted in Anne Showstack Sassoon (2000) *Gramsci and Contemporary Politics: Beyond Pessimism of the Intellect* (London: Routledge).

Smith, A.M. (1998) *Laclau & Mouffe: The Radical Democratic Imaginary* (London: Routledge).

Torfing, J. (1999) *New Theories of Discourse : Laclau, Mouffe, and Zizek* (Oxford: Blackwell).

Tosel, A. (1996) Il Lessico Gramsciano Filosofia della Prassi, *Marxismo Oggi*, 1, 49–67.

Wittgenstein, L. (1953) *Philosophical Investigations*, trans. G.E.M. Anscombe (New York: Macmillan).

Wood, E.M. (1986) *The Retreat from Class: A New 'True' Socialism* (London: Verso).

Towards an Intellectual Reformation: The Critique of Common Sense and the Forgotten Revolutionary Project of Gramscian Theory

ANDREW ROBINSON

One aspect of the work of Antonio Gramsci that has been underplayed in the secondary literature is his critique of common sense. This is crucial, because this critique was a central part of his conception of revolutionary change. It is clear from his *Prison Notebooks* that Gramsci was opposed both to everyday 'common sense', the philosophy of the masses, and to the manipulative and passivity-inducing effects of elite-dominated politics.[1] He was therefore an advocate of a revolution in everyday life, indeed, one of the first such advocates, many years before Situationism and the 'politics of desire' arrived on the scene. When Gramsci writes of the need for an 'intellectual and moral reformation' (sometimes mistakenly translated in English as 'reform', despite Gramsci's frequent allusions to the Reformation as a historical parallel), he has in mind a thoroughgoing transformation and development of people's ways of thinking and acting in everyday life, a transformation fundamental enough to break the grip of bourgeois ideological formations and to transform the subaltern strata from a passive mass into an active historical force. The recovery of Gramsci's revolutionary message is part of the same process as the recovery of the critique of common sense, which has been repressed in most readings of Gramsci.

This article is primarily exegetical, but it is not an exercise in the 'austere historicism' criticised by Morton (2003). Rather, it is an attempt to develop an aspect of Gramsci's theory which has contemporary political relevance, but which has been neglected. While Gramsci was certainly concerned about the specific 'common sense' of his historical context, it is also the case that his analysis has broader resonances which could provide important avenues for research into the politics of everyday life and issues such as ideology, propaganda and pedagogy. Furthermore, these perspectives could potentially deepen the socio-political significance of neo-Gramscian analysis by drawing attention towards everyday life and giving new meaning to key concepts such as hegemony.

I would contend that the concept of common sense has been neglected in the literature on Gramsci. In fact, it is not even discussed in many secondary texts.[2] When it is, it tends to be oversimplified or misunderstood, often in ways which bolster an approach which maintains a distance from everyday life and a focus on elite politics, traditional ideology analysis and so on. For instance, Roger Simon (1991) treats common sense, not as a conception of the world to be overcome, but as an ahistorical 'field' in which social struggles take place. This blunts the critical edge of Gramsci's remarks on common sense. Similarly, when Stuart Hall discusses Gramsci's concept of philosophy, he puts the concept in inverted commas and uses it to refer to exclusively political outlooks (1983: 23, 25, 28), ignoring its matrix in everyday life even while emphasising how it shapes and constrains perceptions. He therefore ends up with a crude conjunctural politicism: 'you lose because you lose because you lose' (Hall 1991: 125). Similarly, Chantal Mouffe portrays common sense as a basis from which a new philosophy can be derived, and thus gives it positive political significance (1979b: 186). In contrast to the exegetical evidence presented below, I can find only two passages (Gramsci 1971: 145, Q15§4; Gramsci 1995: 128, Q5§51) where Gramsci gives such positive connotations to the term 'common sense'. Similarly, José Nun, who has written the most comprehensive study to date of Gramsci's concept of common sense, criticises the idea of such a critique as 'undemocratic' and attempts instead to re-read Gramsci as a pro-common-sense author (1996: 205, 226). The attitude of certain readers of Gramsci can only lead to a tendency to pander to existing beliefs as a way to maximise conjunctural political advantages, which goes against Gramsci's goal of 'intellectual and moral reformation'. The point is not that these readings of Gramsci are flawed because they reappropriate his work in a new context – a necessary part of any effective appropriation – but because they do so in a way that ignores crucial elements of his theory that retain contemporary relevance. In doing so, they blunt the critical force of Gramsci's political project.

Although my approach is not simplistically historicist, I shall adopt a mainly exegetical approach, in order to demonstrate that the strands I advocate are indeed present in Gramsci's work. Because these elements are largely absent from the secondary literature, I am aiming to demonstrate the existence of a 'forgotten' Gramsci whose views open the possibility to more revolutionary and transformative readings of his work. This is in line with Morton's call for 'thinking in a Gramscian way' and searching for a leitmotif in his work (2003: 121, 123; see also the contributions by Finocchiaro and Morton in this volume). I feel that the critique of common sense is a leitmotif of much of the *Prison Notebooks*, and that to 'think in a Gramscian way', one needs to adopt a critical concern to overcome common sense. I would go as far as to suggest that this 'forgotten' Gramsci has a contemporary relevance which other parts of Gramsci's work lack, particularly as regards deepening one's understanding of the operation of oppressive discourse and the ways of effecting substantial social transformation. I am also drawing a distinction between constructive readings, which reappropriate aspects of an author's work in a new context, and straightforward misreadings, which are based on inadequate exegesis. However, the crucial point is that there is a potential agenda for research and theorising embedded in Gramsci's work, which can offer important perspectives to people interested in theorising transformative politics in a contemporary context.

Towards an Intellectual Reformation

Gramsci's relationship to Marxism is itself an example of a creative and recontextualising interpretative appropriation, and his position on the crucial issue of the role of economics and production in constituting social forces varies between different texts. Sometimes, Gramsci maintains a more-or-less orthodox attachment to the last-instance primacy of the economic sphere. On other occasions, far from sticking to the idea of the primacy of production, Gramsci's main starting-point is the idea of 'conceptions of the world and of life', 'modes of thought and action', or, in his unusual vocabulary, 'philosophies'. Instead of a succession of modes of production, Gramsci refers to history as 'the struggle of systems, ... the struggle between ways of viewing reality' (as cited by Nemeth 1980: 167). Instead of referring to modes of production or productive systems, Gramsci tends to use terms such as 'ethico-political system' and 'system of social relations' (1971: 119, Q10I§9). History is therefore reconceived as a series of different ways of thinking and acting, each succeeded by another, which is its immanent critique and transcendent metalanguage. Historical conflicts involve a clash of ethico-political principles of one kind or another, and unless one inquires into how one such set of principles defeats another, one can only describe historical events from the outside and cannot draw causal conclusions (Gramsci 1995: 359, Q10I§13). Gramsci's political writings are in large part an attempt to integrate the economic and 'ethico-political' aspects of social change into a single analytical perspective.

The concept of 'conceptions of the world' is central to Gramsci's analysis. Everyone has a conception of the world of some kind, and this means that 'all men [*sic*] are philosophers', because in 'the slightest manifestation of any intellectual activity whatsoever, in "language", there is contained a specific conception of the world' (Gramsci 1971: 323, Q11§12). This also means that everyone is in a certain sense intellectually and politically active, promoting ways of thinking and acting, which promote particular ethical and/or normative ideas. Gramsci calls his version of Marxism an 'absolute historicism' and 'absolute humanism', adding that it 'puts the will at the base of philosophy' (1971: 345, Q11§59). 'The unity of theory and practice is not just a matter of mechanical fact, but a part of the historical process' (Gramsci 1971: 333, Q11§12). Theory and ideology are therefore central to understanding social phenomena. Every philosophy gives rise to its own ethic, and each ethic motivates adherents to construct a particular social formation which expresses it. Gramsci does not downplay economics completely, since he gives it great importance as an existential sphere in which conceptions of the world emerge and are expressed. However, he denies the view that economic changes have a direct change on social organisation. Between the economic level and the level of elite and mobilisatory politics (the 'politico-military' level), there is always the 'ethico-political' level of the formation, articulation and transformation of conceptions of the world. Transformative action occurs through the formation of a collective will, and this is a process that necessarily occurs on the ethico-political level. For instance, according to Gramsci, economic crisis cannot directly cause revolutions. It can only alter the balance of influence between different conceptions of the world (Gramsci 1971: 184, Q13§17). 'It is not the economic structure which directly determines political activity, but rather the way in which the structure and the so-called laws which govern its development are interpreted' (Gramsci 1977: 49; Bobbio 1979: 33). Economic change is important in revolutions, but it is not the driving force. Rather, it occurs largely as an expression of changes in philosophy as expressed in social relations (Gramsci 1971: 133, Q13§20). It should also be noted that Gramsci downplayed the idea of ideology as 'false consciousness' (1971: 326-327, Q11§12), preferring to see ideas and beliefs as the articulation of needs and feelings into social projects.

Nevertheless, there are different kinds of theory in existence. Some are carefully thought out and express a conception of the world that is integral, expansive and capable of becoming hegemonic. Others are subaltern, and rely to one degree or another on one's subordination to a ruling class. For instance, the badly thought-out philosophies embedded in common sense render the masses subordinate to the influence of ruling classes, and the partial focus established in economic-corporate ideas such as the trade-unionist conception of workers' interests are insufficient to mount a generalised challenge to the capitalist framework within which these interests themselves arise (Gramsci 1977: 109-113; 1978: 76, 164-168). The struggle between ways of viewing reality is not a struggle between equals, and for Gramsci, emancipation in practice must be preceded by ideational emancipation. While all people are philosophers, there is a great difference between coherent, properly considered critical views and the confused and contradictory amalgam that is common sense. Thus, people should be persuaded that, since they necessarily operate as philosophers, they should engage coherently with theoretical issues, and not succumb to the ideological and stultifying influences of capitalism (Gramsci 1971: 28, Q12§1). A crucial point in analysing others' philosophies is that their 'true' philosophy is not necessarily the one they consciously and/or publicly affirm. It is the one they act on in practice (Gramsci 1995: 383, Q10II§31i). The openness involved in Gramsci's analysis of philosophy creates a model of collective action broader than and preferable to those rendered possible by economistic Marxisms and by rational choice theory. For instance, Gramsci portrays class solidarity as arising organically from particular philosophical attachments (1971: 181, Q13§17).

Classes or social groups on the 'ethico-political' (as opposed to the economic and the politico-military) level are for Gramsci defined primarily by their mode of thought and action. 'In acquiring one's conception of the world one always belongs to a particular grouping which is that of all the social elements which share the same mode of thinking and acting' (1971: 324, Q11§12). Everyone has a 'party', in the sense of a group promoting a particular conception of the world (see Sassoon 1980: 240), and all people are 'political beings' and 'legislators', encouraging others to act in particular ways by establishing, reinforcing and acting on 'norms' (1971: 265-266, Q14§13; c.f. 1971: 9, Q12§3). In other words, it is groups of people united by partic- ular conceptions of the world, not classes in an economic sense, which are the main social forces on the ethico-political level (which is the most important level for trans- formative politics and for general socio-cultural analysis). In analysing ways of thinking and acting, Gramsci uses a variety of terms, but many of these are equivalent. I shall follow what I take to be Gramsci's use and deploy the terms 'philosophy', 'ideology', 'conception of the world', 'mode of thought and action' and 'world-view' interchangeably. All of these terms refer to the general way of thinking and acting which determines the specificity of a social class, social group or historical formation.

Gramsci states that 'the first step in emancipating oneself from political and social slavery is ... freeing the mind' (as cited by Ransome 1992: 180). A new society cannot simply be constructed in practice. Rather, it must already be 'ideally active' in the minds of those fighting for change (Gramsci 1985: 39). Subaltern strata linger in a position of subordination partly because their conceptions of the world remain within the framework set by the ruling class. In order to become autonomous and thereby able to change the world, the subaltern strata need to develop a new concep- tion of the world that is not dependent on ruling-class ideas. Gramsci refers to this process as 'intellectual and moral reformation'. Social change can only happen when progressive groups 'work incessantly to raise the intellectual level of ever-growing strata of the population'; it is this above all which changes the 'ideological panorama' of an age (Gramsci 1971: 340, Q11§12). Hence, 'every revolution has been preceded by an intense labour of criticism', including 'the spread of ideas among masses of men who are at first resistant' (1977: 11-12). Every revolution is preceded by a change in philosophical conceptions such as the conception of human- ity (Gramsci 1971: 356, Q7§35; c.f. Gramsci 1985: 249, Q8§3; Gramsci 1971: 394, Q16§9). In forming new political movements, 'great importance is assumed by the question of "language", i.e. the collective attainment of a single cultural "climate"' (Gramsci 1995: 156, Q10II§44). The creation of a new world-view is equivalent to the creation of a new type of political and civil society (Gramsci 1971: 381, Q7§33). When he analyses social movements such as the factory councils, his emphasis is on their effect on intellectual development. For instance, the factory councils were important because they 'gave the masses a "theoretical" consciousness' (Gramsci 1971: 198, Q3§48) and the role of Gramsci's version of the party is 'intellectual and moral reform[ation]' (1971: 133, Q13§1). Despite the emphasis Gramsci places on the unity of a collective will, he also presumes it will express forms of cultural difference (1995: 115, Q8§131ii).

Organic Ideologies

The division between everyday life and elite politics is very important when one considers Gramsci's discussions of 'organic ideology'. Gramsci portrays the forma-tion of organic ideologies as a constant tension between active wills and projects embedded in different political and social movements. Political propaganda does not enter a void; it enters into a situation where conceptions of the world and cultural hierarchies already operate, and its role is rearticulation and dissection of existing ideas (Gramsci 1985: 33). Furthermore, everyday life is the site of the crucial strug-gle around phenomena of activity and passivity. Ruling-class power does not rely on the hegemonic mobilisation of the subaltern strata, but on their being kept passive through processes such as *trasformismo* and actual violence.

However, the resultant relation of domination is incomplete. Since everyone is involved in philosophical and conceptual activity related to their existential and material situation, ruling-class conceptions of the world rarely penetrate in their entirety into subaltern strata. Gramsci draws a distinction between belief-systems which are 'organic', i.e. lived directly within actual social relations (usually linked to social classes and constructed existentially in everyday life, including economic relations and class struggle), and those which are 'arbitrary' or 'superficial', being held without emotional commitment in the context of purely formal relations. 'One must ... distinguish between ... historically organic ideologies ... and ideologies that are arbitrary, rationalistic, or "willed"' (Gramsci 1971: 376-377, Q7§19). One might refer to organic ideologies as containing a strong element of libidinal invest-ment and as being a mobilisation of desire, whereas superficial ideologies have a mediated and weak relation to desire and lack social actuality for this reason. Because they meet psychological needs and play a crucial organising (meaning-producing and activity-inducing) role, organic ideologies have an important histori-cal place (Gramsci 1971: 377, Q7§21), equivalent to that of material forces.[3] Organic ideologies can only be changed or overcome through critical activity, and do not simply give way to rationally-conceived systems of thought (Gramsci 1971: 455, Q11§16). Although they rarely have the coherence of philosophers' philoso-phies, it is only organic and not arbitrary ideologies that have an actual effect on the world. A specialised philosophy or ideology can only become historically effective if it can incorporate itself in reality as if it were an expression of it (Gramsci 1971: 201, Q9§63; c.f. 1995: 75, Q3§140). The historical role of a philosophy can only be assessed through its practical effects, broadly defined, and organicity is the only criterion of the 'realism' of beliefs (Gramsci 1971: 172, Q13§16; 346, Q5§45). There is an irony, however, that the highly abstract forms of continental philosophy are more likely to raise the intellectual level than more immediately practical philosophies such as pragmatism (Gramsci 1971: 373, Q17§22).

It is in the context of this distinction that the better-known contrast between organic and traditional intellectuals gains its meaning. The role of an organic intellectual is to 'change, correct or perfect ... conceptions of the world ... and thus to change ... norms of conduct' (Gramsci 1971: 344, Q10II§17). They are supposed to take particular elements in mass beliefs – the elements Gramsci terms 'good sense' – and shape these into a 'precise and decisive will' and a 'clear and ever-present awareness' (Gramsci 1971: 333, Q11§12). They should feel the 'elementary passions' of the people and aim to develop these feelings into a coherent and rational form (Gramsci 1995: 418, Q10II§11; 450, Q11§66), developing good sense (see below) into a 'precise and decisive will' and a 'coherent ... ever-present awareness' (Gramsci 1971: 333, Q11§12). Organic intellectuals are to 'make the people join in a criticism of themselves and their own weaknesses', to raise the intellectual level of ever-growing strata of people and to 'construct an intellectual-moral bloc which can make possible the intellectual progress of the mass' (Gramsci 1971: 251, Q5§127; 332-333, Q11§12; 340, Q11§12). This bloc is not to be constructed by subordinating intellectuals to common sense, to which it is the 'antithesis', but by raising the intellectual level of the masses. According to Gramsci, Marxism

> affirms the need for contact between the intellectuals and the "simple" ... not in order to restrict scientific activity and preserve unity at the low level of the masses, but precisely in order to construct an intellectual-moral bloc which can make politically possible the intellectual progress of the mass. (1971: 332-3, Q11§12; c.f. 1971: 397, Q16§9)

In one passage, Gramsci emphasises the importance of learning both to feel and to know. 'If the relationship between intellectuals and people-nation ... is provided by an organic cohesion in which feeling-passion becomes understanding and thence knowledge (not mechanically but in a way that is alive) ... then and only then ... can the shared life be realised which alone is a social force – with the creation of the "historical bloc"' (1971: 418, Q11§67). When a new philosophy becomes organic, its adherents form a new 'collective will' or social force.

The role of organic intellectuals is to engage in a two-way dialogue which is sympathetic to subaltern people's needs (Gramsci 1985: 215, Q23§8) but which avoids succumbing to the temptation to glorify existing beliefs. They are to encourage a process in which the teacher is also a learner (Gramsci 1971: 350, Q10II§44) and encourage contact and interchange between intellectual and 'mass' beliefs (Gramsci 1985: 215, Q23§8). A major part of the educative process is to involve the encouragement of critical and analytical abilities, of 'thinking well, whatever one thinks, and therefore acting well, whatever one does', the 'exercise of thought, acquisition of general ideas, habits of connecting causes and effects' and so on (Gramsci 1985: 25). Learning to use concepts and language in effective and trans-formative ways is a crucial part of a Gramscian pedagogical project. Gramsci also calls for activity 'to raise the intellectual tone and level of the mass' (as cited by Williams 1973: 593), 'elaborating, making to think clearly, [and] transforming' (as cited by Merrington 1968: 162), and spreading critical activity.

The envisaged change is to be deep rooted and wide ranging, including new ways of thinking and living, a new morality and philosophy, new forms of language, new philosophical discourses and a new integral philosophy (Gramsci 1985: 41-43; Gramsci 1971: 357, Q7§35; 366, Q10II§12). Every new conception of the world creates a new language, contributing to the development of the broader language by inventing new terms and reworking and metaphorically re-using old ones (Gramsci 1985: 414, Q24§3). The process of change can only occur as a 'molecular' process whereby people gradually free themselves from constraining ideas and influences, but it culminates in a moment of 'catharsis', which involves a decisive break with ruling-class ideas. In a sense, Marxists pursuing Gramsci's project are only 'renovating and making "critical" an already existing activity' (1971: 331, Q11§12), since everyone is already a philosopher of sorts. However, one should not underesti-mate the extent of the transformation Gramsci envisages in everyday beliefs. Work-ers and others are to break down or unlearn their attachments to existing dominant ideologies and are to reconstruct themselves as a historical force which did not previously exist.

An organic or hegemonic social movement as conceived by Gramsci has a wide-ranging energising effect on its supporters and adherents, finding its expression in the emergence of a new culture and a new way of thinking. To show the depth of active energy a movement must release to count as hegemonic, consider Gramsci's remarks on art. An organic or expansive movement is 'irresistible'. Therefore, 'it will find its artists' without the need for artificial manoeuvres. If it fails to do so, this shows that 'the world in question was artificial and fictitious' (Gramsci 1985: 109, Q15§38). This new art is to come 'from deep within', impacting strongly on feel-ings, conceptions and relationships (Gramsci 1985: 207, Q21§5) and broadening horizons in such a way as to generate new creative possibilities for artists (Gramsci 1985: 98, Q23§6). A movement does not become hegemonic simply because it manages to manipulate passive masses into supporting it, nor because it manages to construct cross-class alliances at the level of elite politics. Indeed, a movement that requires an organisational dynamic to grow is by definition not expansive (Gramsci 1985: 211, Q21§5).

Beyond Common Sense

In order to achieve an ideational change, a new philosophy needs to challenge exist-ing mass beliefs. The subaltern strata already have their own philosophy/ies, which

Gramsci terms common sense. He is deeply critical of common sense, accusing it of being confused, contradictory and neophobe and of encouraging various kinds of oppressive discourse. It is uncritical and largely unconscious, dogmatic, anti-dialectical (Gramsci 1971: 435, Q11§22), 'crudely neophobe and conservative' (Gramsci 1971: 423, Q11§13). It is a 'chaotic aggregate of different conceptions' (Gramsci 1971: 422, Q11§13) which 'cannot be reduced to coherence within an individual consciousness, let alone collective consciousness' (Gramsci 1971: 326, Q11§12; c.f. Gramsci 1971: 324, Q11§12; 419, Q11§13), and it is so contradictory that one can find in it 'anything one likes' (Gramsci 1971: 422, Q11§13), leaving adherents open to manipulation by directive figures in their immediate environment (Gramsci 1971: 323-324, Q11§12), particularly by authoritarians who use force and deceit to create an illusion of a unity within common sense (Gramsci 1971: 326, Q11§12). To appeal to common sense as a proof of anything is a nonsense (Gramsci 1971: 423, Q11§13), and the generalisation of common sense judgements leads to arbitrary conclusions (Gramsci 1971: 345, Q10II§17).

Large parts of subalterns' life-worlds are territorialised and constructed by dominant elites, and this often has a profound effect on their identities and attitudes. It can lead to fatalism and the naturalisation of the status quo. Gramsci criticises common sense for assuming that what exists is natural and for reifying institutions. Although much action is indeed habitual, the realisation that it is social rather than natural in origin is a prerequisite for transformative practice (Gramsci 1971: 157-158, Q15§6), and so is the overcoming of the common fetishisation of society as a phantasmagorical abstract being (Gramsci 1971: 187, Q13§36). Far from being natural or spontaneous, common sense is a 'primitive historical acquisition' (Gramsci 1971: 199, Q3§48), reflecting social relations and the influence of particular organic intellectuals. It includes strong tendencies towards fatalism, naturalisation and 'naïve' or 'vulgar' realism (McInnes 1964: 14; Gramsci 1971: 420, Q11§13; 441, Q11§17), and it is often auto-affirming, resisting critique. It tends to neuter critical ideas that are able to enter it (e.g. Gramsci 1971: 352, Q10II§54) and is 'eager for fixed certainties' (Gramsci 1971: 435, Q11§22). Its illusion-inducing effects bar effective social analysis (Femia 1979: 483) and it involves a 'borrowing of conceptions' which binds people intellectually to the leading class (as cited by Merrington 1968: 160). Appeals to common sense in philosophy and theory have 'a certain "reactionary" significance' (Gramsci 1971: 441-442, Q11§17), often being used as an excuse for dogmatism and for ignoring critical refutations (Gramsci 1971: 67-68, Q19§24). Gramsci calls instead for 'an effort through which the spirit frees itself from common sense' (1995: 421-422, Q10II§18).

It is important that philosophical engagement take the form of a critique of common sense (Gramsci 1971: 419, Q11§13). One should be careful not to encourage its uncritical tendencies (Gramsci 1971: 420, Q11§13), and Gramsci is highly critical of authors he thinks support or tail common sense (e.g. Gramsci 1971: 197, Q3§48; 199, Q3§48; 422, Q11§13). For Gramsci, the importance of Marxism breaking with common sense, explaining rather than endorsing it, is the decisive issue in relation to the question of whether Marxism can become hegemonic (Gramsci 1971:

441-442, Q11§17). The threat of relapse into common sense is ever-present and is to be resisted. For instance, one must resist 'the tendency to render easy that which cannot become easy without being distorted' (Gramsci 1971: 43, Q12§2), and one must avoid a situation where 'vulgar common sense has imposed itself on science and not vice versa' (cited in Entwhistle 1979: 27). The reinforcement of common sense has the effect of impeding intellectual development (Gramsci 1995: 353, Q10I§10). Hence, one must avoid such a reinforcement, even while being careful to treat common sense respectfully to avoid entrenching it (Gramsci 1971: 179, Q13§17).

In explaining the pervasiveness of common sense, Gramsci invokes several factors. On one hand, it meets certain emotional needs by providing a force of moral resistance. On the other, it is encouraged by the ruling class's tendency to hold down the intellectual development of the subaltern strata through means such as incorporating organic intellectuals into the existing system. Gramsci's main argument, however, is that subaltern people lack the conceptual abilities to formulate an alternative or to engage critically with new ideas. This is a problem that must be overcome. Whenever a collective will comes into being, 'there comes into being also, in opposition to common sense, a homogeneous – in other words, coherent and systematic – philosophy' (Gramsci 1971: 419, Q11§13). The role of Marxism is to change the 'popular "mentality"' (Gramsci 1971: 348, Q10II§48i), generating 'a new ethical and intellectual unity which has surpassed common sense and become critical' (as cited by Merrington 1968: 160). To perform this role, Marxism itself must change, becoming a philosophy and a way of thinking about human life, rather than simply an analytical perspective. It must also be integral, bearing on all aspects of life, without thereby becoming oppressive. In contrast, Gramsci denounces Catholicism for its inability to provide an integral morality. 'An integral Catholic ... who applied the Catholic norms in every act of his life, would seem a monster', and this is 'the severest ... criticism of Catholicism' (Gramsci 1971: 351, Q10II§54).

Gramsci's critique of common sense partly constructs other aspects of his theoretical edifice. The grammar of the concept of hegemony, for instance, is revealing. The concept occurs in Gramsci's work in at least three different binaries. Firstly, it is used as a synonym for 'direction' and counterposed to 'domination' and to its sub-types (coercion and trasformismo). Secondly, it is contrasted to sectional and economic-corporate kinds of ideology. In this sense, it expresses the idea of a deeply held, wide-ranging organic ideology, as distinct from a narrower set of claims focused on immediate economic interests. On the hegemonic as distinct from the economic-corporate level, questions are posed in universal terms, and deal with the whole superstructure of society and not only with economic issues (Gramsci 1971: 181, Q13§17). According to Gramsci, the social position of an ideology is a result of whether it has its own philosophy or is subordinate to a larger one (Gramsci 1971: 157, Q15§6). A hegemonic world-view contains its own social vision elaborated from the impulses of a particular social group, whereas a class with an economic-corporate conception pursues its interests and impulses within a framework set (and limited) by another class. Whereas partial or economic-corporate conceptions create parties that tend to seek concessions within the existing system, integral philosophies tend to create integral states (i.e. new kinds of society) (Gramsci 1995: 34, Q20§2; 37, Q6§188). In order to be hegemonic in this sense, a philosophy must have undergone sufficient qualitative development and to have become a new integral, organic and expansive conception of the world. Thirdly, hegemony is also used in a binary with 'subalternity'. In Gramsci's vocabulary, a subordinate group is subjected to domination, whereas a subaltern group is controlled even more deeply, by means of its partial acceptance of another group's conception of the world. This is particularly the case if the subaltern group accepts the other group's ideas fatalistically, without an active hegemony and a tendency to raise the intellectual level.

Common sense operates as a mode of entrapment that ties the subaltern strata to the ruling class. Nevertheless, some parts of subaltern conceptions of the world escape dominant philosophies and form a node of resistant ideas and themes within subaltern strata. Gramsci terms these elements 'good sense'. Although 'good sense' is minimal and insufficient to construct a new philosophy, Gramsci sees it as a route through which dissident ideas might enter and transform the conceptions of the world held by the subaltern strata (Gramsci 1971: 326-327, Q11§12). It is an embryonic autonomous conception of the world that appears sporadically, usually during crises and mobilisations. Gramsci portrays good sense sometimes as an amalgam of good ideas which just happen to have sneaked into common sense, and sometimes as a nascent worldview developed in engagement with one's actual circumstances, particularly at work. Subaltern people superficially affirm ruling-class beliefs and think they are acting on them, as indeed they often are in periods of passivity. But good sense, which is often 'kept hidden for fear of common sense' (Gramsci 1995: 557, Q11§56), is actually in contradiction with common sense, so that one can even say that workers and others have two consciousnesses or ideologies (Gramsci 1971: 333, Q11§12).

Good sense operates as a critique of common sense from within, providing a route into common sense for critical and Marxist conceptions. It is not, however, a full philosophy in its own right. For instance, it tends to be negative rather than positive (c.f. Boggs 1976: 71). It is a starting-point rather than an end-point of transformation, and it is to be 'educated' and developed into a critical and coherent world-view (Gramsci 1971: 168-189, Q13§23, Q13§14). However, in spite of its incompleteness, Gramsci praises it for its progressive role. 'The beginnings of the new world, rough and jagged though they always are, are better than the passing away of the world in its death-throes and the swan-song that it produces' (Gramsci 1971: 343, Q11§12). An example of good sense is a generalised but amorphous hostility to *signores* or bosses (Gramsci 1971: 272-273, Q3§46). Because of good sense, Marxism need not take the doomed path of simply confronting mass beliefs. There is an element in mass beliefs which can be 'educated' and developed into a critical and coherent world-view (Gramsci 1971: 198-199, Q3§48).

Conclusion: Intellectual and Moral Reformation Today

To conclude, therefore, it is important to restore to readings of Gramsci's work an element of commitment to a revolution in everyday life and to radical transformations in popular belief-systems. The bulk of this piece has been exegetical, but I would also emphasise that the elements I am stressing in Gramsci's work are more relevant today than ever. Transformist and coercive systems are increasingly operative but are also weakened by their existential impact. The anti-capitalist movement has mounted a 'politico-military' challenge to bourgeois power (in Gramsci's sense of confronting opposed political forces in a particular conjuncture), but it has not yet developed the means to draw ever-growing strata of the population into the nascent new society it is constructing. One needs now more than ever to raise the question of constructing new ways of thinking and acting which can escape the bourgeois trap on a psychological and cognitive as well as a social level and which can provide the basis for lasting changes which destroy capitalist oppression.

The issue of 'common sense' is relevant to contemporary issues in many ways, and can be applied to understanding diverse contemporary problems. When examining the ideological influence of populist pro-capitalist media, for instance, it is important to emphasise not only the corporate control of the media and the steady flow of disinformation, but also the emotional attachments and 'common sense' assumptions which arise from a committed exposure to material espoused by right-wing outlets. Strong in-group/out-group distinctions around issues such as crime, immigration and religious identity are recurring forces in politics around the world, including the recent re-election of George W. Bush in the United States, an outcome widely attributed to widespread uncritical attachment to neoconservative religious and nationalist beliefs in certain sections of American society. These issues are neither about politics in the traditional 'politico-military' sense, nor issues of economics and the production structure. They are issues of what Gramsci calls the 'ethico-political' level, requiring an analysis and critique of 'common sense'. Gramsci's approach offers researchers useful ways of examining and engaging with such phenomena, and it is in such potential research approaches that the importance of this article lies.

Acknowledgements

The author would like to thank Andreas Bieler, Adam Morton and Simon Tormey as well as two anonymous referees for helpful comments and suggestions.

Notes

1. Quotes cited as being from Gramsci – but referenced to secondary texts – are translations from the Italian editions of the *Prison Notebooks* by the authors of the secondary texts, and are not available in English editions, to the present author's knowledge. Following the convention established in this volume, reference to the Gramsci anthologies is accompanied by a citation of the notebook number (Q) and section (§).

2. Credit is, however, due to Femia (1975), Nun (1996) and Nemeth (1980) for significant attempts to rectify the absence of discussions of 'common sense' in the secondary literature.

3. The word 'organic' often has connotations of 'economic' in Gramsci's work, and Gramsci assumes that organic ideologies are outgrowths of the material structure in fundamental ways, whereas arbitrary philosophies are not. He also supposes that this link to production determines whether or not arbitrary philosophies can become organic. However, his operationalisation of the concept suggests that an ideology proves itself to be organic, and therefore to have a link to the production structure, if it is deeply felt and arises in everyday life on a mass scale. Its organicity in the sense of being widespread and passionately felt is proof of its historical vitality, which in turn demonstrates its material relevance.

References

Bobbio, N. (1979) Gramsci and the conception of political theory, in: Mouffe, C. (Ed.), *Gramsci and Marxist Theory*, pp. 21–47 (London: Routledge).

Boggs, C. (1976) *Gramsci's Marxism* (London: Pluto Press).

Entwhistle, H. (1979) *Antonio Gramsci: Conservative Schooling for Radical Politics* (London: Routledge).

Femia, J. (1975) Hegemony and consciousness in the thought of Antonio Gramsci, *Political Studies*, 23(1), 29–48.

Femia, J. (1979) The Gramsci phenomenon: some reflections, *Political Studies*, 27(3), 472–483.

Gramsci, A. (1971) *Selections from the Prison Notebooks*, ed. & trans. Q. Hoare & G. Nowell-Smith (London: Lawrence and Wishart).

Gramsci, A. (1977) *Selections from Political Writings 1910-1920*, ed. Q. Hoare, trans. J. Matthews (London: Lawrence and Wishart).

Gramsci, A. (1978) *Selections from Political Writings, 1921-1926*, trans. & ed. Q. Hoare (London: Lawerence and Wishart).

Gramsci, A. (1985) *Selections from Cultural Writings*, ed. D. Forgacs & G. Nowell-Smith, trans. W. Boelhower (London: Lawrence and Wishart).

Gramsci, A. (1995) *Further Selections from the Prison Notebooks*, ed. & trans. D. Boothman (London: Lawrence and Wishart).

Hall, S. (1983) The great moving right show, in: Hall, S. & Jacques, M., *The Politics of Thatcherism*, pp. 19–39 (London: Lawrence and Wishart).

Hall, S. (1991) Postscript: Gramsci and us, in: Simon, R., *Gramsci's Political Thought: An Introduction*, rev. ed., pp. 114–130 (London: Lawrence and Wishart).

Hall, S. & Jacques, M. (Eds) (1983) *The Politics of Thatcherism* (London: Lawrence and Wishart).

McInnes, N. (1964) Antonio Gramsci, *Survey*, 53, 3–15.

Merrington, J. (1968) Theory and practice in Gramsci's Marxism, in: Miliband, R. & Saville, J., *The Socialist Register*, pp. 145–176 (London: Merlin Press).

Morton, A.D. (2003) Historicising Gramsci: situating ideas in and beyond their context, *Review of International Political Economy*, 10(1), pp. 118–146.

Mouffe, C. (Ed.) (1979a) *Gramsci and Marxist Theory* (London: Routledge).

Mouffe, C. (1979b) Hegemony and ideology in Gramsci, in: Mouffe, C., *Gramsci and Marxist Theory*, pp. 168–204 (London: Routledge).

Nemeth, T. (1980) *Gramsci's Philosophy: A Critical Study* (Brighton: Harvester).

Nun, J. (1996) Elements for a theory of democracy: Gramsci and common sense, *Boundary 2*, 14(3), pp. 197–229.

Ransome, P. (1992) *Antonio Gramsci: A New Introduction* (Hemel Hempstead: Harvester Wheatsheaf).

Sassoon, A.S. (1980) *Gramsci's Politics* (London: Croom Helm).

Simon, R. (1991) *Gramsci's Political Thought: An Introduction*, rev. ed. (London: Lawrence and Wishart).

Williams, R. (1973) Base and superstructure in Marxist cultural theory, *New Left Review* (I), 182, pp. 3–16.

Reading Gramsci in an Era of Globalising Capitalism

MARK RUPERT

In recent years, the neo-Gramscian research programme in International Relations (IR) has been seriously challenged. Often cited in this regard is the influential critique by Randall Germain and Michael Kenny (1998). While such challenges can be re-invigorating and healthy for those obliged once again to think through and defend fundamental positions (see the exemplary defence by Morton 2003), I fear that their effect on debates within the larger subfield has been to obscure the ways in which a dialectical reading of Gramsci – one which seeks to interpret and recon- struct his work in terms of its relevance for our contemporary context of globalising capitalism – can be intellectually illuminating and politically enabling.

In particular, I want to suggest that it is possible to read Gramsci – and through him, the tradition of historical materialism – in such a way that we are enabled to realise a potentially transformative politics of solidarity in a world where capitalist relations are extending and deepening, but which is nonetheless plural. Although not without its tensions and limitations, Marxian theory provides critical leverage for understanding the structures and dynamics of capitalism, its integral if complex relationship to the modern form of state and the class-based powers it enables and the resistances these entail. Gramsci's rich if eternally inchoate legacy also suggests a conceptual vocabulary for a transformative politics in which a variety of anti-capitalist movements might coalesce in order to produce any number of future possible worlds whose very possibility is occluded by capitalism. In the present context of globalising capitalism and neo-imperialism, such resistance has taken the form of a transnational confluence of movements for global justice and peace (see Rupert 2003, 2004). A Gramscian-inflected historical materialism can help us to understand these movements as potentially containing the germ of new post-liberal and conceivably post-capitalist political cultures and forms of political practice. But before such possibilities can come into view, we must exert critical leverage upon the reifications of social life generated by capitalist relations and practices.

Capitalism, Social Power and Reification

One of the enduring insights of Marxian theory is that the seemingly apolitical economic spaces generated by capitalism – within and across juridical states – are permeated by structured relations of social power deeply consequential for political life and, indeed, for the (re)production of social life as a whole. These powers may be ideologically depoliticised – and thus rendered democratically unaccountable – in liberal representations separating a naturalised and privatised economy from the formally political sphere. The operation of this economy (and the implicit social powers residing within it) may then be represented as something approaching a universal social good, the engine of economic growth and a generalised prosperity (Rupert 2000: ch. 3; also Steger 2002). However another of these enduring Marxian insights is that social power relations are also *processes* – dynamic, contradictory and contestable.

On a dialectical Marxian view, capitalism entails liberation from the relations of direct politico-economic dependence characteristic of feudalism and other pre-capitalist forms, and hence presents possibilities for social individuation and 'political emancipation' within the parameters of republican forms of state. But capitalism simultaneously limits the historically real emancipatory possibilities it brings into being by (re-)subjecting persons to social domination through the compulsions of market dependence and the disabling effects of fetishism and its reification of social power relations. These dialectics of freedom and unfreedom, the powers they generate and resistances they engender, have produced families of capitalist historical structures which are fraught with tension and possibilities for change. Whether any such possibilities are realised, and in what particular ways, depends upon open-ended political struggles in which the power relations of capitalism will necessarily be implicated.

The critical leverage of a Marxian critique of capitalism is generated by its explicit focus on the social power relations that inhere in, and yet are obscured by, the structures and practices of capitalist production and exchange. Under historical conditions of capitalism, social relations are mediated by things – commodities. Although the social division of labour under capitalism has brought together and collectively empowered human producers as never before, it simultaneously divides and disables them by representing their social relations as naturalised relations of exchange between commodities (the *locus classicus* is Marx 1977: ch. 1). To the extent that social relations are subsumed into a world of putatively independent objects – 'things' – communities of human producers are correspondingly disempowered. Inhabitants of the capitalist market, the subjects of capitalist modernity, are represented to themselves as abstract individuals who, as such, are largely unable to discern – much less communally to govern – the social division of labour in which they are embedded. The social division of labour takes on the appearance of objectivity, an uncontrollable force of nature, the mystical market whose price signals and compulsions individuals defy at our peril. Concomitantly, capitalism's fetishism and reification serve to mystify social power relations by making power appear as a property of things which may be possessed (or not) by abstract individuals: 'Like everything else in the bourgeois world, social power too is "mediated by things".'

> In a society where social relations take the form of relations between things, one must command those things in order to command people ... Power is externalised, residing now in objective forms outside of people rather than in their differential subjective [social] identities ... And it is this objectification which enables power to be exercised by individuals *as* individuals rather than as personifications of a community. It is no longer inscribed in their particular social personalities but instead becomes a *thing* which can be privately *possessed*, in principle by anyone. Its essential character as a relationship of persons is obscured by the 'material' forms through which it is mediated. (Sayer 1991: 66–67)

The implications for democracy are deeply ironic. For even as capitalism realises 'political emancipation' through the development of the liberal republic in which citizens are formally equal, it effectively reifies, privatises and de-politicises class-based social powers (by associating them with ownership of 'private property') and thereby evacuates from the purview of political democracy much of the substance of social life, vitiating democracy's promise of social self-determination (see Marx 1975; Sayer 1991: ch. 2; Thomas 1994; Wood 1995; Dryzek 1996).

Behind these mystifications, capitalist social relations generate the possibility of asymmetrical social powers distributed according to class. Socially necessary means of production are constituted as private property, exclusively owned by one class of people. The other class, whose exclusion from ownership of social means of production is integral to the latter's constitution as private property, are then compelled to sell that which they do own – labour-power, their capacity for productive activity – in order to gain access to those means of production and hence – through the wage – their own means of survival. As consumer of labour-power, the capitalist may control the actual activity of labour – the labour process – and appropriate its product, which is then subsumed into capital itself. In Jeffrey Isaac's apt summary, 'the capitalist class thus possesses two basic powers: the power of control over investment, or appropriation; and the power to direct and supervise the labour process' (1987: 126; the *locus classicus* is Marx 1977: 291–292; see also Bowles & Gintis 1986: 64–91; Wood 1995: 28–31, 40–44). As *employers*, capitalists and their managerial agents attempt to assert control over the transformation of labour-power – the abstract, commodified capacity for labour – into actual labour. They seek to maximise the output of workers in relation to wages paid for labour-power, and may lengthen the work day or transform the labour process itself in order to do so (Marx 1977: 948–1084).[1] In the social position of *investors*, their decisions directly determine the social allocation of labour and resources – the pace of aggregate economic activity and the shape of the social division of labour – and indirectly limit the scope of public policy through the constraint of 'business confidence' and the implicit threat of 'capital strike' and transnational flight (Block 1977: 16; Bowles & Gintis 1986: 88–90). Insofar as these social powers are effectively privatised – associated with private ownership and exchange of property among juridically equal individuals in an apparently de-politicised economic sphere – they are ideologically mystified and democratically unaccountable (Thomas 1994; Wood 1995).

Anti-democratic and disabling as they might be, these class-based powers are neither uncontestable in principle nor uncontested in fact. Like all relations of social power, capitalist power relations are reciprocal, constituting a 'dialectic of power' subject to ongoing contestation, renegotiation and restructuring (see Isaac 1987). They represent, in short, historically particular forms of social power. As such, class powers must be actualised in various concrete sites of social production where class is articulated with other socially meaningful identities resident and effective in those historical circumstances. Capitalist power over waged labour has been historically articulated with gendered and raced forms of power: separation of workplace from residence and the construction of ideologies of feminised domesticity rationalising unpaid labour; ideologies of white supremacy rationalising racial segregation and inequality; gendered and raced divisions of labour; and so forth. These relations of race and gender have had important effects on class formation (e.g. Barrett 1988; Brenner 1993; Goldfield 1997). This implies that in concrete contexts class cannot be effectively determining without itself being determined. However this is not to say, in some pluralist sense, that class is only one of a number of possible social identities all of which are equally contingent. Insofar as productive interaction with the natural world remains a necessary condition of all human social life (Marx 1977: 290), I would maintain that understandings of social power relations which abstract from the social organisation of production must be radically incomplete.

Common Sense, Historical Bloc, and Transformative Politics

If Marx left us with incisive theorisations of capitalism, its core structures and constitutive tensions, it was the Italian political theorist and communist leader Antonio Gramsci who contributed to the historical materialist tradition a conceptual vocabulary with which to enable processes of transformative politics. Marx suggested that socialist transformation might emerge out of the confluence of capitalism's endemic crisis tendencies, the polarisation of its class structure and the intensified exploitation of the proletariat and, most importantly, the emergence of the latter as a collective agent through the realisation of its socially productive power, heretofore developed in distorted and self-limiting form under the conditions of concentrated capitalist production (Marx 1977). Gramsci accepted in broad outline Marx's analysis of the structure and dynamics of capitalism (Gramsci 1971: 34, Q12§2; 201–202, Q9§67), but was unwilling to embrace the more mechanical and economistic interpretations of Marx circulating in the international socialist movement (see his swinging critique of Bukharin's crude materialism, 1971: 419–472, Q11§*passim*).[2]

For Gramsci theory and practice are *internally related* such that progressive social change does not automatically follow in train behind economic developments, but must instead be produced by historically situated social agents whose actions are enabled and constrained by their social self-understandings (Gramsci 1971: 164–165, Q13§18; 172, Q13§16; 326, Q11§12; 375–377, Q11§63, Q7§21; 407–408, Q7§24; 420, Q11§13; 438, Q11§15).[3] 'The majority of mankind are philosophers in so far as they engage in practical activity and in their practical activity (or in their guiding lines of conduct) there is implicitly contained a conception of the world, a philosophy' (1971: 344, Q10II§17). As integral aspects of human social self-production, reflecting the internal relation of theory and practice, these 'popular beliefs ... are themselves material forces' (1971: 165, Q13§18). Thus, for Gramsci, popular 'common sense' becomes a critical terrain of political struggle (1971: 323–334, Q11§12; 419–425, Q11§13). His theorisation of a social politics of ideological struggle – which he called 'war of position' to distinguish it from a Bolshevik strategy of frontal assault on the state (1971: 229–239, Q1§134, Q1§133, Q13§24, Q7§16, Q6§138; 242–3, Q13§7) – contributed to the historical materialist project of de-reifying capitalist social relations (including narrowly state-based conceptions of politics, e.g. 1971: 268, Q8§130) and constructing an alternative – more enabling, participatory, intrinsically democratic and open-ended – social order out of the historical conditions of capitalism.

Popular common sense could become a ground of struggle because, for Gramsci, it is not univocal and coherent, but an amalgam of historically effective ideologies, scientific doctrines and social mythologies. This historical 'sedimentation' of popular common sense 'is not something rigid and immobile, but is continually transforming itself, enriching itself with scientific ideas and with philosophical opinions which have entered ordinary life. [It] is the folklore of philosophy' (Gramsci 1971: 326, Q11§12). As such, it is 'fragmentary, incoherent and inconsequential, in conformity with the social and cultural position of those masses whose philosophy it is' (1971: 419, Q11§13). Gramsci understood popular common sense not to be monolithic or univocal, nor was hegemony an unproblematically dominant ideology which simply shut out all alternative visions or political projects. Rather, common sense was understood to be a syncretic historical residue, fragmentary and contradictory, open to multiple interpretations and potentially supportive of very different kinds of social visions and political projects. And hegemony was understood as the unstable product of a continuous process of struggle, 'war of position,' 'reciprocal siege' (1971: 182, Q13§17; 210, Q13§23; 239, Q6§138; 323–34, Q11§12; 350, Q10II§44; 419–425, Q11§13).

Gramsci's political project thus entailed addressing the popular common sense operative in particular times and places, making explicit the tensions and possibilities within it as well as the socio-political implications of these, in order to enable critical social analysis and transformative political practice. 'First of all', Gramsci says of the philosophy of praxis,

> it must be a criticism of 'common sense', basing itself initially, however, on common sense in order to demonstrate that 'everyone' is a philosopher and that it is not a question of introducing from scratch a scientific form of thought into everyone's individual life, but of renovating and making 'critical' an already existing activity. (1971: 330–331, Q11§12)

His aim was 'to construct an intellectual-moral bloc which can make politically possible the intellectual progress of the mass and not only of small intellectual groups', and thereby 'to create the conditions in which this division [leaders/led] is no longer necessary', and in which 'the subaltern element' is 'no longer a thing [objectified, reified] but an historical person ... an agent, necessarily active and taking the initiative' (1971: 332–333, Q11§12; 144, Q15§4; 337, Q11§12; also 346, Q11§59; 349, Q10II§44; 418, Q11§67). Instead of a Bolshevik vanguardism which would deliver to the (objectively preconstituted and cognitively disabled) working class an historical vision formulated from an Archimedean point populated by professional revolutionaries, at the core of Gramsci's project was a critical pedagogy.[4] This took as its starting point the tensions and possibilities latent within popular common sense, and sought to build out of the materials of popular common sense an emancipatory political culture and a social movement to enact it – not just another hegemony rearranging occupants of superior/subordinate social positions, but a *transformative* counter-hegemony.

Gramsci's historical materialism understands history as a complex and contradictory story of social self-production under specific social circumstances. In line with more dialectical interpretations of Marx, Gramsci denies that there exists any transhistorical human nature, and insists that what we are in any given place and time is produced through the 'complex of social relations' in which historically situated persons live their lives, (re-) produce their social existence, and develop their self-understandings:

> man becomes, he changes continuously with the changing of social relations ...
> Each individual is the synthesis not only of existing relations, but of the history of these relations ... The 'societies' in which a single individual can take part are very numerous, more than would appear. It is through these 'societies' that the individual belongs to the human race. (1971: 355, Q7§35; 353, Q10II§54)

The meaning of this social history, then, resists reduction to simple formulae: 'The experience on which the philosophy of praxis is based cannot be schematised; it is history in all its infinite variety and multiplicity' (1971: 428, Q11§25). But while history is infinitely complex, from within the context of capitalist modernity – with its dialectical tensions between social unification and separation – it is socially possible to imagine grounds for emancipatory collective action and social self-determination. Gramsci's historical materialism thus envisions a process of 'becoming which ... does not start from unity, but contains in itself the reasons for a possible unity' (Gramsci 1971: 356, Q7§35).

> The unity of history (what the idealists call unity of the spirit) is not a presupposition, but a continuously developing process. Identity in concrete reality determines identity in thought, and not vice versa ... every truth, even if it is universal, and even if it can be expressed by an abstract formula of a mathematical kind (for the sake of the theoreticians), owes its effectiveness to its being expressed in the language appropriate to specific concrete situations. If it cannot be expressed in such specific terms, it is a Byzantine and scholastic abstraction, good only for phrase-mongers to toy with. (Gramsci 1971: 201, Q9§63)

In Gramsci's words, 'Politics in fact is at any given time the reflection of tendencies in the structure, but it is not necessarily the case that these tendencies must be realised' (1971: 408, Q7§24). 'In reality one can "scientifically" foresee only the struggle, but not the concrete moments of the struggle, which cannot but be the results of opposing forces in continuous movement, which are never reducible to fixed quantities since within them quantity is continually becoming quality' (1971: 438, Q11§15). I understand all of this to mean that the class-based relations of production under capitalism create the *possibility* of particular kinds of collective agency, but this potential can only be realised through the political practices and struggles of concretely situated social actors, practices which must negotiate the tensions and possibilities – the multiple social identities, powers and forms of agency – resident within popular common sense. This interpretation is, I believe, fully consistent with the relational social ontology at the core of Gramsci's thought:

> one could say that each one of us changes himself, modifies himself to the extent that he changes and modifies the complex relations of which he is the hub. In this sense the real philosopher is, and cannot be other than, the politician, the active man [*sic*] who modifies the environment, understanding by environment the *ensemble* of relations which each of us enters to take part in. If one's own individuality is the *ensemble* of these relations, to create one's personality means to acquire consciousness of them and to modify one's own personality means to modify the *ensemble* of these relations. (Gramsci 1971: 352, Q10II§54, original emphasis)

Gramsci was, of course, a Marxist, and assigned to class identity a relatively privileged position in his vision of transformative anti-capitalist politics:

> in reality, only the social group that poses the end of the state and its own end as the target to be achieved can create an ethical state – i.e., one which tends to put an end to the internal divisions of the ruled, etc., and to create a technically and morally unitary social organism … The content of the political hegemony of the new social group which has founded the new type of state must be predominantly of an economic order: what is involved is the reorganisation of the structure and the real relations between men on the one hand and the world of the economy or of production on the other. (Gramsci 1971: 259, Q8§179; 263, Q8§141; also Gramsci 1971: 139–40, Q8§132; 148, Q13§21; 151, Q13§33; 227, Q3§119)

Yet Gramsci's Marxism was a historicism which explicitly disavowed the notion that historical materialism represented trans-historical or universal truth. He derided as 'metaphysics' not just speculative idealism but 'any systematic formulation that is put forward as an extra-historical truth, as an abstract universal outside of time and space', explicitly including in this critique the 'metaphysical materialism' represented by Bukharin (1971: 437, Q11§31). Rather, Gramsci insisted that the 'philosophy of praxis' (his prison code for historical materialism, implicitly emphasising the (re-)unification of theory and practice) was a *situated knowledge*, constructed within and relevant to the historical relations of capitalism in particular times and places: 'the philosopher of praxis … cannot escape from the present field of contradictions, he cannot affirm, other than generically, a world without contradictions, without immediately creating a utopia' (1971: 405, Q11§62). Upon the historical supercession of capitalism, then, historical materialism would be superceded by other forms of knowledge relevant to their own socio-historical context (1971: 201, Q9§63; 248–249, Q5§127; 404–407, Q11§62; 436–437, Q11§14; 445–446, Q11§17). This understanding of historical materialism as situated knowledge implies, at the very least, the potential for productive political dialogue with other forms of situated knowledge constructed in contexts where capitalism has been articulated with various kinds of social identities and relations not reducible to class.

Despite Gramsci's insistence that a counter-hegemonic bloc should be led by anti-capitalist forces (1971: 259, Q8§179; 263, Q6§88), his vision of this historical bloc in terms of a dialogic process creates openings for engagement with other situated knowledges in ways which, his relational ontology implies, will reshape the identities of all participants in the conversation. Gramsci emphasises the transformative potential of such a relational vision by interpreting politics – entailing the historical problem of leaders/led – in terms of education (1971: 242, Q13§7; 247, Q13§11), which to the extent that it is successful is transformative of the teacher/student relation along with the parties embedded within that relation.

An historical act can only be performed by 'collective man', and this presupposes the attainment of a 'cultural-social' unity through which a multiplicity of dispersed wills, with heterogeneous aims, are welded together with a single aim, on the basis of an equal and common conception of the world ... This problem can and must be related to the modern way of considering educational doctrine and practice, according to which the relationship between teacher and pupil is *active and reciprocal so that every teacher is always a pupil and every pupil a teacher* ... Every relationship of 'hegemony' is necessarily an educational relationship and occurs not only within a nation, between the various forces of which the nation is composed, but in the international and world-wide field, between complexes of national and continental civilisations. (Gramsci 1971: 349–50, Q10II§44, emphasis added)

The political-educational process he envisions should be distinguished from indoctrination insofar as the former entails reciprocal development and seeks to enable the student to produce new truths independent of his or her teacher and, in the process, to teach the teacher, thereby transforming their relation:

learning takes place especially through a spontaneous and autonomous effort of the pupil, with the teacher only exercising a function of friendly guide – as happens or should happen in the university. To discover a truth oneself, without external suggestions or assistance, is to create – even if the truth is an old one. It demonstrates a mastery of the method, and indicates that in any case one has *entered the phase of intellectual maturity in which one may discover new truths*. (Gramsci 1971: 33, Q12§1, emphasis added)

The relation teacher/student (and leader/led) is then reciprocal but (in the context of capitalist modernity) initially asymmetrical: Gramsci aims at developing the reciprocity of the relation until the asymmetry approaches the vanishing point. I am suggesting, in other words, that Gramsci's political project aims at overcoming the historical division between leaders and led through 'active and reciprocal' processes of transformative dialogue as an integral part of the reconstruction of social relations and identities. This is why, I believe, he emphasises (contrary to the mechanical operations of economistic Marxisms) that the core of his pivotal concept of 'historical bloc' entails 'a necessary reciprocity between structure and superstructure, a reciprocity which is nothing other than the real dialectical process' (1971: 366, Q10II§12).

How then to account for his insistence that this process should be led, initially at least, by class-identified social forces (1971: 139–140, Q8§132; 148, Q17§37; 151, Q13§33; 227, Q3§119; 259, Q1§47; 263, Q6§88) and that the counter-hegemonic historical bloc should be 'one hundred percent homogeneous on the level of ideology' in order to effect a social transformation (1971: 366, Q10II§12; also, less categorically, 158, Q15§6; 168, Q13§23; 328, Q11§12; 445, Q11§17; but compare the seemingly much more rigid formulation in 1971: 265, Q6§136)? It is interesting to observe that the assertion of 'necessary reciprocity' between structure and super-structure quoted in the paragraph above occurs immediately following Gramsci's suggestion that an historical bloc must be 'one hundred percent homogeneous on the level of ideology' etc., and hence implies a critique of economism (sharply made elsewhere in the *Prison Notebooks*: see Gramsci 1971: 158–168 Q13§18, Q13§23, 419–472 Q11§13–34) which would undercut a simple class-reductionist interpretation of what he meant by 'homogeneous'. Rather than reading Gramsci as straightforwardly (and, in light of his larger project, perversely) reasserting the economistic Marxist eschatology of the 'universal class' as historical messiah, I would make sense of these claims in the context of the relational theory of transformative process sketched out here. I understand Gramsci to be suggesting that, in a capitalist social context, the necessary condition for any sort of transformative project whatever is a re-opening of political horizons effectively foreclosed by capitalist social relations and their associated self-understandings. Whatever else they may be or become (i.e., 'history in all its infinite variety and multiplicity'), transformative politics from within a capitalist context must necessarily entail shared anti-capitalist commitments in order to open up future possible worlds which are obscured by the social identities of abstract individualism and disabling ideologies of fetishism and reification produced by capitalism.

But the counter-hegemonic historical bloc should not be 'homogeneous' in the sense of annihilation of meaningful political difference, a unitary and uniform class-based identity imposed by a party uniquely in possession of a full understanding of history (although see Gramsci 1971: 265, Q14§13 for a passage which, if abstracted out of the larger relational context I am suggesting here, might be construed in this way). Homogeneity in this strongest sense would entail a self-defeating refusal to engage with, learn from and reciprocally develop potential allies, a stance of 'intransigence' which Gramsci derisively identifies with 'economistic superstition' (1971: 164, Q13§18).

> It is clear that this aversion on principle to compromise is closely linked to economism. For the conception on which this aversion is based can only be the iron conviction that there exist objective laws of historical development similar in kind to natural laws, together with a belief in a predetermined teleology like that of a religion. (Gramsci 1971: 167–168, Q13§23)[5]

If the historical supercession of capitalism is to be achieved, this will entail a relational transformation not just of the social-structural environment but of the participants in the struggle themselves. Gramsci's vehicle for the realisation of this kind of transformation was the historical bloc, led/educated – initially at least – by a class-identified political party:

> Clearly it will be necessary to take some account of the social group of which the party in question is the expression and most advanced element. The history of a party, in other words, can only be the history of a particular social group.

But this group is not isolated; it has friends, kindred groups, opponents, enemies. The history of any given party can only emerge from the complex portrayal of society and state (often with international ramifications too). (Gramsci 1971: 151, Q13§33)

Although every party is the expression of a social group, and of one social group only, nevertheless in certain given conditions [a counter-hegemonic bloc] certain parties [the party of the non-owners of capital] *represent a single social group precisely insofar as they exercise a balancing and arbitrating function between the interests of their group and those of other groups, and succeed in securing the development of the group which they represent with the consent and assistance of the allied groups.* (Gramsci 1971: 148, Q13§21, emphasis added).

In other words, the party of those subordinated under capitalism's class-based power relations can realise its potential as such only by transcending a narrow, instrumental or sectarian approach to politics and by attaining hegemonic leadership of a bloc of social forces committed to attaining post-capitalist futures (also Gramsci 1971: 180–182, Q13§17). Gramsci's historical bloc is not a one-way street, nor is it based on an instrumental understanding of compromise in which the constituent groups and their core interests remain essentially the same even as they accommodate one another. Rather the counter-hegemonic historical bloc involves the transformation of all parties actively involved in its construction, including the leading party:

The development of the party into a state [that is, a new form of collective social self-determination, 'an integral state, and not into a government technically understood'] reacts upon the party and requires of it a continuous reorganisation and development, just as the development of the party and state into a conception of the world, i.e., into a total and molecular (individual) transformation of the ways of thinking and acting, reacts upon the state and party, compelling them to reorganise continually and confronting them with new and original problems to solve (Gramsci 1971: 267, Q17§51).

Since every party is only the nomenclature for a class, it is obvious that the party which proposes to put an end to class divisions will only achieve complete self-fulfillment when it ceases to exist because classes, and therefore their expressions, no longer exist (1971: 152 Q14§70).

The goal of this process is not the permanent institutionalisation of the rule of one particular, preconstituted social group or its party over all others, but the transformation of capitalist social relations and their characteristic structural separations of state/society, politics/economics, theory/practice and so on, in order to enable the devolution of implicitly class-based political rule into a more generalised social self-determination – a future for which the democratisation of economic relations (the 'regulated society,' Gramsci 1971: 257, Q6§12; 263, Q6§88) would be a necessary condition. 'The [new, integral] state's goal is its own end, its own disappearance, in other words the re-absorption of political society into civil society' (Gramsci 1971: 253, Q5§127; also 260, Q1§46; 263, Q6§88).

In light of all this, I suggest that Gramsci's counter-hegemonic bloc may be understood as 'homogeneous' to the degree that it develops a common rejection of capitalism's abstract individuals in favour of more socially-grounded relational ontologies, process-oriented visions of social reality, and acknowledgements of the historical situatedness of political knowledge and practice. Once developed from within popular common sense, these elements of a 'homogeneous – in other words coherent and systematic – philosophy' (Gramsci 1971: 419, Q11§13) constitute the necessary common ground for forging an anti-capitalist bloc which would, if successful, construct new forms of political community and open doors to a rich variety of possible futures all of which are occluded by capitalism's reification of social life. Once this post-capitalist political horizon was approached, the anti-capitalist bloc would lose its historical reason for existence and its social condition of intelligibility. It would transform itself in ways appropriate to the new social context and new identities it had brought into being, and would thus be superceded by new forms of social self-determination.

What then am I to make of Gramsci's distinction between effective and historically organic ideologies on the one hand, and, on the other 'arbitrary, rationalistic, or "willed"' ideologies based on empty rhetoric and fleeting polemic (Gramsci 1971: 376–377, Q7§19)?[6] I am deeply skeptical of any interpretation of this distinction that is premised on economistic notions of base and superstructure. Gramsci's central concept of historical bloc, as I understand it, is predicated on reinterpreting the Marxian base/superstructure metaphor in terms of an internal relation in which each is – as an aspect of their mutually constitutive relation – already present in the other and neither is understandable apart from their inter-relation (e.g. Gramsci 1971: 377, Q7§19, Q7§21). This is the dialectical underpinning for Gramsci's claims that 'popular beliefs ... are themselves material forces' (Gramsci 1971: 165, Q13§18) and that 'historical bloc' entails 'a necessary reciprocity between structure and superstructure, a reciprocity which is nothing other than the real dialectical process' (Gramsci 1971: 366, Q10II§12). Concretely, then, while supercession of the historical circumstances of capitalism would require anti-capitalist commitments in order to effectuate a transformative politics, those politics are not themselves reducible to class nor need they have an exclusive point of origin in the 'economy' – which is, after all, but one of the reified forms of appearance characteristic of capitalist social reality as a whole. Gramsci's 'totalitarianism', then, is not a totalitarianism of class dictatorship but rather a view toward the transformation of capitalist social reality in its totality, overcoming separations of politics/economics, theory/practice, leaders/led, and so on (e.g. 1971: 335, Q11§12; 366, Q10II§12), a politics encompassing civil society, economy and state in order to re-integrate and transform the social life which has been fragmented, reified, naturalised and foreclosed under capitalism. Reconceptualising politics in this way re-opens processes of social self-determination which might lead to an infinite variety of post-capitalist futures. Therefore any social movement whose self-understanding and mode of political practice challenges the reified structural boundaries and atomised self-understandings characteristic of capitalism appears to me as 'organic', potentially part of a transformative counter-hegemonic bloc.

> What matters is that a new way of conceiving the world and man is born and that this conception is no longer reserved to the great intellectuals, to professional philosophers, but tends rather to become a popular, mass phenomenon, with a concretely world-wide character, capable of modifying (even if the results include hybrid combinations) popular thought and mummified popular culture. (Gramsci 1971: 417, Q15§61)

Conclusion

This is, I confess, not an innocent reading of Gramsci (I doubt whether any such thing is possible). Rather, my reading is motivated by a desire to reappropriate his thinking in order to enable a politics of solidarity in the increasingly unified but nonetheless plural world of globalising capitalism. I do not mean to suggest by this that Gramsci's thinking entirely escapes the potential pitfalls of Marxian teleology (see, e.g. Gramsci 1971: 417, Q15§61), only that there are resources within his thought for auto-critique and continual re-opening of political possibility. And Gramsci offers these resources without committing the obverse error of abstracting from capitalism and its historically specific relations. In the present context of globalising capitalism and neo-imperialism, such dialectical resources are no less important than they were when Gramsci wrote.

A Gramscian-inflected historical materialism enables an understanding of globalising capitalism, its relations of power and structures of governance, as the product of struggles – at once material and ideological – among concretely situated social agents. As the emergent neoliberal historical bloc has sought to (re)produce its social powers on an increasingly global scale, they have encountered recurrent bouts of more-or-less explicitly political resistance from a variety of social agents (some explicitly class-identified but many others not) who have challenged neoliberal representations and called into question not just the agenda of the neoliberal globalisation, but the legitimacy of the implicitly capitalist social powers, social positions, and identities underlying it (Rupert 2000, 2003, 2004). When viewed in terms of a dialectical reading of Gramsci, these struggles may be seen as reassertions of situated knowledges and process-based understandings of social reality, antithetical to the abstract individualism residing in capitalism's core, and embodying possibilities for critical engagement, dialogue, and transformative politics in an era of globalising capitalism.

Acknowledgements

I am grateful to the many people who have contributed in various ways to the development of the arguments I sketch out here. I am especially appreciative of the astute guidance offered by Adam D. Morton and Andreas Bieler and to two anonymous referees.

Notes

1. On the latter tendency as it was instantiated in struggles surrounding Fordist workplace regimes, see Rupert 1995.
2. Following the convention established in this volume, reference to the Gramsci anthologies is accompanied by a citation of the notebook number (Q) and section (§).
3. The concept of internal relations is central to a Marxian dialectic. An internal relation is one in which the inter-related entities take their meaning from (or are constituted within) their relation, and are unintelligible (on non-existent) outside of the context of that relation. Carol Gould contrasts these with external relations, 'in which each *relatum* is taken as a self-subsistent entity, which exists apart the relation and appears to be totally independent of it' (Gould 1978: 38).
4. Gramsci explicitly criticises the presumption, characteristic of Bukharin's Bolshevik primer, of a trans-historical, objective standpoint (1971: 444–445, Q11§17). I must note, however, Gramsci's ambiguous relation to Leninism: on the one hand, he admired the historical activism manifested by the Bolshevik Party in the Russian revolution and saw it as a potent antidote to the quietism induced by mechanical economism ('The Revolution against Capital,' 1977: 34–37; also 1971: 365, Q10II§12; 382, Q7§33); on the other hand, there are resources in Gramsci's more dialectical theory which can be mobilised for a critique of anti-democratic Bolshevik vanguardism, as I am suggesting here. For Gramsci's more dialectical construction of 'democratric centralism', see 1971: 189–190, Q13§26. Gramsci's ambivalent relationship with Leninism is a central theme in Boggs 1984.
5. Positions that Gramsci himself assails in his critique of Bukharin, especially see Gramsci 1971: 434–448, Q11§14–31.
6. This distinction of Gramsci's was brought to my attention by Adam D. Morton but also see Andrew Robinson's contribution in this volume.

References

Barrett, M. (1988) *Women's Oppression Today: Problems in Marxist Feminist Analysis* (London: Verso).

Block, F. (1977) The Ruling class does not rule: notes on the marxist theory of the state, *Socialist Revolution*, 33, pp. 6–28.

Boggs, C. (1984) *The Two Revolutions: Antonio Gramsci and the Dilemmas of Western Marxism* (Boston: South End).

Bowles, S. & Gintis, H. (1986) *Democracy and Capitalism: Property, Community and the Contradictions of Modern Social Thought* (New York: Basic Books).

Brenner, J. (1993) The best of times, the worst of times: US feminism today, *New Left Review* (I), 200, pp. 101–159.

Dryzek, J. (1996) *Democracy in Capitalist Times: Ideals, Limits and Struggles* (Oxford: Oxford University Press).

Germain, R. & Kenny, M. (1998) Engaging Gramsci: International Relations theory and the new Gramscians, *Review of International Studies*, 24(1), pp. 3–21.

Goldfield, M. (1997) *The Color of Politics: Race and the Mainsprings of American Politics* (New York: New Press).

Gould, C. (1978) *Marx's Social Ontology: Individuality and Community in Marx's Theory of Social Reality* (Cambridge, MA: MIT Press).

Gramsci, A. (1971) *Selections from the Prison Notebooks*, ed. & trans. Q. Hoare & G. Nowell-Smith (New York: International Publishers).

Gramsci. A. (1977) *Selections from the Political Writings 1910–1920*, ed. Q. Hoare, trans. J. Matthews (New York: International Publishers).

Isaac, J. (1987) *Power and Marxist Theory: A Realist View* (Ithaca, NY: Cornell University Press).

Marx, K. (1975 [1843]) On the Jewish Question, in: Marx, K., *Karl Marx: Early Writings*, trans. R. Livingstone and G. Benton, pp. 211–241 (New York: Vintage).

Marx, K. (1977) *Capital*, vol. 1 (New York: Vintage).

Morton, A.D. (2003) Historicising Gramsci: situating ideas in and beyond their context, *Review of International Political Economy*, 10(1), pp. 118–146.

Rupert, M. (1995) *Producing Hegemony: The Politics of Mass Production and American Global Power* (Cambridge: Cambridge University Press).

Rupert, M. (2000) *Ideologies of Globalization: Contending Visions of a New World Order* (London: Routledge).

Rupert, M. (2003) Globalising common sense: a Marxian-Gramscian (re-)vision of the politics of governance/resistance, *Review of International Studies*, 29(Special Issue), pp. 181–198.

Rupert, M. (2004) Anti-capitalist convergence? Anarchism, socialism, and the global justice movement, in: Steger, M. (Ed.), *Rethinking Globalism*, pp. 121–135 (Lanham, MD: Rowan and Littefield).

Sayer, D. (1991) *Capitalism and Modernity: An Excursus on Marx and Weber* (London: Routledge).

Steger, M. (2002) *Globalism: The New Market Ideology* (Lanham, MD: Rowan & Littlefield).

Steger, M. (Ed.) (2004) *Rethinking Globalism* (Lanham, MD: Rowan & Littlefield).

Thomas, P. (1994) *Alien Politics: Marxist State Theory Retrieved* (London: Routledge).

Wood, E.M. (1995) *Democracy Against Capitalism: Renewing Historical Materialism* (Cambridge: Cambridge University Press).

Gramsci and Left Managerialism

KEES VAN DER PIJL

As Gramsci argues in the *Prison Notebooks*, there is no class without 'organic' intellectuals who spell out the challenges facing it and chart its possible directions for development. When that class is historically progressive, these particular intellectuals and their mode of thinking constitute a pole of spontaneous attraction for the intellectual stratum at large (Gramsci 1975: 42, Q1§44).[1] With the help of this notion of the organic intellectual, Gramsci sought to discard the illusion of the autonomous, 'free-floating' intellectual who supposedly stands above social conflict; without organic intellectuals, a class cannot achieve *hegemony*, the consent of the broader set of social forces it leads in its quest to become the directive force in social development (Femia 1998: 109). The concept of 'organic intellectual' was Gramsci's attempt to give positive content to Engels' famous statement that 'in this day and age, "pure" intellectuals only exist on the side of reaction'.

Now what if we ask the question, *for which class* was Gramsci an organic intellectual himself – and not take for granted that this would have been the working class? Gramsci's thinking moved through several stages, but the *Prison Notebooks* are the key reference here. These writings, as few will dispute, revolve around the question *how to conquer and retain power in a complex society whilst avoiding adventurism and violence.* This task specifically deals with the 'managerial' aspect inherent in the vanguard concept of the party relative to the working class. Therefore, Gramsci's concerns in this area, I would argue, are organically related to the tasks of the managerial-technical *cadre* of contemporary capitalism. As this stratum grows in size and in terms of the centrality of its interventions, the resonance of Gramsci's ideas increases as well – that is, if the line of development is towards the Left.

Gramsci stands in the tradition of the organic intellectuals of the modern cadre, the strand of neo-Machiavellian elitism, represented by Pareto, Michels and notably Mosca. These thinkers did speak for the ascendant technocracy of their day, but they were also concerned with the specific *role of the new middle class in disseminating ideas that would bend democratic aspirations of the wider population in a particular direction* – away from socialism, that is. In that sense they were precursors of what today is called, significantly, 'Gramscianism of the Right' (cf. Nederveen Pieterse 1992: 22–32): the Irving Kristols, Francis Fukuyamas, and other 'neo-cons' in the United States today. Gramsci on the other hand, whilst concerned with the Machiavellian problematic of political science and with the circulation of ideas within the critical middle layer in the social structure, is of course a thinker of the Left. There is also a second connection to Machiavelli that runs deeper: this concerns the anti-metaphysical philosophical position, Machiavelli's humanism, which resonates so strongly in Gramsci (Femia 1998: 3, 89).

Today, as a new generation of cadre are being trained in the universities against the background of an unravelling of the neoliberal orthodoxies of the 1980s in the face of ecological crisis, war and inflation, Gramsci's thinking is developing a new 'organic' quality. As testified by the world-wide movement against capitalist globalisation in the 1990s and equally by the terrorist violence perpetrated by discarded US proxies, resistance to global capitalist discipline and its cultural hegemony is on the ascendant. For at least a segment of the cadre, the avoidance of violent excesses whilst trying to inflect the mood of the popular masses acquires a fresh urgency. For those who see themselves as future managers of global society (whether as state managers, teachers or development consultants in multilateral organisations or NGOs), the affinity of the Gramscian approach to their future tasks and present concerns is obvious. It is this affinity that I want to argue in the present contribution.

Class Antecedents of Neo-Machiavellianism

The growth of a capitalist market economy passed through two major phases – one of real market economy (a capitalism of small producers), and one of advanced, corporate capitalism eventually extending its discipline over the whole of society. Under the conditions of the former, market exchange binds producers into a division of labour realised blindly, so that the process of socialisation of labour very much remains confined to the national economy. Socialisation refers to the unification of divided labour into a functional unity; under liberal capitalism, this functional unification is entrusted partly to the actual state, but partly also left to the self-employed professional middle classes, the 'notables' of society – the notaries, actuaries, and in the ideological sphere, priests, novelists and others shaping and/or upholding the normative structure. In the type of society we are thinking about, commercialism remains very much fringe phenomenon surrounding a largely landed, agricultural economy, safely embedded in traditional values. France is the typical country here; within its social structure, the broadly speaking 'bourgeois' element in which are included the self-employed 'old notables', still in the early 1920s was numerically stronger than the wage-earning proletariat (cf. Rosenstock-Huessy 1961: 403; cf. Gramsci 1971: 105, Q17§37).

Now as the processes of concentration and centralisation of capital develop through crises in which small producers are expropriated, a rival context of socialisation to that upheld by the state and the old notables begins to emerge in the context of large corporations and parallel social structures. The market no longer is the only mechanism by which the division of labour is validated and social cohesion assured; capital begins to contain the division of labour within itself. Capital, after all, is a form of socialisation of labour, both at the level of the firm, which brings together a complex structure of labour-at-work in a single private jurisdiction; and at the level of the network of all firms connected by market relations, in competition.

Confining ourselves to the middle stratum between capital and labour, the effect of the changes in the structure of the capitalist economy on society is the parallel rise of a managerial-technical cadre. This cadre differs from the old notables in that they are no longer typically self-employed, and their authority is not an extension of the state in the old sense. They are paid a salary, they are employed by large-scale corporations and by the state and quasi-state organisms which mutate away from the old notables' state to a technocratic structure of power supporting the private sector. The new cadre tasks include, (a) the management of complex labour processes under the discipline of capital; (b) the provision of qualified workers capable of performing in them; (c) upholding the legitimacy of an order in which collective labour remains subordinate to the direction by others than the producers themselves; and (d) training and reproducing themselves as a class (Bihr 1992; Boltanski 1982).

The need for a special category of people to perform these tasks resides in a further aspect of socialisation, *alienation*. By this we understand that socialisation in a class society develops as a process divorced from conscious direction by its subjects. It is mediated, dependent on people performing an intermediary role, which includes a moment of mystification. The managerial, planning function assigned to the cadres by capital is made possible by the expropriation of skills and knowledge from the workers, just as capital expropriates the material product of labour in exchange for wages. Therefore the cadre, and the various fractions into which they dissolve and realign, constitute a central force-field *within which* the struggles over the deepening and widening of capitalist discipline are fought out. In these struggles, the cadre are more sensitive to the pressures emanating from the actual working class because under the veil of alienation that covers over contemporary society, cadre and workers constitute a salaried collective, self-managing a complex economy and society (I have argued this at greater length in van der Pijl 1998: ch.5).

Now since the rise of the cadre is a product of the concentration/centralisation of capital which in turn presupposes the expropriation of small owners, the sociological profile of the cadre tends to be 'petty bourgeois' – they are the children of dispossessed small shopkeepers, farm owners or, of course, old notables being replaced by the expanding state/corporate sector. In this sense, paradoxically, the 'new' cadre tend to reproduce the mind-set of a bygone age: that of small-scale market economy. Hence we should not be surprised to find among the broadly defined managerial–technical cadre, a weakly developed sense of class solidarity, an adherence to notions of abstract individual judgement, and a sensitivity to individual social status and privilege (cf. Bourdieu 1979: 465).

In the twilight of the crisis of the old notables and the rise of the new cadre, a strand of thinking emerged which articulated the resistance to the combined advance of industrial society and the labour movement, to capital *and* labour so to speak. Friedrich Nietzsche in this sense expresses, in Deppe's phrase, 'the pessimistic mood of young bourgeois intellectuals' in the *Belle Epoque* (1999: 109). Indeed, Nietzsche's diatribes against the equalisation tendency of modern society which elevates the dumb masses ('the herd') to a position of power, and his heroisation of a supposed superman, the *Übermensch*, articulate key aspects of this transition. In *The Will to Power*, Nietzsche specifically rails against the new middle class when he writes that

> today, in the era in which the state has acquired an absurdly fat belly, in all fields and disciplines, there are, in addition to the workers proper, also 'representatives' ... Our modern life is extremely costly because of this mass of intermediaries; in a city of antiquity on the other hand ... one acted for oneself and would have given nothing for such a modern representative or intermediary – except then, a kick in the ass! (Nietzsche 1959: 59, aphorism 75)

Nietzsche's was not the voice of a lone thinker. The idealisation of Antiquity and the early Renaissance as pre-industrial paradises, was a powerful current at the time – in Richard Wagner, Jacob Burkhardt, John Ruskin, Dante Gabriel Rossetti and many others in the arts and the history of art. The re-discovery of the political thinker of the *late* Renaissance, Machiavelli, was part of the same conjuncture. Facing the concrete challenge posed by the rapidly growing urban working classes, a group of thinkers moved beyond Romanticism to apply Machiavellianism to the changed circumstances, more particularly defining the role of the ascendant cadre as a new *elite*. The founder of this school of neo-Machiavellian elitists, Gaetano Mosca, speaks, when discussing who will meet the challenge of the masses, of the 'educated classes', and more generally, of a *political class* (Livingston in Mosca 1939: xi, xli).

Like the other elitists, Mosca really focuses on the mediating role of the social class which acts as a bridge between the rulers and the masses. It is 'the second stratum of the ruling class', which constitutes the channel through which information about the lower classes is passed on to the ruling class, and which in turn provides the legitimation for the latter's rule. It also serves as a training and recruiting ground for rejuvenating the ruling class in the longer run (Mosca 1939: 410; Parry 1969: 33). The spiritual despotism of the ruling class, which makes physical despotism superfluous, cannot do without the intellectual role of the cadre (cf. Femia 1998: 102). Indeed as Gramsci notes, the successive editions of Mosca's book were written at two junctures in Italian history, 1895 and 1923, when the political class disintegrated without being able to find the terrain on which to reconstitute itself (Gramsci 1975: 956, Q8§24; 972, Q8§52; 1978–79 Q19§5).

The cadre, then, in Mosca's understanding, provide the masses with a worldview, a *political formula*, constructed around theories and ethical concepts that will make rule acceptable to a much broader part of the population. It rests on a 'social type', which may be a nation or any other 'imagined community' such as a religion or a civilisation (Anderson 1983); and which serves to coordinate a multiplicity of wills and aims, and to achieve common ends (Livingston in Mosca, 1939: xv, xxix). But as Mosca underlines,

> political formulas are [not] mere quackeries aptly invented to trick the masses into obedience ... they answer a real need in man's social nature; and this need, so universally felt, of governing and knowing that one is governed not on the basis of mere material and intellectual force, but on the basis of a moral principle, has beyond any doubt a practical and a real importance. (Mosca 1939: 71)

In a striking anticipation of Gramsci's notion of the social foundations of hegemony, Mosca proposes to account for the stability of a regime by looking at the ratio between the number and strength of the social forces that it controls or conciliates; and the number and strength of the social forces that it fails to represent and faces as adversaries. Those periods of history are the most benevolent and productive, in which law, habit, custom and morals combine to create a legally entrenched system of balanced social relations (Livingston in Mosca 1939: xix–xx).

Mosca's work inspired his contemporary, Vilfredo Pareto (there were actually accusations of plagiarism). To Gramsci, Pareto's 'elite' is the equivalent of Mosca's 'political class' (Gramsci 1975: 956, Q8§24). While Mosca was still a traditional conservative, Pareto gravitated towards Fascism and he accepted many honours from it late in life. Pareto was a 'cadre' himself: a descendant of a Genoese patrician family, and a mathematician and engineer by training, he was a manager in an iron and steel factory from 1873 to 1890. Writing in self-imposed 'exile' from practical work, Pareto like Nietzsche, articulates concerns which are particularly alive among the declining old middle class, the younger descendants of which are groping for a new role in a changed capitalist society – a role which leaves classical liberalism behind and moves into the age of imperialism and mass politics. With respect to this cadre role, Pareto sees the danger of socialism precisely in that it *can mobilise an elite of its own by educating a segment of the working class* (Deppe 1999: 193, cf. 207).

A further important figure among the neo-Machiavellians, the Frenchman Georges Sorel, has a biography drawn straight from the transformation of old into new middle class. Sorel's father went bankrupt as a small businessman, and the son became a civil engineer trained at the École Polytechnique in Paris. Working for the French state in the road and bridge construction department, mostly in the provinces and in Algeria, Sorel resigned in 1892, at 45, to devote himself entirely to writing, just as Pareto had done. In many ways, Sorel remains a petty bourgeois in outlook. Robert Michels, a descendant of one of Germany's aristocratic banking dynasties, a pupil of Mosca's and, like Mosca, a professor at the University of Turin when Gramsci studied there (he famously wrote about the oligarchic tendency of party cadre) qualified Sorel as 'old-fashioned, very bourgeois ... irreconcilable, intolerant ... [and with] a deep mistrust of the Jews' (as cited by van Stokkom 1990: 38; note that Jews at the time 'stood for' urban life and capitalism). Sorel's great talent but vengeful personality put his legacy at the disposal of highly varying political currents, all of them violently anti-'humanistic' though. Like Nietzsche, Sorel had a magical effect on bourgeois and petty-bourgeois intellectuals because, again, he captures the sense of crisis whilst simultaneously, offering a Manichean vision of liberation (Deppe 1999: 223).

The fact that James Burnham, the author of *The Managerial Revolution* of 1941, two years later published a study of the elitists under the title *The Machiavellians*, may remind us of the connection between managerialism and this strand of political science (Burnham 1941, 1943). In Europe the connection was made by Fascism, which Boltanski has analysed in terms of 'the alliance, within each class, of fractions in decline and ascendant fractions' (Boltanski 1982: 102), especially in the middle class, the old notables and the new cadre.

Gramsci as a Neo-Machiavellian

Gramsci's life as an intellectual moved through several stages (Levy 1987: 392). He first was a witness to the workers' council tradition in Turin. But whilst appreciating the Russian soviet movement optimistically as a revolt 'against the social hierarchies generated by universal suffrage and bureaucratic careerism', he noted in 1919 already that in Western Europe, these hierarchies were resistant to a socialist breakthrough precisely because they had a powerful grip also on the working classes – thus prefiguring a central theme in his later work (Gramsci 1977: 79–80).

In the actual Russian revolution, the Bolsheviks approached the existing soviets in the spirit of the 'elitist' programme laid down in Lenin's *What Is to Be Done* of 1902. Vanguardism typically emerges in the normative vacuum striking people in the aftermath of the process of original expropriation prior to capital accumulation, as they are driven from a landed existence into sprawling industrial cities, sometimes via the trenches. The 'masses' at such junctures are truly a mass, a dislocated, disarticulated multitude united only in negative terms, driven by a state/party cadre committed to seizing power. The constructive intellectual moment of their struggles will be minute and abstract, and the Bolshevik version of vanguardism can be displaced by a mullah version as in Iran whilst all the other classical aspects of 'revolution' are in place – as happened in 1979 (cf. Hough 1990: 48). Following the Russian revolution, the other limit of Bolshevism was revealed when the new leadership found that 'bourgeois specialists' were indispensable to the functioning of modern society, and it will be remembered that one of Stalin's functions was head of the 'Workers' and Peasants' Inspection' which was set up to control them through repression. In prison, Gramsci noted that the Stalinist revolution from above and its forced industrialisation strategy (which he then still ascribes to Trotsky, its original advocate),

> consisted in an 'over'-resolute (and therefore not rationalised) will to give supremacy in national life to industry and industrial methods, to accelerate, through coercion imposed from the outside, the growth of discipline and order in production, and to adapt customs to the necessities of work.' He concludes that, 'given the general way in which all the problems connected with this tendency were conceived, it was destined necessarily to end up in a form of Bonapartism. (Gramsci 1971: 301, Q22§11)

Reformism on the other hand, provided the middle ground on which workers who have become de-radicalised by the dull compulsion of industrial existence, and the growing middle layer of cadre (technical, managerial), can develop a common platform. Bernstein, the organic intellectual of the reformist strand, had a much better grasp of the process of socialisation of labour than most Marxists, and accurately claimed that capitalist development engenders a multiplication of functions performed for capital and a corollary change in the character of the intermediate groups (Bernstein 1981: 60). But his position on colonialism that drew the fire of Rosa Luxemburg, made him a *persona non grata* for the revolutionaries in the labour movement. Gramsci was scornful of the reformist tendency in the labour movement, and in particular mocked Bernstein's claim that Marx 'mistakenly' relied on Hegel. Yet to the Gramsci of the *Prison Notebooks*, the awareness that advanced capitalist society is a complex structure with a wide range of class 'intermediaries' is likewise the starting point of the analysis. The mere numerical presence of this cadre element and the complexity of its situation in the structures of socialisation that hold society together, rules out any precipitate seizure of power by the working-class party. A revolution in such a society must be preceded instead by the winning over of the many intermediate strata of cadre, or 'intellectuals', in a struggle over cultural-political hegemony – just as the Enlightenment preceded the French revolution. Historical change, in Gramsci's view, has two interrelated sources: 'a struggle between social classes' and a struggle between 'contending world-views created by intellectuals … which are incorporated by classes' (Levy 1987: 391). Gramsci's real counterpart as a forward-looking cadre intellectual is Max Weber, who also seeks to understand how in a capitalist society receiving its innovative impulses from America (mass production, Fordism), the configuration of classes can be regrouped around the industrial pole. But whereas Weber's aim is to incorporate a cadre into a 'rational' arrangement under capitalist hegemony, Gramsci's strategic concern is of course to win over the cadre to the workers' cause (Rehmann 1998: 14; cf. Rupert 1995).

Now if the rationalised state can be ruled by convincing and deploying the cadre, the question arises: How is the consent of the masses obtained if the rationality of modern rule is conveyed to them not as such, rationally, but by 'formulas' premised on alienation and referring to an ideological community that is not (yet) championed on account of its rationality, but as an imagined community such as the nation? Pareto speaks of two strands in collective thought: one is made up of the residues, the basic instincts; the other, the 'derivations', rationalisations guided by emotions. In paragraph 1868 of his *Trattato*, he writes: 'The feelings which express themselves in derivations that transcend experience and reality, have great effect as motive forces to action. This fact explains', he continues, 'the origin of a phenomenon that Georges Sorel has observed and highlighted very well: Social doctrines that have great effectiveness (especially the emotions that are expressed in them) assume the form of myths' (as cited by Deppe 1999: 197). But Sorel goes beyond the individualistic, mathematised economics on which Pareto's sociology is premised. His concept of 'myth' is not a synthesis of consumer preferences but an autonomous, social-psychological force (Augelli and Murphy 1997: 27; cf. Gramsci on Pareto's mathematical logic, Gramsci 1975: 1663, Q14§9).

The neo-Machiavellians, then, played their role in devising a theory about how politicians crafted a 'mythology' revolving around notions of rebirth and struggle, a romanticised politics based on an aestheticisation of reality. To mobilise the masses, reality is not at all conceived realistically, but rendered in a spirit of pessimistic rejection (even though labelled 'realism'). The motif of a Spenglerian final demise, and of *war* as a last stand is prominent in this mythology. It can be used to great effect in an organic crisis, whether Fascism in the 1930s or the 'war on terror' today.

Now Gramsci does not simply borrow the concept of myth in its Sorelian sense; he is too much aware of the real complexity of society (civil plus political society) under advanced capitalism to believe that an explosive coming together of collective feeling that is not firmly anchored in the existing structures of socialised labour, internalised by the cadre and intuitively grasped by the masses, would ever be sufficient to establish a new order. Revolutionary myths lacking the internal consistency that can only derive from the real constellation of forces, even if conceived dynamically, leave the 'collective will in the primitive and elementary phase' and 'may at once cease to exist, scattering into an infinity of individual wills which in the positive phase then follow separate and conflicting paths' (Gramsci 1971: 128, Q13§1). Nevertheless he reveals his parentage as a cadre thinker of his age in his use of the language of politics as war. Politics can take the form of a war of movement (manoeuvre), war of position ('trench warfare'), and subterranean war (guerrilla). The well-off classes can afford to maintain and deploy 'shock troops' (*arditi*) to break through stalemates, etc. (Gramsci 1975: 121–123, Q1§133–1334). Of course in advanced capitalism, only the protracted war of position is a realistic option. If one wants to define revolutionary politics in war terms, it is best compared to *colonial war*, which involved conquest and control, and not to war as such, that is, the mere destruction of the enemy's power (Gramsci 1975: 122, Q134).

The Gramscian Legacy in Contemporary Social Science

When a class is no longer on the ascendant, the spontaneous attraction which the core ideas of its intellectuals exert on the intellectual stratum at large, dissipates. Today, the discipline of capital is mediated in the intellectual sphere by a demand for ideological conformity which reveals its 'willed' and artificial hegemony by imposing strictures on academic freedom, as in the early Cold War. Thus the rules of neo-positivist methodology and Weberian value neutrality that we may associate with Cold-War Fordism (cf. the qualification of Ayer's *Language, Truth and Logic* as the 'Summa Theologia' of post-war managerial society; Hewison 1981: 43) were embraced in academia more or less spontaneously in the 1960s. But the demise of national Fordism/Keynesianism and perhaps the implication of behaviourism and positivism in the war in Vietnam (Chomsky 1969), undermined the spontaneous attraction, and philosophy today has to be imposed as a regime (*'costrizione'*) (Gramsci, 1975: 42, Q1§44). In today's universities, outside funding and the partic- ular conditions imposed on it in the sphere of methodology, bring this out clearly if never in a watertight way. There is no denying that the younger generation of schol- ars is forced, by the new conditionalities of its employment, to adopt a 'consultancy' profile rather than commit itself to any particular strand of thought. Postmodernism, the fluidity of knowledge and its multi-applicability, may be considered the most direct ideological expression of this trend. Knowledge, Lyotard argues in his para- digmatic essay on the topic, changes in nature in the post-industrial stage of society; not truth, but performance becomes the criterion of its effectiveness. Postmodernism according to Lyotard is 'incredulity towards meta-narratives' (1984: xxiv), in the place of which he expects the ascent of 'a pragmatics of language particles'.

Of course this may be a 'natural' attitude for the new cadre employed in manage- ment consultancies and other relays of neoliberal discipline. They after all have to be acceptable to clients who would not hire somebody committed to a meta-narrative other than the silent 'grand theory' governing all contemporary reason, neo-liberal micro-economics; so some care as to where actually the 'language particles' perco- late is in order. But as the ascent of neoliberalism seems to be levelling off, a peren- nial problem of the cadre re-emerges as well – its acceptance of capitalist discipline and the subordination of its outlook and interest definition to those of the ruling class. Indeed, 'expert labour is potentially both panacea and serious problem. Experts can "walk" – join or become the opposition – or quite easily pour the intellectual equiv- alent of "sand" into the corporate gearbox', in the course of 'the long-running battle for control over expert labour in the face of heightened uncertainty and risk' (Chumer et al. 2000: xxiii).

If we see the academic social sciences as the reproductive apparatus of the contemporary cadre, and the Gramscian legacy as a key component of the cadre mind-set, one would expect that the number and range of applications of Gramsci's thinking in the social sciences would both increase over time. In my own area, International Relations (IR) and Global Political Economy (GPE), there certainly has developed a strong new interest in the uses of Gramsci's thinking from the early 1980s (see the contributions by Rupert, Bieler, Cutler, Pasha and William Robinson in this volume). In that sense the neo-Gramscian strand in contemporary IR/GPE may be interpreted as the theoretical condensation of a particular 'walk' taken by one segment of the post-war cadre, that is, those involved in one way or another, in the attempt to regulate and mitigate the impact of the transnationalisation of capital and its disruptive effects on society across the globe. The biography of Robert W. Cox, who pioneered the neo-Gramscian strand of thought in IR/GPE, in this light fits the pattern of Pareto, Sorel and others: a career in the ILO in Geneva from 1948 to 1972, ultimately as director of the International Institute of Labour Studies, followed by a return to academia (see Cox 1977: 415; Cox 1987, 2002, and the intellectual autobiography with Tim Sinclair, 1996).

Stephen Gill, in his introductory chapter to a key edited collection on the development of the Gramsci legacy in international studies, explicitly indicates how the research agenda that he identifies, may contribute to 'the development of transnational counter-hegemonic historic blocs' (Gill 1993: 17). Whether the intermediary stratum that would contribute to such a process actually relies on Gramsci explicitly is not necessary for this to materialise. But the spread of Gramsci as a key reference (in titles and/or abstracts) can be documented as broadly fitting the ascent and establishment of an IR/GPE neo-Gramscian approach. Johnna Montgomerie has looked at this for the period from 1945 to the present, surveying databases in several languages and comprising some 40,000 social science academic papers (Table 1).

Table 1.   Rise and spread of Gramsci's ideas across the social sciences (academic papers with Gramsci in the title and/or abstract)

	1945–1970	1971–1980	1981–1990	1991–2004
Total	19	157	316	386
New areas	Political philosophy Italian Studies	Education	Linguistics Jazz/Theatre Peasant studies International political economy Geography Other country studies Religions	Gender Literature Fisheries Urban studies African culture Aging Masculinity Muslim Brotherhood Anarchism Accounting Internet Library studies

Source: adapted from Montgomerie (2004).

Even if this can be used as an illustration only, one may deduce from it that the application of Gramsci's ideas is no longer confined to Italian studies and political philosophy, but runs across the social sciences, and increasingly so. If many of today's students in the social sciences, but also in medicine and engineering, are looking for opportunities to engage in a struggle for survival of the most vulnerable segments of global society, as I think they are, this would suggest that at least a segment of the cadre are taking the Gramscian legacy seriously. The reason for this is, as I have argued, that Gramsci as an organic intellectual speaks for this class first of all. His theoretical position touches on the core modern cadre role; and this role is becoming more important in a context of struggle, actually on both sides (hence, Gramscism of the Left *and* of the Right). As Bob Deacon claims in a study on the subject, this applies to ongoing struggles in the context of global social policy:

> a war of position ... IS being fought within and between international organi-
> sations; ... through the support given to labour movements and their represen-
> tatives in ministries of labour ... a connection to local social forces can be
> developed; and ... international [NGOs] and their complex connections to local
> civil society are part of this war of position. (Deacon 1997: 218)

Perhaps this is not much in the way of 'revolution' in the early-twentieth-century sense of the word. Rather it suggests processes which require a much longer dura-tion across a range of mediating structures, and which cannot be speeded up, at least not in the sense of 'leaping over phases of history', to use Marx's phrase. Even so, one may read this as a pointer to a set of connections, linking ongoing ideological struggles within the global state and quasi-state structures, with academic debates involving the Gramsci legacy, and hence with interest among students being trained for cadre roles. This is never a static, or even fully crystallised state of affairs. It depends on the real balance of forces, a balance that today is characterised by the rise of a world-wide anti-capitalist globalisation movement. It may be, then, that Gramsci's political-intellectual development (but in a reverse order), can help us to visualise how the protracted process of epochal transformation from a society alien-ated under capital, to a self-conscious, autonomous society, may be expected to evolve. First, as a war of position largely within a managerial cadre stratum, with each 'party' drawing strength from different sides making up the wider balance of forces in the global arena – capital and the property-owning bourgeoisie on the one hand, and the world-wide mass of humanity exploited by it on the other. Next, as struggles in which certain elements on the anti-capitalist side begin to assume 'vanguard' roles in rolling back capitalist discipline in a more irreversible way, adopting a war of manoeuvre posture and eliminating excessive forms of private appropriation and speculation. Finally, reaching a stage of conscious self-organisa-tion of humanity, the workers' councils tradition would finally come into its own, transcending not just the alienation of production relations, but also that of represen-tative politics and inter-national relations. However, by that time, we will be well into the 'long run', about which Keynes made his famously grim remark.

Acknowledgements

The author wishes to thank Johnna Montgomerie, PhD candidate at the University of Sussex, for research assistance. He also gratefully acknowledges the comments and suggestions for improving this article of two anonymous referees.

Notes

1. Following the convention established in this volume, reference to both the critical edition and the Gramsci anthologies is accompanied by a citation of the notebook number (Q) and section (§).

References

Anderson, B. (1983) *Imagined Communities: Reflections on the Origin and Spread of Nationalism* (London: Verso).

Augelli, E. & Murphy, C.N. (1997) Consciousness, myth and collective action: Gramsci, Sorel and the ethical state, in: Gill, S. & Mittelman, J.H. (Eds) (1997) *Innovation and Transformation in International Studies*, pp. 25–38 (Cambridge: Cambridge University Press).

Bernstein, E. (1981 [1899]) *De voorwaarden tot het socialisme en de taak der sociaal-democratie* [1899], intro. B. Tromp, trans. L. Inberg (Amsterdam: Arbeiderspers).

Bihr, A. (1992) *Entre bourgeoisie et proletariat. L'encadrement capitaliste* (Paris: L'Harmattan).

Boltanski, L. (1982) *Les cadres. La formation d'un groupe social* (Paris: Minuit).

Bourdieu, P. (1979) *La distinction. Critique sociale du jugement* (Paris: Minuit).

Burnham, J. (1941) *The Managerial Revolution, or, What is Happening in the World Now* (London: Putnam).

Burnham, J. (1943) *The Machiavellians, Defenders of Freedom* (London: Putnam).

Chomsky, N. (1969) *American Power and the New Mandarins* (Harmondsworth: Penguin).

Chumer, M., Hull, R. & Prichard, C., (2000) Introduction: situating discussions about 'Knowledge', in Prichard, C., Hull, R., Chumer, M. & Willmott, H., (Eds), *Managing Knowledge: Critical Investigations of Work and Learning*, pp. x–xxx (London: Macmillan).

Cox, R.W. (1977) Labor and hegemony, *International Organization*, 31(3), pp. 385–344.

Cox, R.W. (1987) *Production, Power, and World Order: Social Forces in the Making of History* (New York: Columbia University Press).

Cox, R.W. & Schechter, M.G. (2002) *The Political Economy of a Plural World: Critical Reflections on Power, Morals and Civilisation* (London: Routledge).

Cox, R.W. & Sinclair, T.J. (1996) *Approaches to World Order* (Cambridge: Cambridge University Press).

Deacon, B., Hulse, M. & Stubbs, P. (1997) *Global Social Policy: International Organisations and the Future of Welfare* (London: Sage).

Deppe, F. (1999) *Politische Denken im 20. Jahrhundert. Die Anfänge* (Hamburg: VSA).

Femia, J. (1998) *The Machiavellian Legacy: Essays in Italian Political Thought* (Basingstoke: Macmillan).

Gill, S. (1993) Epistemology, ontology, and the 'Italian School', in: Gill, S. (Ed.), *Gramsci, Historical Materialism and International Relations*, pp. 21–48 (Cambridge: Cambridge University Press).

Gill, S. (Ed.) (1993) *Gramsci, Historical Materialism and International Relations* (Cambridge: Cambridge University Press).

Gill, S. & Mittelman, J.H. (Eds) (1997) *Innovation and Transformation in International Studies* (Cambridge: Cambridge University Press).

Gramsci, A. (1971) *Selections from the Prison Notebooks*, ed. & trans. Q. Hoare & G. Nowell-Smith (New York: International Publishers).

Gramsci, A. (1975) *Quaderni del carcere*, ed. V. Gerratana, 4 vols (Turin: Einaudi).

Gramsci, A. (1977) *Selections from Political Writings 1910–1920*, ed. Q. Hoare, trans. J. Matthews (New York: International Publishers).

Hewison, R. (1981) *In Anger: British Culture in the Cold War* (New York: Oxford University Press).

Hough, J.F. (1990) *Russia and the West: Gorbachev and the Politics of Reform* (New York: Simon & Schuster).

Levy, C. (1987) Max Weber and Antonio Gramsci, in: Mommsen, W.J. & Osterhammel, J. (Eds), *Max Weber and His Contemporaries*, pp. 382–402 (London: Allen & Unwin).

Lyotard, J.F. (1984) *The Postmodern Condition: A Report on Knowledge*, trans. G. Bennington & B. Massumi (Manchester: Manchester University Press).

Montgomerie, J. (2004) *Tracking Gramsci: The Proliferation of the Gramscian Approach in Themes and Numbers*, reesearch note, Centre for Global Political Economy; ⟨http://www.cgpe.org⟩.

Mommsen, W.J. & Osterhammel, J. (Eds) (1987) *Max Weber and His Contemporaries* (London: Allen & Unwin).

Mosca, G. (1939 [1895]), *The Ruling Class*, ed. & intro. A. Livingston, trans. H. Kahn (New York: McGraw-Hill).

Nederveen Pieterse, J. (1992) Christianity, politics and Gramscism of the right: introduction, in: Nederveen Pieterse, J. (Ed.), *Christianity and Hegemony: Religion and Politics on the Frontiers of Social Change*, pp. 1–32 (Oxford: Berg).

Nietzsche, F. (1959[1906]), *Der Wille zur Macht. Versuch einer Umwertung aller Werte*, ed. P. Gast with E. Förster-Nietzsche (Stuttgart: Alfred Kröner Verlag).

Parry, G. (1969) *Political Elites* (London: Allen & Unwin).

van der Pijl, K. (1998) *Transnational Classes and International Relations* (London: Routledge).

Prichard, C., Hull, R., Chumer, M. & Willmott, H. (Eds) (2000) *Managing Knowledge: Critical Investigations of Work and Learning* (London: Macmillan).

Rehmann, J. (1998) *Max Weber: Modernisierung als passive Revolution: Kontextstudien zu Politik, Philosophie und Religion im Übergang zum Fordismus* (Berlin, Argument Verlag).

Rosenstock-Huessy, E. (1961 [1931]) *Die Europäischen Revolutionen und der Character der Nationen*, 3rd ed. (Stuttgart: Kohlhammer).

Rupert, M. (1995) *Producing Hegemony: The Politics of Mass Production and American Global Power* (Cambridge: Cambridge University Press).

van Stokkom, B. (1990) *Georges Sorel: De ontnuchtering van de Verlichting* (Zeist, Kerkebosch).

Class Struggle over the EU Model of Capitalism: Neo-Gramscian Perspectives and the Analysis of European Integration

Neo-Gramscian perspectives, first introduced by Robert Cox within International Political Economy (Cox 1981, 1983), were initially applied to the study of hegemony and the transformation of world order. Since the mid-1990s, a historical materialist approach to European integration, drawing on a range of different, yet related, neo-Gramscian perspectives, started to emerge. After first attempts by Cox (1993), Gill (1992) and Holman (1992), more comprehensive neo-Gramscian analyses of individual instances of integration followed (van Apeldoorn 2002, Bieler 2000, Bieler & Morton 2001a, Bieling & Steinhilber 2000, Cafruny & Ryner 2003). This article provides a critical engagement with these perspectives, dealing with their core theoretical assumptions as well as empirical analyses. It will do so with a specific focus on how scholars have drawn on the work of Antonio Gramsci and developed concepts suitable for today's empirical investigations. This follows closely Morton's suggestion that while one has to appreciate the specific historical circumstances of Gramsci's concepts, these concepts can, nonetheless, be transferred to other historical periods and fruitfully employed in empirical research. By thinking in a Gramscian way about the history of ideas, they can be situated in and beyond their context at the same time (Morton 2003a).

From early on, the study of European integration has been dominated by neo-functionalist and intergovernmentalist theories. Critics point to the conceptual determinism of these theories – the notion of economic spill-over in the case of the former, state-centrism in the case of the latter – leading to an ahistorical analysis, as well as their exclusive focus on form, i.e. the institutional set-up of the emerging European polity, at the expense of the content, i.e. the rationale underlying European integration (van Apeldoorn 2002: 34–44; van Apeldoorn et al. 2003; Bieler 2000: 3–8). Moreover, both sets of approaches neglect the social relations of production. Instead, they take the separation of the state and market, characteristic of capitalism, as their ahistoric starting point of investigation. Thus, the inner connection between the political and the economic cannot be problematised and the historical specificity of capitalism is overlooked (Burnham 1995: 136).

In the next section, Open Marxism is introduced as a historical materialist alternative to established approaches. While its focus on class struggle is welcomed, its state-centric analysis of developments at the international, European level is criticised. This sets the stage for an outline of an alternative historical materialist approach drawing on neo-Gramscian perspectives and conceptualising class struggle as a transnational phenomenon in times of globalisation. Then, recent neo-Gramscian empirical research with a specific focus on the struggle over the emerging European model of capitalism will be presented, before the conclusion summarises the results of the article and raises several shortcomings of neo-Gramscian perspectives for future research.

Open Marxism and the Analysis of European Integration

A range of perspectives on European integration, which can be grouped together under the label 'Open Marxism' (see the contributions in Bonefeld 2001a; Bonefeld 2002; Carchedi 1997; Moss 2000), have recently emerged. In contrast to established approaches, Open Marxism starts an analysis through a focus on the social relations of production. Instead of fetishising 'state' and 'market' as ahistoric 'things', both are treated as different forms expressing the very same social relations of production. By looking at the way these relations are organised in capitalism, it can be explained why state and market appear to be separate (Holloway & Picciotto 1977: 78). Based on the institution of private property, society is split between the bourgeoisie, i.e. those who own the means of production, and labour, i.e. those who only have their labour power to sell. Thus, economic exploitation is not politically enforced, but the result of the 'free' sale and purchase of labour power. Furthermore, Open

Marxism is opposed to economic deterministic, base/superstructure explanations. Determinism is avoided through a focus on class struggle, which by 'definition is uncertain and outcomes remain open' (Burnham 1994: 225).

This emphasis on open-ended class struggle and on overcoming the separation of the political and the economic is expressed in Open Marxist analyses of European integration. EMU, for example, is considered to be an attempt to ensure that monetary policy remains removed from politics. This should not, however, be understood as a separation of the economic from the political. Rather, by isolating neoliberal economic policies and abolishing the possibility of devaluation through the introduction of a single currency, those countries with lower rates of productivity can only compete with more productive countries through the extraction of more surplus value at the point of production; i.e. a higher level of worker exploitation through lower wages, longer working days and labour market flexibilisation (Bonefeld 2001b: 89; Carchedi 1997: 95–101). By indicating that it is actually labour, which bears the costs of EMU, it is also clear how a class analysis 'helps reveal the true nature of the project' (Carchedi & Carchedi 1999: 128). 'EMU merely provides a supranational anchor for the purpose of a politics of austerity' (Bonefeld 2002: 134). Thus, the intensification of exploitation of labour in order to secure the continuation of capitalist accumulation is identified as the social purpose visible in the revival of European integration.

Nevertheless, Open Marxism's ability to account for structural change is limited. While the character of the accumulation of capital and, thus, class struggle is considered to be global in substance (Holloway 1994: 30), the conditions of exploitation are standardised at the national political level. The form of class struggle at the global level is the interaction of states, which 'are interlocked internationally into a hierarchy of price systems' (Burnham 1995: 148). In other words, class struggle is only in substance but not in form understood as taking place at the global level. This reminds one of state-centric mainstream approaches and their shortcomings (Bieler & Morton 2003: 475). This state-centrism is also apparent in Open Marxist analyses of European integration. Carchedi, for example, analyses capitalist accumulation as the result of competition between different national capitals, competing with each other for the extraction of surplus value at the international level. The future form of the EU 'will continue to be shaped by inter-capitalist rivalries (centring upon the relations among Germany, France and the United Kingdom)' (Carchedi 1997: 108–109). Moss applauds Moravcsik's state-centric explanation of European integration and only recommends to amend analysis of domestic preference formation, which emphasises the interests of domestic producers and governments, with a focus on geopolitics, political ideology and class (Moss 2000). In short, globalisation as processes of structural change beyond the state system cannot be conceptualised and transnational class formation is overlooked by Open Marxism.

A Neo-Gramscian Approach to European Integration

Drawing on the work of the Italian Marxist Antonio Gramsci (1971), neo-Gramscian perspectives conceptualise the historical specificity of capitalism by taking the sphere of production as the starting-point of their analysis. Importantly, production is to be understood in a wide sense including the production and repro-duction of knowledge, institutions and the social relations involved in the produc-tion of physical goods (Cox 1989: 39). Similar to Open Marxism, state and market are comprehended as two different forms of the same social relations of production (Bieler & Morton 2003: 476). Moreover, the social relations of production are considered to engender social forces as the most important collective actors. Impor-tantly, this focus on production is closely informed by Gramsci's rejection of econo-mism in all its forms, including the idea that communism will come about as a result of an inevitable, automatic historical development. 'For the conception upon which the aversion is based can only be the iron conviction that there exist objective laws of historical development similar in kind to natural laws, together with a belief in a predetermined teleology like that of a religion' (Gramsci 1971: 168, Q13§23).[1] Hence, a neo-Gramscian analysis emphasises class struggle 'as the heuristic model for the understanding of structural change' (Cox with Sinclair 1996: 57–58) and, thus, acknowledges that there are always several possible outcomes.

Class can be identified by relating social forces to their place in the production process. The capitalist mode of production is organised around wage labour and private property, leading to the opposition between capital and labour (see above). The work of van der Pijl has been crucial in expanding upon this basic characterisa-tion of the capitalist social relations of production. Drawing on Marx, van der Pijl outlined the capital fractions approach, considering the different functional forms of capital within the overall process of surplus accumulation. He concludes that due to their different position in the production process, finance capital is likely to have different interests than industrial capital (van der Pijl 1984: 4–20). Robert Cox further developed the capital fractions approach by identifying different class fractions through an analysis of the level at which production is organised. Because of the partial transnationalisation of national production and financial systems due to globalisation, he argues that 'it becomes increasingly pertinent to think in terms of a global class structure alongside or superimposed upon national class structures' (Cox 1981: 147; see also Cox 1993: 259–260). Therefore, and here neo-Gramscian perspectives crucially go beyond Open Marxism, there is not only class struggle between capital and labour at the national level, but also between national capital and labour and transnational forces of capital and labour (van Apeldoorn 2002: 26–34; Bieler 2000: 10–11). At the European level, it is possible to distinguish between European transnational forces, engendered by production structures organised across borders within Europe, and global forces of capital and labour, stemming from production structures across the world (van Apeldoorn 2002: 47; Holman 1992: 15–16). At a general level, it can be hypothesised that transnational capital and labour are likely to support neo-liberal restructuring at the national level, because their busi-ness relies on open borders. On the other hand, national capital and labour may oppose neo-liberalism, since they depend on state protectionism against international competition. At the European level, European transnational forces may favour strong internal integration combined with some protection against outside competition, while truly global social forces may prefer fully open borders. Nevertheless, an analysis of the production structure only allows the identification of the core actors and the formulation of research hypotheses. The uncovering and explanation of actual strategies of social forces remains the task of an empirical investigation. The position within the sphere of production shapes the behaviour of social forces, it does not determine it. The latter would imply an economism, which Gramsci rejected.

This is where further inspiration can be drawn from Gramsci linked to his thinking on the agency–structure problem. An emphasis on class struggle and a rejection of economism implies the possibility for agency to make a difference within certain constraining structural limits. Conceived within a dialectical conception of past and present, where the past involves the sphere of necessity, and the present the realm of freedom, Gramsci offers an understanding of the relationship between structure and agency. Employed by neo-Gramscian perspectives, this takes the form of an acknowledgment of the impact of the social relations of production, forms of state and world order, resulting from strategies in the past, on agency in the present. In turn, there is also comprehension of the open-endedness of agency at the same time. 'What emerges within this historicist conception of philosophy and history, therefore, is a concern with the structural conditions of existence, the realm of necessity, initially inherited from the past forms of thought and action, as well as concern for the realisation of agency, the realm of freedom, that is both determined and determining' (Bieler & Morton 2001b: 19). In other words, understanding structure as the result of strategies in the past, makes it possible to reflect on the freedom of action in the present. 'Structure ceases to be an external force which crushes man [*sic*], assimilates him to itself and makes him passive; and is transformed into a means of freedom, an instrument to create a new ethico-political form and a source of new initiatives' (Gramsci 1971: 367, Q10II§6i). Returning to globalisation, this dialectical understanding of structure and agency also overcomes the understanding of globalisation as external pressure to which actors can only respond and adjust. Instead, it helps us to identify the forces behind globalisation, i.e. transnational capital, and the particular social purpose they pursue, i.e. neo-liberal restructuring. Whether they are able to push through their particular interests is a matter of social struggle.

The rejection of economism, the related focus on open-ended class struggle, as well as the dialectical perspective on agency-structure, all highlight the independent role Gramsci attributed to ideas. This is his third main contribution employed by neo-Gramscian scholarship. As Gramsci points out, 'it is on the level of ideologies that men [*sic*] become conscious of conflicts in the world of economy' (Gramsci 1971: 162, Q13§18). Two different functions of ideas can be distinguished. On the one hand, they can be considered to be a part of the overall structure in the form of 'intersubjective meanings'. Hence, ideas establish the wider frameworks of thought, 'which condition the way individuals and groups are able to understand their social situation, and the possibilities of social change' (Gill & Law, 1988: 74). On the other hand, ideas may be used by actors as 'weapons' in order to legitimise particular policies and are important in that they form part of a hegemonic project by organic intellectuals (see below). While recent constructivist contributions to European integration can only outline the variety of different discourses present (e.g. Rosamond 2002), through a reference to Gramsci's definition of 'organic ideas', neo-Gramscian perspectives can comprehend the material structure of ideas and, thus, analyse why certain ideas have become predominant at a particular time (Bieler 2001: 95–99). Only those ideas are organic that 'organise human masses, and create the terrain on which men [*sic*] move, acquire consciousness of their position, struggle, etc.' (Gramsci 1971: 377, Q7§21). The connection between human masses, i.e. social forces, and ideas is provided by organic intellectuals, emerging from and representing particular fractions of social forces (Gramsci 1971: 5, Q12§1). They do not simply produce ideas, but they concretise and articulate strategies in complex and often contradictory ways, which is possible because of their class location, i.e. proximity to the most powerful forces in production. As Morton (2003b: 30) asserts, this understanding 'links the social function of intellectuals to the world of production within capitalist society, without succumbing to economic determinism, whilst still offering the basis for a materialist and social class analysis of intellectuals'. It is the task of organic intellectuals to organise the social forces they stem from and to develop a 'hegemonic project', which is able to transcend the particular economic-corporate interests of their social group by binding and cohering diverse aspirations, interests and identities into an historical bloc. Such an historical bloc is at one level an alliance of various fractions of social forces. At another level, however, it indicates the integration of a variety of different class interests, of ideas and material properties, that are propagated throughout society 'bringing about not only a unison of economic and political aims, but also intellectual and moral unity ... on a "universal" plane' (Gramsci 1971: 181–182, Q13§17). Once successful, an historical bloc establishes a position of hegemony, where its rule relies predominantly on the consent of the ruled, not on open force (Cox 1981: 139). The focus on the role of ideas as part of a hegemonic project implies that the definition of globalisation as the transnationalisation of production and finance has to be amended with neo-liberalism as its ideological component (Cox 1993: 266–267; Rupert 2000: 54).

Taking all these concepts together: (1) the rejection of economism and the related open-ended nature of historical development; (2) the dialectical understanding of the relationship between structure and agency; and (3) the conceptualisation of ideas as the representation of specific material interests, which makes it possible to analyse how different interests and ideas are involved in specific instances of class struggle, it is clear why neo-Gramscian perspectives are a critical theory, which 'does not take institutions and social and power relations for granted but calls them into question by concerning itself with their origins and how and whether they might be in the process of changing' (Cox 1981: 129). This makes it possible to analyse the social purpose underlying various social forces' activities (van Apeldoorn 2002: 11–13; Bieler 2000: 8). In the next section, neo-Gramscian work on the revival of European integration since 1985 and the continuing contestation over the social purpose of the future EU model of capitalism will be presented to illuminate these theoretical points.

The Revival of European Integration in the mid-1980s: A Historical Materialist Analysis

In comparative political economy, there is currently a debate about different models of capitalism and their respective viability within conditions of globalisation. A distinction is frequently made between an Anglo-American model of capitalism, based on the free market economy and neo-liberal economics; a consensual model of capitalism, including traditional social democratic concepts; and a state-led model of capitalism, frequently associated with authoritarian forms of state in South-East Asia and dirigiste France (e.g. Coates 2000: 6–11; Schmidt 2002: 107–146). Due to their focus on the social purpose of European integration since the mid-1980s in relation to the current struggle over the future EU economic–political model, neo-Gramscian perspectives can refer to these models as ideal types, against which the course of the EU is charted (van Apeldoorn 2002: 13).

In 1985, the Commission published its famous White Paper 'Completing the Internal Market', which proposed 300 (later reduced to 279) measures designed to facilitate progress towards the completion of the Internal Market by 1992 through the abolition of non-tariff barriers. The Single European Act (SEA) of 1987, which institutionalised the Internal Market programme, spelled out the goals of the four freedoms, i.e. the free movement of goods, services, capital and people. The rationale underlying the Internal Market programme was clearly of a neo-liberal nature (Grahl & Teague 1989). A bigger market was supposed to lead to tougher competition resulting in higher efficiency, greater profits and eventually, through a trickle-down effect, in more general wealth and jobs. National markets were deregulated and liberalised, national companies were privatised. An emerging common competition policy was meant to secure the market against state intervention or ownership even in areas such as telecommunications, public procurement and energy. The Treaty of Maastricht was signed in 1991. Amongst other changes, it laid out the plan for EMU, including a single currency to be administered by a supranational and independent European Central Bank (ECB). In January 1999, 11 member states carried out this step, when they irrevocably fixed their exchange rates. The underlying rationale of EMU is embodied in the statutory role of the ECB and the convergence criteria. As for the former, a common monetary policy is now dealt with by the independent ECB. The primary target of the ECB and its interest rate policy, as spelled out in the Treaty of Maastricht, is the maintenance of price stability and low inflation. Economic growth and employment are only secondary objectives. Gill describes this as an instance of 'new constitutionalism', which is a 'move towards construction of legal or constitutional devices to remove or insulate substantially the new economic institutions from popular scrutiny or democratic accountability' (Gill 1992: 165; see also Gill 2001: 47). The convergence criteria, most importantly, obliged member states to have a government budget deficit of no more than 3 per cent of GDP and government debt of no more than 60 per cent of GDP. They did not include a criterion on unemployment. This was of secondary importance and thought to be solved through the trickle-down effect. EMU member countries had to implement tough austerity budgets in order to meet the criteria in the run-up to EMU. Within EMU, continuation of neo-liberal budget policies has been ensured through the Stability and Growth Pact, adopted at the Amsterdam European Council summit in June 1997. It committed members to stay within the neo-liberal convergence criteria even after the start of EMU on 1 January 1999 and, through the requirement to adhere to the Broad Economic Policy Guidelines including a general commitment to a balanced budget, further emphasised the overriding focus on low inflation (Jones 2002: 37–40).[2] In sum, both the Internal Market and EMU firmly put the EU on the road towards a neo-liberal Anglo-American model of capitalism.

When analysing which social forces are behind this move towards neo-liberalism within the EU, a neo-Gramscian analysis turns towards the social relations of production. Transnational capital is well organised at the European level. Especially the ERT, founded in 1983 and currently consisting of 45 CEOs, played a crucial role in the revival of European integration. In January 1985, the ERT chairman Wisse Dekker (Philips) published the report 'Europe 1990: An Agenda for Action'. Three days later, the new President of the Commission Jacques Delors gave a speech to the EP with very similar contents. In fact, the Commission White Paper on Completing the Internal Market, published in June 1985, resembled very much Dekker's report. The only real difference was the postponement of the deadline from 1990 to 1992 (Balanya et al. 2000: 21). Nevertheless, as van Apeldoorn's (2002: 78–82 and 115–157) detailed analysis of the different projects behind the Internal Market programme reveals, neo-liberalism had initially not been the only possible basis. Two further projects can be identified. A neo-mercantilist project was mainly supported by transnational European firms, which predominantly produced for the European market, but were still not fully global players. They hoped that the completion of the Internal Market would be complemented with a European industrial policy and some form of protectionism against global competition. The second alternative was a social democratic project, initiated by Jacques Delors. For social democrats and several trade unions, the European level seemed to offer the possibility of market re-regulation at a higher level. The eventual outcome of the struggle between these three projects constituted a compromise, aptly labelled 'embedded neo-liberalism' by van Apeldoorn (2002: 158–189). By meeting some of the concerns for a European industrial policy with the chapters on 'Trans-European [infrastructure] networks' and 'Research and Technological Development' and for a Social Europe with the Social Protocol, the Treaty of Maastricht co-opted social forces from the other two projects into the predominantly neo-liberal compromise.

The ERT should, however, not be misunderstood as a lobby group next to other lobby groups. From a neo-Gramscian perspective, the ERT is an institution which provides a platform for organic intellectuals, who formulate a coherent hegemonic project for transnational European capital, which is at the same time able to transcend the particular interests of this capital fraction in order to attract wider social forces towards the formation of a historical bloc (van Apeldoorn 2002: 104–107). Embedded neo-liberalism can be understood as the hegemonic project of transnational European capital. The fact that it is so influential is not because the ERT is merely the more effective lobbying machine. Instead, it is firstly because, following the neo-Gramscian conceptualisation of ideas, the neo-liberal ideas, underpinning embedded neo-liberalism, correspond positively to the general shift towards neo-liberalism, which is itself a part of the structural change of globalisation since the mid-1970s and early 1980s (Gamble 2001). Secondly, in line with a neo-Gramscian understanding of structure and agency, embedded neo-liberalism has gained predominance within the EU, because this project has been backed up by the increasing structural power of transnational capital, i.e. it was firmly rooted in material structures. Partly driving the move towards the Internal Market programme in 1985, but especially also in response to it, European production has become increasingly transnationalised. While the annual average of inward FDI flows into the EU between 1989 and 1994 was $76,634 million, inward FDI in 2000 was $617,321 million (UN 2001: 291). The corresponding figures for outward FDI are $105,194 million as an annual average between 1989 and 1994, and $772,949 million in 2000 (UN 2001: 296). Neo-Gramscian analyses of the widening of European integration since the mid-1990s, including the accession of Austria, Finland and Sweden in 1995 and ten Mediterranean and Central and Eastern European countries in 2004, similarly demonstrate neo-liberal restructuring as the underlying social purpose, pushed especially by transnational European capital (see, for example, Bieler 2000, 2002; Bohle 2000; Holman 2001; Shields 2003).

Conclusion

To summarise, this essay has demonstrated that through an adoption of Gramsci's rejection of economism, his dialectical analysis of the agency-structure problem, and his way of conceptualising the material structure of ideas, neo-Gramscian perspectives are able to analyse European integration as an open-ended historical development. This includes identifying the social purpose underlying European integration, as well as understanding it as part of a structural change of the international system through its emphasis on transnational class formation. It was outlined how the revival of European integration since the mid-1980s, driven to a large extent by transnational capital, has moved the EU towards the neo-liberal Anglo-American model of capitalism. There are, however, several shortcomings of neo-Gramscian analyses to date. They are the concern of this conclusion.

Neo-Gramscian perspectives can incorporate the structural changes related to globalisation in their analyses. Little work, however, has been conducted about the impact of the national as well as European institutional set-ups on European integration. The main actors are deduced from the social relations of production. Their chances of success in their particular institutional environment, however, are not conceptualised. A neo-Gramscian perspective accepts that social forces operate within and through different forms of state concerned with the relationship between civil society and the state (Cox 1989: 41). What is generally lacking, however, is a conceptualisation of the structural impact these institutions have on social forces. A potential way of overcoming this shortcoming is to engage with Jessop's 'strategic-relational' approach to the state. As an institutional ensemble the state can be understood as the framework within which various different strategies are possible. As such, however, the state 'can never be considered as neutral. It has a necessary structural selectivity' (Jessop 1990: 268), favouring certain social forces and strategies over others. Empirical research should not only investigate which actors pursue which strategy for what purpose, but how this strategy relates to the structural environment and what are the related chances of success (Bieler 2005). Related to this neglect of institutional form is the danger, as Strange maintains, that too strong a focus on social content makes neo-Gramscian perspectives overlook the possibilities for change within existing institutional forms. Euro-Keynesianism combined with a radical Euro-corporatism could provide an alternative within the current institutional set-up. This is even more so since the employment chapter, adopted as part of the Treaty of Amsterdam in 1997, implied a stronger level of accountability of the ECB and a potential related change in policy emphasis towards growth and employment (Strange 2002: 359–360).

This point refers to the more general criticism of neo-Gramscian perspectives that too little attention has been paid to the potential of resistance to neo-liberalism. As early as 1994, Drainville had bemoaned the emphasis given to the apparent strength of neo-liberal hegemony at the expense of projects of resistance (Drainville 1994: 124). Within neo-Gramscian studies of the revival of European integration since the mid-1980s too much attention has been given to the way neo-liberalism was established and too little has been said about the potential for alternatives. While neo-liberalism has been dominant over the last two decades, it should not be forgotten that hegemonic projects such as 'embedded neo-liberalism' always need to be re-confirmed and are constantly contested. In short, hegemony is never solid but open to change. First neo-Gramscian analyses of instances of resistance have been conducted in relation to the struggle of the Zapatistas in Mexico (Morton 2002) as well as the anti-globalisation movements in Europe within the European Social Forum in Florence in 2002 (Bieler & Morton 2004), but much more work needs to be done in respect of European integration.

Moreover, not only resistance in general, but also labour and trade unions and their potential role within resistance to neo-liberalism has been neglected. Van Apeldoorn simply states that the 'process of transnational class formation so far has been restricted to the capitalist class' and that labour would remain weak at the European level (van Apeldoorn 2002: 33; see also 46). This overlooks, firstly, that class is identified by individuals' position in the production process, not whether they have developed a common consciousness and class activity at a political level (Ste. Croix 1981: 44). As there is a transnational production structure in certain sectors in the EU, there is also a transnational class fraction of labour. Secondly, the potential of resistance by labour and actual first steps of organisation at the European level are denied and excluded from the beginning. Again, first studies have been conducted especially in relation to trade unions' positions on EMU and on the related future development of the EU model of capitalism (see Bieler 2003a, 2003b, Bieling & Schulten 2003, Ryner & Schulten 2003, Strange 2002), but much more research is needed to understand the full potential of labour's resistance to neo-liberal restructuring within the EU.

Finally, increasing neo-Gramscian scholarship on European integration brings with it the danger of the formation of a school of thought. This, as Morton (2001) outlines, implies the danger of internal self-referencing and a general loss of the critical dimension. Scholars from Amsterdam have been crucial in the development of neo-Gramscian perspectives on European integration. The fact, however, that they refer to themselves as the 'Amsterdam School' (van Apeldoorn et al. 2003: 37, 38) and speak about a specific Amsterdam Project (van Apeldoorn 2004, Overbeek 2004) is rather worrying in this respect.

Acknowledgements

I am indebted to Kamran Matin, Adam David Morton, two anonymous referees, and the participants of the workshop *Images of Gramsci: Connections and Contentions in Political Theory and International Relations*, held at the School of Politics, University of Nottingham, UK (24–25 October 2003), for comments on earlier drafts.

Notes

1. Following the convention established throughout this volume, reference to the Gramsci anthologies is succeeded by the notebook number (Q) and section (§) to facilitate easier cross-checking of citations.
2. France and Germany are currently in breach of the Pact. While this indicates the power of larger countries in the EU, it does not imply a general departure from the price stability macroeconomic policy course of the EU at this point.

References

van Apeldoorn, B. (2002) *Transnational Capitalism and the Struggle over European Integration* (London: Routledge).

van Apeldoorn, B. (2004) Theorising the transnational: a historical materialist approach, *Journal of International Relations and Development*, 7(2), pp. 142–176.

van Apeldoorn, B., Overbeek, H. & Ryner, M. (2003) Theories of European integration: a critique, in: Cafruny, A.W. & Ryner, M. (Eds), *A Ruined Fortress? Neoliberal Hegemony and Transformation in Europe*, pp. 17–45 (Lanham, MD: Rowman and Littlefield).

Balanyá, B., Doherty, A., et al. (2000) *Europe Inc.: Regional and Global Restructuring and the Rise of Corporate Power* (London: Pluto Press).

Bieler, A. (2000) *Globalisation and Enlargement of the European Union: Austrian and Swedish Social Forces in the Struggle over Membership* (London/New York: Routledge).

Bieler, A. (2001) Questioning cognitivism and constructivism in IR theory: reflections on the material structure of ideas, *Politics*, 21(2), pp. 93–100.

Bieler, A. (2002) The struggle over EU enlargement: a historical materialist analysis of european integration, *Journal of European Public Policy*, 9(4), pp. 575–597.

Bieler, A. (2003a) Labour, neo-liberalism and the conflict over economic and monetary union: a comparative analysis of British and German trade unions, *German Politics*, 12(2), pp. 24–44.

Bieler, A. (2003b) Swedish trade unions and economic and monetary union: the European Union membership debate revisited?, *Cooperation and Conflict*, 38(4), pp. 385–407.

Bieler. A. (2005) European integration and the transnational restructuring of social relations: the emergence of Labour as a regional actor?, *Journal of Common Market Studies*, 43, pp. 461–484.

Bieler, A. & Morton, A.D. (Eds) (2001a) *Social Forces in the Making of the New Europe: The Restructuring of European Social Relations in the Global Political Economy* (London: Palgrave).

Bieler, A. & Morton, A.D. (2001b) The Gordian knot of agency-structure in international relations: a neo-Gramscian perspective, *European Journal of International Relations*, 7(1), pp. 5–35.

Bieler, A. & Morton, A.D. (2003) Globalisation, the state and class struggle: a 'critical economy' engagement with open Marxism, *British Journal of Politics and International Relations*, 5(4), pp. 467–499.

Bieler, A. & Morton, A.D. (2004)'Another Europe is possible?' Labour and social movements at the European social forum, *Globalizations*, 1(2), pp. 303–325.

Bieling, H.-J. & Steinhilber, J. (Eds) (2000) *Die Konfiguration Europas: Dimension einer kritischen Integrationstheorie* (Münster: Westfälisches Dampfboot).

Bieling, H.-J. & Schulten, T. (2003) 'Competitive restructuring' and industrial relations within the European Union: corporatist involvement and beyond, in: Cafruny, A.W. & Ryner, M. (Eds), *A Ruined Fortress? Neoliberal Hegemony and Transformation in Europe*, pp. 231–259 (Lanham, MD: Rowman and Littlefield).

Bohle, D. (2000) EU-Integration und Osterweiterung: die Konturen einer neuen europäischen Unordnung', in: Bieling, H.-J. & Steinhilber, J. (Eds), *Die Konfiguration Europas: Dimension einer kritischen Integrationstheorie*, pp. 304–330 (Münster: Westfälisches Dampfboot).

Bonefeld, W. (Ed.) (2001a) *The Politics of Europe: Monetary Union and Class* (Basingstoke: Palgrave).

Bonefeld, W. (2001b) European monetary union: ideology and class, in: Bonefeld, W. (Ed.), *The Politics of Europe: Monetary Union and Class*, pp. 64–106 (Basingstoke: Palgrave).

Bonefeld, W. (2002) European integration: the market, the political, and class, *Capital and Class*, 77, pp. 117–142.

Burnham, P. (1994) Open Marxism and vulgar international political economy, *Review of International Political Economy*, 1(2), pp. 221–231.

Burnham, P. (1995) State and market in international political economy: towards a Marxian alternative, *Studies in Marxism*, 2, pp. 135–159.

Cafruny, A.W. & Ryner, M. (Eds) (2003) *A Ruined Fortress? Neoliberal Hegemony and Transformation in Europe* (Lanham, MD: Rowman and Littlefield).

Carchedi, G. (1997) The EMU, monetary crises, and the single european currency, *Capital and Class*, 63, pp. 85–114.

Coates, D. (2000) *Models of Capitalism: Growth and Stagnation in the Modern Era* (Cambridge: Polity).

Cox, R.W. (1981) Social forces, states and world orders: beyond international relations theory, *Millennium: Journal of International Studies*, 10(2), pp. 126–155.

Cox, R.W. (1983) Gramsci, hegemony and international relations: an essay on method, *Millennium: Journal of International Studies*, 12(2), pp. 162–175.

Cox, R. W. (1989) Production, the state, and change in world order, in: Czempiel, E.-O. & Rosenau, J.N. (Eds), *Global changes and Theoretical Challenges: Approaches to World Politics for the 1990s*, pp. 37–50 (Lexington, MA: Lexington Books).

Cox, R.W. (1993) Structural issues of global governance: implications for Europe, in: Gill, S. (Ed.), *Gramsci, Historical Materialism and International Relations*, pp. 259–289 (Cambridge: Cambridge University Press).

Cox, R.W. & Sinclair, T. (1996) *Approaches to World Order* (Cambridge: Cambridge University Press).

Czempiel, E.-O. & Rosenau, J.N. (Eds) (1989) *Global Changes and Theoretical Challenges: Approaches to World Politics for the 1990s* (Lexington, MA: Lexington Books).

Drainville, A. (1994) International political economy in the age of open Marxism, *Review of International Political Economy*, 1(1), pp. 105–132.

Gamble, A. (2001) Neo-liberalism. *Capital and Class*, 75, pp. 127–134.

Gill, S. (1992) The emerging world order and European change: the political economy of European Union, in: Miliband, R. & Panitch, L. (Eds), *The Socialist Register: New World Order?*, pp. 157–196 (London: Merlin Press).

Gill, S., ed. (1993) *Gramsci, Historical Materialism and International Relations* (Cambridge: Cambridge University Press).

Gill, S. (2001) Constitutionalising capital: EMU and disciplinary neo-liberalism, in: Bieler, A. & Morton, A.D. (Eds), *Social Forces in the Making of the New Europe: The Restructuring of European Social Relations in the Global Political Economy*, pp. 47–69 (London: Palgrave).

Gill, S. & Law, D. (1988) *The Global Political Economy: Perspectives, Problems and Policies* (London: Harvester and Wheatsheaf).

Grahl J. & Teague, P. (1989) The cost of neo-liberal Europe, *New Left Review*, 174, pp. 33–50.

Gramsci, A. (1971) *Selections from the Prison Notebooks*, ed. & trans. Q. Hoare & G. Nowell-Smith (London: Lawrence and Wishart).

Holloway, J. (1994) Global capital and the national state, *Capital and Class*, 52, pp. 23–49.

Holloway, J. & Picciotto, S. (1977)Capital, crisis and the state, *Capital and Class*, 2, pp. 76–101.

Holman, O. (1992) Transnational class strategy and the new Europe, *International Journal of Political Economy*, 22(1), pp. 3–22.

Holman, O. (2001) The enlargement of the European Union towards Central and Eastern Europe: the role of supranational and transnational actors, in: Bieler, A. & Morton, A.D. (Eds), *Social Forces in the Making of the New Europe: The Restructuring of European Social Relations in the Global Political Economy*, pp. 161–184 (London: Palgrave).

Jessop, B. (1990) *State Theory: Putting the Capitalist State in its Place* (Cambridge: Polity).

Jones, E. (2002) *The Politics of Economic and Monetary Union* (Lanham, MD: Rowman and Littlefield).

Miliband, R. & Panitch, L. (Eds) (1992) *The Socialist Register: New World Order?* (London: Merlin Press).

Morton, A.D. (2001) The sociology of theorising and neo-Gramscian perspectives: the problems of 'school' formation in IPE, in: Bieler, A. & Morton, A.D. (Eds), *Social Forces in the Making of the New Europe: The Restructuring of European Social Relations in the Global Political Economy*, pp. 25–43 (London: Palgrave).

Morton, A.D. (2002) 'La Resurrección del Maiz': globalisation, resistance and the Zapatistas, *Millennium: Journal of International Studies*, 31(1), pp. 27–54.

Morton, A.D. (2003a) Historicising Gramsci: situating ideas in and beyond their context, *Review of International Political Economy*, 10(1), pp. 118–146.

Morton, A.D. (2003b) The social function of Carlos Fuentes: a critical intellectual or in the 'shadow of the state'?, *Bulletin of Latin American Research*, 22(1), pp. 27–51.

Moss, B.H. (2000) The European Community as monetarist construction: a critique of Moravcsik, *Journal of European Area Studies*, 8(2), pp. 247–265.

Overbeek, H. (Ed.) (2003) *The Political Economy of European Employment: European Integration and the Transnationalization of the (Un)employment Question* (London: Routledge).

Overbeek, H. (2004) Transnational class formation and concepts of control: towards a genealogy of the Amsterdam project in international political economy, *Journal of International Relations and Development*, 7(2), pp. 113–141.

van der Pijl, K. (1984) *The Making of an Atlantic Ruling Class* (London: Verso).

Rosamond, B. (2002) Imagining the European economy: 'competitiveness' and the social construction of 'Europe' as an economic space, *New Political Economy*, 7(2), pp. 157–177.

Rupert, M. (2000) *Ideologies of Globalization: Contending Visions of a New World Order* (London: Routledge).

Ryner, M. & Schulten, T. (2003) The political economy of labour-market restructuring and trade union responses in the social-democratic heartland, in: Overbeek, H. (Ed.), *The Political Economy of European Employment: European Integration and the Transnationalization of the (Un)employment Question*, pp. 176–198 (London: Routledge).

Schmidt, V.A. (2002) *The Futures of European Capitalism* (Oxford: Oxford University Press).

Shields, S. (2003) The 'charge of the right brigade': transnational social forces and the neoliberal configuration of Poland's transition, *New Political Economy*, 8(2), pp. 225–244.

Ste Croix, G.E.M. de (1981) *The Class Struggle in the Ancient Greek World from the Archaic Age to the Arab Conquests* (London: Duckworth).

Strange, G. (2002) Globalisation, regionalism and labour interests in the new IPE, *New Political Economy*, 7(4), pp. 343–365.

UN (2001) *World Investment Report 2001: Promoting Linkages* (New York: United Nations).

Gramsci, Law, and the Culture of Global Capitalism

A. CLAIRE CUTLER

This article is inspired by the insight that the works of Antonio Gramsci provide an 'invitation' to think critically about law (Kennedy 1982: 32), and in particular, about international law. Although Gramsci did not engage in any extensive analysis of law and his existing analysis was framed in the context of early twentieth-century domestic Italian criminal and constitutional laws, his conception of law has a significance that goes beyond temporal, geographical or disciplinary limitations (but see Bellamy 1990). Indeed, this article argues that developing an understanding of Gramsci's conception of law is crucial to 'engaging' Gramsci in the manner of an immanent critique contemplated by Gramsci himself. Moreover, such analysis is argued to provide crucial insight into the role of international law in the constitution of the contemporary global political economy and in framing the conditions of possibility for the latter's revolutionary transformation.

This article argues that the global political economy is undergoing a process of juridification in which a commodified legal form provides the template for economic and social regulation. Domestic and global orders are increasingly linked to and disciplined through law by the logic of capital. However, while rooted in the present, this analysis seeks to learn from Gramsci's understanding of 'absolute historicism'. Absolute historicism recognises that 'the present is a *criticism* of the past besides [and because of] "surpassing" it,' while the past is 'a complex of the living and the dead' whose preservation will be determined in the 'dialectical process [that] cannot be determined *a priori*' (Gramsci as cited by Morton 2003: 130). In contrast, 'austere historicism' 'reduces past forms of thought to their precise historical context' (Morton 2003: 128), thus denying the dialectical relation between the present and the past, as well as the historical effectivity of philosophical critique. Absolute historicism recognises, as did Gramsci, that while there are clear limits to transposing understandings of the past onto the present, ideas may have a significance beyond their specific historical circumstances. As Joseph Femia has noted, they may have a 'permanent value,' transcend 'particular contexts,' and leave a '"residue" … which cannot be explained by the historical context' (Femia 1981: 115, 124 quoting Gramsci). The philosophy of praxis requires reading Gramsci 'fresh' (Haug 1999: 108) 'with the seriousness of real criticism' (Anderson 1972: 72) contemplated by immanent critique. To the extent that the present contains traces of the past and that the past is linked historically and dialectically to the present, this article is written in the spirit of respect for both the living and the dead in Gramsci.

Indeed, Gramsci's conception of law provides valuable insight into the nature of the relationships between law, society and political economy and about the historical effectivity of law. Perhaps, even more importantly, Gramscian conceptions, as developed in the disciplines of Law and International Relations (IR), highlight 'elements of continuity and change' and what is 'new' about the current configuration of social forces in the world (Sassoon 2001: 6). Drawing upon and developing Gramsci's conception of law, this article examines the specific form that law takes under contemporary conditions of postmodernity and late capitalism. It presents the commodity form of law as the specific form of law in the current historical conjuncture, which is framed in terms of Gramsci's conceptions of historical bloc and hegemony. In developing our understanding of the nature and role of law in the expansion of global capitalism the article identifies crucial openings for resistance, and contestation and explores the possibilities for emancipatory politics both through law and against law.

Before moving to consider these claims, however, it will be useful to review Gramsci's conception of law and to provide a larger analytical and theoretical context for the analysis. The next section thus addresses Gramsci's conception of law, while the following sketches the analytical and theoretical foundations for understanding the form law takes under conditions of late capitalism and postmodernity. Subsequent sections will then address Gramsci's conceptions of historical bloc and hegemony as applied to the global political economy.

The Praxis Conception of Law

Gramsci developed the fragments of what may be called a *praxis conception of law* that is rooted in his understanding of historical materialism as the philosophy of praxis. While more will be said of this in subsequent sections, Gramsci conceived of law as working both coercively and consensually within the state, in securing and advancing the economic interests of the dominant class and in disciplining and educating the subaltern into the ideology of conformity. For Gramsci, 'the Law is the repressive and negative aspect of the entire positive, civilising activity undertaken by the State' and 'the state represents the coercive and punitive force of juridical regulation of a country' (Gramsci 1971: 246, Q13§11; 267, Q17§51).[1] However, law is also an integral element of civil society and performs an educative role 'turning necessity and coercion into "freedom"' (Gramsci 1971: 242, Q13§7); 'through "law" the state renders the ruling group "homogeneous", and tends to create a social conformism which is useful to the ruling group's line of development' (Gramsci 1971: 195, Q6§84). The 'double face of law', consensual and coercive (Benney 1983: 205; Cain 1983), forms a dialectic specific to the bourgeois conception of law, which Gramsci posited to be an ethical conception:

> The revolution which the bourgeois class has brought into the conception of law, and hence into the function of the state, consists especially in the will to conform (hence ethicity of the law and of the state). The previous ruling classes were essentially conservative in the sense that they did not tend to construct an organic passage from the other classes into their own, i.e. to enlarge their own sphere 'technically' and ideologically: their conception was that of a closed caste. The bourgeois class poses itself as an organism in continuous movement, capable of absorbing the entire civil society, assimilating it to its own cultural and economic level. The entire function of the state has been transformed; the state has become an 'educator', etc. (Gramsci 1971: 260, Q1§47)

Law partakes of both the coercive arm of the state and the consensual domain of civil society. The ethical, integral or perfect state, one in which the 'whole of society' is assimilated, 'would perfect this conception of the state and of law, so as to conceive the end of the state and of law – rendered useless since they will have exhausted their function and will have been absorbed by civil society' (Gramsci 1971: 260, Q8§2). Gramsci here hints that the dialectic of the double face of law could thus be ultimately resolved in the ethical, integral state, which contemplates the very negation of law (and state) through law (and through state). Central to this theorisation is the praxis conception of law.

Gramsci rejected doctrinal conceptions of law that traced laws' pedigree and efficacy to transcendent and universal characteristics or principles. His conception of law 'must be an essentially innovative one not to be found, integrally, in any pre-existing doctrine' (Gramsci 1971: 246, Q13§11). Rather, Gramsci conceived of law in practice and in lived experience; a conception 'freed from every residue of transcendentalism and from every absolute; in practice, from every moral fanaticism' (Gramsci 1971: 246, Q13§11). Reasoning that in the ethical state the 'passage from necessity to freedom takes place through the society of men and not nature' (Gramsci 1971: 407, Q11§62) he favoured the common law over systems based on codes deemed eternal, perpetual or to be based upon absolute truth. In addressing the role of law in guiding and educating society, Gramsci (1971: 196, Q6§84) emphasised the significance of the 'organic continuity' of law, 'which is realistic and always close to concrete life in perpetual development'; this 'organic continuity requires a good archive, well stocked and easy to use, in which all past activity can be reviewed and "criticised"'.

This praxis conception of law, in founding law's transformative force in practical experience, reveals Gramsci's commitment to 'absolute' as opposed to 'austere' historicism, discussed above. Indeed, for Gramsci absolute historicism *is* the 'philosophy of praxis' (Gramsci 1971: 465, Q11§27), which marries thought and action in revolutionary praxis. As Chantal Mouffe (1979: 7) observed, Gramsci's historicism re-establishes the 'indissoluble link between theory and practice at the heart of Marxism', of revolutionary theory, and of understanding ideas as historical forces.

For Gramsci (1971: 427, Q11§26), the philosophy of praxis 'is realised through the concrete study of past history and through present activity to construct new history'. Law, like ideas, becomes an historical force when it cements society and economy together, binding subordinate groups to the interests, purposes and beliefs of the dominant class. However, Gramsci did not provide a detailed analysis or theorisation of the way in which law becomes an historical force. As Mark Benney (1983: 197) has noted, Gramsci's failure to arrive at a settled conception of the state left 'certain ambiguities in his conception of law'. While this matter will be more fully addressed later when analysing the relation between law and state, Gramsci did not explicate the significance of law as part of the structure or superstructure of the capitalist state. Nor did he address the transformative role of law in contributing to the hegemony or unity of theory and practice in 'a single coherent conception of the world' (Gramsci 1971: 333, Q11§12) when 'structure ceases to be an external force which crushes man, assimilates him to itself and makes him passive; and is transformed into a means of freedom, an instrument to create a new ethico-political form and a source of new initiatives' (Gramsci 1971: 367, Q10II,§6i). Gramsci's analysis is suggestive of the economic/material and cultural/ideological roles of law in advancing the interests of the ruling classes and in forming the integral and ethical state, which would ultimately displace both law and state. However, his analysis requires elaboration.

In order to capture law's significance as an historical force it is necessary to ground the analysis in the specific context that the legal form takes in bourgeois political economy, for law takes on a form that is specific to a particular set of historical and material circumstances. The next section thus presents law in its commodity form as the dominant legal form for the contemporary historical context.

The Commodity Form of Law

While law has figured prominently, historically, in effecting changes in political economy, as probably noted most acutely by Karl Marx, it takes on a distinctive form and significance in different historical conjunctures. Operating as a system of customary rights and prerogatives inherited through birth in the feudal period, law subsequently underwent transformations with the advent of absolutist and later constitutional states (Thompson 1975). Law formed an integral part in each transition in society and political economy. Indeed, Perry Anderson (1974: 405) notes that 'juridical property can never be separated either from economic production or politic-ideological power' because 'its absolutely central position within any mode of production derives from its linkage between the two'. However, as Marx suggested in *Capital* (1976: ch.1) and others have developed further (Pashukanis 1978), law takes on a distinctive form under capitalism that mirrors and is homologous with the 'commodity form'. It is thus first necessary to develop an understanding of the commodity form under capitalism before the legal form may be analysed.

Marx reasoned that commodities have a particular usefulness or 'use-value' that differs from commodity to commodity. However, commodities also have another characteristic that derives from their dual nature as 'objects of utility and bearers of value' (Marx 1976: 138). This is their 'exchange-value', which in its most developed form is the 'money-form'. Isaac Balbus (1977: 573–574) described the nature of the two forms as 'an abstraction from, and masking of, the qualitatively different *contents* of the objects and the concrete human needs to which they correspond'. The use-value of an object reflects its value as a qualitatively distinct object that embodies a particular amount of human labour. In contrast, the exchange-value no longer embodies the particular qualities or labour involved in the production of the object, because the exchange-value is rendered in terms of money, which Marx (1973: 239) argued equalised very different commodities. In this sense, all objects, no matter how qualitatively distinctive. entail a common form upon their entry into the commodity form when they are exchanged for money. Balbus (1977: 574) described the logic of the commodity form as 'that of a *double movement from the concrete to the abstract, a double abstraction of form from content, a twofold transmutation of quality into quantity*'. These movements and transformations thus constitute the commodity as an economic form no longer characterised by qualitative attributes or by the human labour that went into creating it, but by its exchange or money value. Marx theorised that these abstractions masked the link between commodities and their human creators, alienating the labourer from the fruits of labour. The abstraction of form from content and the transformation of quality into quantity separate the labourer from the product of labour, infusing the product, now a commodity, with the appearance of independence from its producer with a life of its own. This Marx (1976: 163–164) identified as the fetishism of commodities, which he believed explained the 'metaphysical subtleties', 'mystery', and 'enigmatic character' of commodities under capitalism.

Developing this analysis, Balbus (1977: 573) theorised that under capitalism law takes on a specific form and posited 'an essential *identity* or homology between the legal form and the very "cell" of capitalist society, the commodity form'. Just as the commodity form creates the appearance that all products are equal, the legal form creates an appearance of equality between peoples as legal subjects. In the moves to abstract and concretise, the law, like the commodity form under capitalism, creates the appearance of equality which masks and conceals class and social inequalities. It removes capitalist property relations from the sphere of politics by configuring the laws governing property as part of the domain of civil society, economic markets and free and equal exchange between juridical equals. This ultimately neutralises and depoliticises what Marx regarded as relationships that are by definition coercive, exploitative and inherently *political* (see Marx 1972a,b; Pashukanis 1978; Cutler 2003).

Duncan Kennedy (1985: 976–977) has noted that 'what is important about the commodity system is its *legal structure*, rather than the physical or technological arrangement of the productive process'. The commodity system presupposes laws of contract and property that legitimate and enforce private ownership of the means of production and exchange. These laws neutralise the commodity system by presenting the communal protection of private property rights and entitlements as natural incidents of the rationalised commodity form.

In instantiating distinctions between the private and public law domains, the law formalises the private/public distinction, emptying the private sphere of political content (Wood 1995). Commodity production and exchange, as with all other economic activity, is relegated to the private sphere of civil, 'economic law' that neutralises their political and distributional significance. Law operates to simultaneously materialise and mystify the social relations of production and exchange as it reproduces the fetishised commodity form in a fetishised legal form. In its fetishised form, the law presents as formally rational and equitable an economic and political system that is at root coercive, oppressive and inherently inequitable. The legal form, in simultaneously creating illusory forms of equality and precluding genuine equality, is thus a 'specifically "bourgeois" form' (Balbus 1985: 580).

The commodity form of law forms the template for legal and social regulation today and is being generalised through processes of globalisation and juridification. Globalisation involves 'the intensification of worldwide social relations, which link distant localities in such a way that local happenings are shaped by events occurring many miles away and vice versa' (Giddens 1990: 64). Globalisation of law involves the *juridification* of economy and society as legal and juridical concepts, institutions and ideologies are used with increasing extensity and intensity, in terms of their expanded geographical and substantive scope and their deep penetration into local political/legal/social orders. Juridified relations substantiate and legitimate increasingly more diverse claims to political authority and identity and reflect the specificity of the association between legal regulation and the social relations underlying capitalism.

Gramsci's praxis conception of law provides a useful point of entry into understanding the centrality of the commodity form of law to processes of juridification.

It directs attention to the practical and theoretical linkages of law, capital and the state under a particular historical bloc. The praxis conception of law suggests that bourgeois law takes its form from capital, or more specifically, from the fetishised commodity form created by capitalist productive relations. This form is given life and consecrated by the state in constitutional, criminal and civil laws protecting individual, private property rights and securing the stability of possession. Insofar as laws such as constitutional and administrative laws then secure the authority of state, the influence of law and state is reciprocal. So too is the influence between law and capital reciprocal, for just as law is given its form by capital, capital is given its form by laws that enable its accumulation, disposition, alienation, and so on (Cain 1994). This reciprocal constitution of law and capital may be reasonably apparent in the context of the state where institutions of government and civil society give shape to dominant practices and ideology in the form of laws. However, this relation becomes more complicated when one attempts its capture, globally and transnationally, where governmental and civil-societal relations and institutions are skeletal. Indeed, this raises the important problem of locating law and the issue of whether Gramsci's conceptions of historical bloc and hegemony travel to IR to inform an understanding of the role of international law in the global political economy. The following section submits that they do in fact travel, but with some adjustments.

Historical Bloc, Hegemony, and International Law

Two different but related obstacles conspire to make the development of a praxis conception of international law difficult. One derives more generally from dominant conceptualisations of law, while the other is of particular relevance to international law. The former concerns the problem of locating law as part of the structure or superstructure of capitalism, while the latter addresses the anarchy problematic in international relations, which contests the possibility of international law in the absence of governmental/state authority. The former will be addressed first.

Locating Law

A differentiation between the economic base and the political and ideological superstructure of capitalism has created important limitations to developing a praxis conception of law. When combined with the location of law in the superstructure, this limitation has impeded the development of an adequate understanding of the historical effectivity and materiality of international law. Law as part of the superstructure can hardly be regarded as an historical force or as Santos (1995) observed, as a site for emancipatory politics. In addition, for both conventional and unconventional IR and legal theorists, disciplinary differentiations between economics and politics and between private and public international law have impeded the development of a historical materialist critique of international law (Cutler 2003). The dominant fetishised belief that private international economic law, the law that constitutes global capitalism, is part of the sphere of private, apolitical, economic activity provides a powerful impediment to its praxis conception.

While there is some ambiguity in Gramsci's position on the differentiations between the base and superstructure of capitalism and between economic and political activity, his conception of an historical bloc offers an important analytical concept for transcending these differentiations. Gramsci (1971: 366–367, Q10II§6i) observed that 'structures and superstructures form an "historical bloc"' which he defined as 'the complex, contradictory and discordant *ensemble* of ... the social relations of production'. An historical bloc comprises a 'unity between nature and spirit (structure and superstructure), unity of opposites and of distincts' (Gramsci 1971: 137, Q13§10). However, ambiguity appears when Gramsci seems to give priority to the base by presenting the superstructure as its 'reflection'. In the very next breath, though, he refers to their necessary 'dialectical' and 'reciprocal' relationship: 'the necessary reciprocity between structure and superstructure, a reciprocity which is nothing other than the real dialectical process' (Gramsci 1971: 366, Q10II§12). This analysis has led some to regard the base and superstructure in Gramsci's work to be interactive and mutually constitutive (Hunt 1993). In this regard, it is instructive to recall that Gramsci, in a critique of 'free trade economism' cautioned that the differentiation between politics and economics/civil society is not a natural one, but an analytical one based upon 'a theoretical error' developed by liberalism: the distinction 'is made into and presented as an organic one, whereas in fact it is merely methodological' (Gramsci 1971: 160–161, Q13§18). He continued that the idea that economics 'belongs to civil society, and that the state must not intervene to regulate it' is in fact a form of state regulation: 'it must be made clear that *laissez faire* too is a form of state "regulation", introduced and maintained by legislative and coercive means. It is a deliberate policy, conscious of its own ends, and not the spontaneous, automatic expression of economic facts' (Gramsci 1971: 160, Q13§18). Indeed, Duncan Kennedy (1982: 34) argued that Gramsci's concept of historical bloc is a totalising conception in which economic, social, political, cultural and other ideological forces 'form a single, indivisible whole'. Steven Spitzer (1983: 105) similarly provides an insightful analysis of analytical efforts to 'flatten out' the distinction between the base and superstructure of capitalist society in order to facilitate an understanding of the relationships between structures, people and the law. He identifies in Gramsci an emphasis on 'law's active, shaping, embedded, and "lived" character'.

In this regard, the conception of an historical bloc as developed in the work of Robert Cox (1996) is most useful in capturing the complexities of the lived and embedded nature of international law. Conceptualising an historical bloc as the overall configuration of productive, institutional and ideological forces of a given historical period assists in integrating an understanding of the historical significance, materiality and effectivity of international law. The contemporary historical bloc may be characterised as postmodern and late capitalist, materially, institutionally and ideologically.

Materially, postmodern and late capitalist legal regulation are juridifying and commodifying increasing dimensions of existence. Very briefly, postmodernity in law is reflected in legal pluralism, interlegality and the porosity of law as multiple legal orders operate subnationally, nationally, regionally and transnationally, cross-secting and overlapping. These regimes simultaneously occupy the same space, linking local and domestic political economies and societies through the creation and expansion of legal regimes governing regional and international trade, commerce, banking, insurance, transportation, investment, finance, dispute resolution, human rights, the environment and criminality (Santos 1995, 1987). Late capitalism in law is reflected in the increasing recourse to law to facilitate the displacement of welfare states by competition states through deregulation and privatised legal codes and procedures, in the intensification and expansion of legal disciplines facilitating transnational capital accumulation, and in the related tendency to flexible production and 'soft law' re-regulation of labour relations, consumer protection, environmental practices, and corporate ethics (Harvey 1990; Robinson 2004).

Institutionally and ideologically, postmodern and late capitalist formulations of law inform the activities of key international and regional governmental organisations and associations, including the United Nations, the International Monetary Fund (IMF), the World Bank (WB) and the Organisation of Economic Cooperation and Development (OECD), the United Nations Commission on International Trade Law (UNCITRAL), the World Trade Organisation (WTO), the North America Free Trade Agreement (NAFTA), and the European Union (EU). These institutions form crucial sites for generating both the material and ideological bases for the continuing expansion of global capitalism. In addition, less visible but increasingly important private associations, such as the International Chamber of Commerce (ICC), the International Law Commission (ILC), the Trilateral Commission (TC), transnational business corporations, cartels and private business, accounting, tax, and lawyers associations participate in the constitution of the laws that govern the global political economy (Trubek et al. 1994; Cain & Harrington 1994). These institutions and associations are globalising the commodity form of law through private regulatory frameworks that assess legality according to criteria of economic efficiency and effective market discipline (Cutler et al. 1999). They contribute to the discursive and ideological significance of international law as the creator of the mythology and common sense understandings that undergird the perceived legitimacy of the contemporary historical bloc. This understanding constitutionalises neoliberal market discipline, global competitiveness and economic efficiency as the grundnorms of an increasingly transnational historical bloc (Gill 2003). Central to these developments are the concept and practice of hegemony, to which attention now turns.

Transnational Hegemony

A related obstacle to formulating a praxis conception of international law concerns the transferability of Gramsci's understanding of hegemony to global and transnational relations. Gramsci's conceptualisation of hegemony was clearly bound up with the state and civil society and raises the issue of whether hegemony is conceivable outside the state (and civil society) where international anarchy is said to prevail (Germain & Kenny 1998). In many ways this objection restates the anarchy problematic articulated by neo-Realists in IR, which posits the impossibility of law, normativity and governance in the absence of a state and civil society capable of their articulation. However, before addressing this concern it is important to develop an understanding of Gramsci's conception(s) of hegemony.

Gramsci (1971: 12, Q12§1; 59, Q19§24; 181–182, Q13§17) used the concept of hegemony to depict a 'function' 'which the dominant group exercises throughout society' and identified the significance of 'intellectual, moral and political', as well as economic hegemony. While there is 'persistent slippage' in Gramsci's alternate associations of hegemony with the coercive arm of the state or with the consensual domain of civil society, Gramsci clearly regarded both as central to the constitution of hegemony (Anderson 1972: 25). This is evident in his association of the ascendant class with both 'domination' and 'intellectual and moral leadership' and his explication of *trasformismo*, by which the ruling group constitutes itself through the absorption of subordinate groups (Gramsci 1971: 57, Q19§24). *Trasformismo* is the process by which opposition and resistance to hegemony is absorbed into the dominant ideology, resulting in the 'decapitation' and 'annihilation' of the opposition (Gramsci 1971: 58–59, Q19§24). Central to this transformation is the coercive arm of the state, as well as the institutions of civil society that develop ideological support for the ruling class.

A praxis conception of law indicates the centrality of legal institutions and ideologies to the constitution of the hegemonic class. In this regard, it is crucial to note that hegemony is a process (Benney 1983: 194). It is a process through which a class or group establishes the conditions necessary to establish control, not just through force, but through ideologically capturing popular support as the articulator of the public interest or common sense (Mouffe 1979). Law forms, as Nikos Poulantzas notes, the mechanism for 'cementing together the social formation under the aegis of the dominant class'. Law participates in the organisation of consent, 'including insofar as it masks the state monopolisation of physical force, the mechanisms of ideological inculcation' (Poulantzas 1978: 82, 88). Law operates hegemonically through processes of naturalisation, rationalisation and universalisation (Litowitz 2000: 222; Kennedy 1982). Indeed, these processes form the essence of juridified social relations under capitalism and, while they may be relatively transparent in the domestic context of states (and their civil societies), they are contentious in IR. As Germain and Kenny (1998) noted, the globalisation of Gramsci requires a conceptualisation of a *global civil society* that is organically related to a *global state*. However, it is here submitted that this merely restates the anarchy problematic and the alleged analytical and theoretical problems of governance in the absence of government. Important studies reveal that while global civil societal and governmental mechanisms may be rudimentary, they are succeeding rather well in facilitating the transnational expansion and consolidation of capitalism and a transnational capitalist class (van der Pijl 1998; Robinson 2004; Rupert 2000; Gill 2003).

Indeed, today in the fields of international economic and business law the privatisation and marketisation of regulations governing labour relations, human rights, the environment, corporate ethics and a variety of other substantive areas is naturalised as the common sensical and, indeed, the best way to approach legal regulation. Neoliberal economic theories of law are marshaled to establish the inherent efficiency, the organic nature and hence the economic rationality of private marketised regulation. Private codes of conduct, non-binding statements of principle, and 'soft' legal regulations proliferate in both local and global politico-legal orders. Increasingly, economistic, marketised and commodified criteria for enforcement establish the legal standard. This is international law taking the commodity form under late capitalism.

Once naturalised and rationalised, private legal ordering and the commodity form of law are then universalised through the operations of multi and transnational law, tax, accounting, insurance and financial firms, private business associations, international commercial arbitrators, as well as international organisations engaged in the unification, harmonisation and globalisation of law (Picciotto & Mayne 1999). They function as the 'organic intellectuals', elsewhere (Cutler 2003) referred to as the *mercatocracy*, or merchant class, who transmits the logic of the commodity form throughout the world as a universal, rational, and natural system of ordering.

Global institutions are participating in the institutionalisation of the hegemony of private legal ordering under neoliberal market ideology. As officials of the World Economic Forum have noted, 'globalisation has established the supremacy of the market in an unprecedented way' (Klaus Schwab & Claude Smadja as cited by Rupert 2000: 145). The Secretary General of the United Nations, Koffi Annan, launched the Global Compact which invites business corporations to enter into voluntary arrangements governing labour, human rights and environmental practices in an effort to give neoliberal globalisation a 'human face'. Significantly though, the legal response is a growing system of private, non-binding rules of conduct. Moreover, what are being held out as an emergent global system of law and a universal commercial code are neither global and universal in interest representation nor distributional consequences. Rather, juridified relations are taking the shape of Anglo-American law based very closely upon commercial practices of First World and primarily American corporate values and interests. In addition, to the extent that juridification is taking a non-binding, 'soft' form of law, one must consider whether law is operating dialectically to juridify certain relations in hard legal disciplines (enforcement under WTO, NAFTA, the EU), and to de-juridify others (corporate social responsibility; corporate environmental and labour practices) in 'soft law' and voluntary legal regimes (enforcement under the ICC, UNCITRAL and private arbitrations).

By naturalising, rationalising and universalising, the commodity form, international law assists in mystifying and concealing the very private interests that are being advanced, promoted, and rewarded as communal interests. Gramsci (1971:

12, Q12§1; 195–196, Q6§84) emphasised how an important element of hegemony is the ability of the ruling class to have its parochial interests accepted and protected 'spontaneously' as communal interests. This communalisation of private interests is the ultimate expression and constitutionalisation of Adam Smith's presumption concerning the 'natural' and, indeed, defining human tendency to 'truck, barter, and exchange'. Indeed, it becomes the defining condition of an increasingly one-dimensional society under the culture and commodity form of global capitalism.

The Praxis Conception of International Law and the Culture of Global Capitalism

This article has argued that Gramsci's praxis conception of law and related conceptions of historical bloc and hegemony may be usefully applied to developing an understanding of the significance of international law in the constitution of the global political economy. As a dialectical formulation, a praxis conception of international law may be seen as giving rise to forces of both domination and potential emancipation. This is important in the context of understanding the various operations of law, for the law works to create, consecrate and conceal asymmetries of power and influence in the world. However, it also has the potential of transforming these relations through revelation of the fetishism and mystification of the legal and commodity forms. Indeed, the Gramscian conceptions of historical bloc and hegemony provide insights into new elements of transformation in world order and crucial openings for resistance, contestation and emancipation. They assist in understanding the processes by which the contemporary world order is being reconfigured as marketised and commodified social forms and relations with both local and global reach. Juridification (and de-juridification) is proposed as the analytical link between local and global politico-legal orders and as the process that is instantiating a commodified legal form as the template of economic and social regulation. Juridification is the process by which law becomes hegemonic and defines the current historical bloc. The next step is to theorise the relationship between legal hegemony and resistance.

One might begin by noting that the hegemony of neoliberalism is incomplete and rests upon a continuing ability of the mercatocracy to represent the communalisation of its private interests as rational and as common sense. Indeed, growing fractures in the hegemony of law are increasingly evident. The homology between the commodity form and the legal form is imperfect. As Spitzer (1983: 106) observes, 'law is always at least somewhat at odds with the mode of production in which it is found'. Thus we find laws reflecting elements of an earlier mode of production persisting in the face of an altered mode of production (as in the feudal Poor Laws which persisted under capitalism and later were replaced by the Poor Law reforms of 1834 that were more reflective of the capitalist mode of production). One explanation of this disjunction lies in the lagging behind of law in the face of dynamic economic and social changes. However, this does not account for the constitutive role of law as praxis and as an integral element in the constitution of the dominant mode of production. Thus another explanation draws upon Poulantzas' (1978: 84–85) formulation of this disjunction as 'legality shot through with illegality':

> Every juridical system includes illegality in the additional sense that gaps, blanks, or 'loopholes' form an integral part of its discourse. It is a question here not merely of oversights or blind spots arising out of the ideological operation of concealment underlying the legal order, but of express devices that allow the law to be breached.

While capitalism needs law, it requires a particular type of law. This law must bite hard to protect capital, but not so hard that capital flees; law must thus be capable of biting both hardly and softly.

Today, there are tensions between juridified and de-juridified relations and between hard and soft legal disciplines which reflect the dialectical operation of international law. This variability in legal disciplines suggests the potential for resistance, particularly at the local level where hegemonic laws are produced, enforced, interpreted and reproduced and where common sense understandings about power and authority may be challenged. Resistance and contestation are thus linked to the dialectical operation of and the double face of law. The global promulgation of private non-binding codes of corporate conduct and 'soft' legal discipline are illustrations of *trasformismo*. They are promoted as the efficient and rational means for giving globalisation a 'human face', but this mythology conceals their nature as safety valves for capital. Similarly, hard legal disciplines enforcing private property rights in the trade, investment, financial and intellectual property regimes, purport to create an equal playing field for all, but through the concealing move of law constitutionalise private regimes of accumulation. The most acute example may be found in the interface of indigenous identity claims and the intellectual property regime where *trasformismo* is reframing collective rights to identity into property rights subject to dispossession through hard legal disciplines.

However, there is increasing evidence of subordinate groups organising and expressing their opposition to privatised legal regimes, which may construct an alternative counter-hegemony. Resistance to international intellectual property law is mounting in India, Malaysia, Nepal, Indonesia, Thailand, Sri Lanka, Bangladesh and the Philippines, as well as in Nigeria, where indigenous peoples are organising and demanding compensation and remedies for rights dispossessed by transnational mining, logging, pharmaceutical and oil corporations. Other examples of local resistance to the globalisation of neoliberal market civilisation may also be found in the mobilisation of labour in Asia, Latin America and North America; challenges by citizen groups in Canada and the United States to corporate taxation laws and policies that shift tax burdens to individuals; Islamic social movements; opposition to structural adjustment policies in Bangladesh and Zimbabwe; and civil-society mobilisation in the anti-globalisation protests in Seattle during the WTO ministerial conference in 1999. These are indications of fractures in the discipline of neoliberal economic law and the commodity form of capitalism. Mark Rupert (2000) cautioned that right-wing populist opposition to neoliberal discipline in the United States has been recognised and is generating *trasformismo* in efforts by world leaders and international organisations to 'sustain globalisation' by giving it a 'human face'. However, he also noted (Rupert 2000: 153) that 'resistance to globalisation has opened up possibilities for new forms of political practice which are not circumscribed by the territorial state or by the conventional separation of politics from the economy'. Indeed, Gramscian conceptions of historical bloc, hegemony and the related conception of *trasformismo* provide fruitful analytical and theoretical approaches to understanding the significance of law in the constitution and potential re-constitution of world order. Under global capitalism the commodity form of international law is central to the production and reproduction of commodified and marketised definitions of culture and civilisation. The praxis conception of international law identifies important openings for contestation of this one-dimensional market civilisation both through and against law. The distinction is critical, for the dialectical, double face of law opens up the possibility of praxis that through law negates law.

Acknowledgements

The constructive comments and suggestions of the editors and two anonymous referees for this journal were gratefully received.

Notes

1. Following the convention established in this volume. reference to the Gramsci anthologies is accompanied by a citation of the notebook number (Q) and section (§).

References

Anderson, P. (1974) *Lineages of the Absolutist State* (London: Verso).
Anderson. P. (1972) The antinomies of Antonio Gramsci, *New Left Review* I,100, pp. 5–78.
Babb, H. (Ed. & Trans.) (1951) *Soviet Legal Philosophy* (Cambridge, MA: Harvard University Press).
Balbus, I. (1977) Commodity form and legal form: an essay on the 'relative autonomy' of the law, *Law & Society*, 11, pp.571–588.
Bellamy, R. (1990) Gramsci, Croce and the Italian political tradition, *History of Political Thought*, 11(2), pp. 313–337.
Benney, M. (1983) Gramsci on law, morality, and power, *International Journal of Sociology of Law*, 11(2), pp. 191–208.
Cain, M. (1994) The symbol traders, in: Cain, M. & Harrington, B. (Eds) (1994) *Lawyers in a Postmodern World: Translation and Transgression*, pp. 13–48 (Buckingham: Open University Press).
Cain, M. (1983) Gramsci, the state and the place of law, in: Sugarman, D. (Ed.), *Legality, Ideology, and the State*, pp. 95–117 (London: Academic Press).
Cain, M. & Harrington, B. (Eds) (1994) *Lawyers in a Postmodern World: Translation and Transgression* (Buckingham: Open University Press).
Cox R.W. & Sinclair, T.J. (1996) *Approaches to World Order* (Cambridge: Cambridge University Press).
Cutler, A.C. (2003) *Private Power and Global Authority: Transnational Merchant Law in the Global Political Economy* (Cambridge: Cambridge University Press).

Cutler, A.C., Haufler, V. & Porter, T. (Eds) (1999) *Private Authority in International Affairs* (New York: State University of New York Press).

Femia, J. (1981) An historicist critique of "revisionist" methods for studying the history of ideas, *History and Theory*, 20(2), pp. 113–134.

Germain, R.D. & Kenny, M. (1998) Engaging Gramsci: International Relations theory and the new Gramscians, *Review of International Studies*, 24(3), pp. 3–21.

Gill, S. (2003) *Power and Resistance in the New World Order* (Houndsmill: Palgrave Macmillan).

Giddens, A. (1990) *Sociology* (Oxford: Polity Press).

Gramsci, A. (1971) *Selections from the Prison Notebooks of Antonio Gramsci*, ed. & trans. Q. Hoare & G.-N. Smith (New York: International Publishers).

Harvey, D. (1990) *The Condition of Postmodernity: An Enquiry into the Origins of Cultural Change* (Cambridge, MA: Blackwell Publishers).

Haug, W. (1999) Rethinking Gramsci's philosophy of praxis from one century to the next, *Boundary 2*, 26(2), pp. 101–117.

Hunt, A. (1993) *Explorations in Law and Society: Toward a Constitutive Theory of Law* (London: Routledge).

Kennedy, D. (1985) The role of law in economic thought: essays on the fetishism of commodities, *The American University Law Review*, 34, pp. 939–1001.

Kennedy, D. (1982) Antonio Gramsci and the legal system, *American Legal Studies Forum*, 6(1), pp. 32–37.

Litowitz, D. (2000) Gramsci, hegemony, and the law, *Brigham Young University Law Review*, 2, pp. 515–551.

Marx, K. (1976) *Capital: A Critique of Political Economy*, volume 1, trans. B. Fowkes (Harmondsworth, England: Penguin Books).

Marx, K. (1973) *Grundrisse: Foundation of the Critique of Political Economy*, trans. M. Nicolaus (Harmondsworth, England: Penguin Books).

Marx, K. (1972a) On the Jewish question, in: Tucker, R. (Ed.), *The Marx-Engels Reader*, pp. 24–51 (New York: Norton).

Marx, K. (1972b) The German ideology, in: Tucker, R. (Ed.), *The Marx-Engels Reader*, pp. 110–164 (New York: Norton).

Morton, A.D. (2003) Historicising Gramsci: situating ideas in and beyond their context, *Review of International Studies*, 10(1), pp. 118–146.

Mouffe, C. (1979) Hegemony and ideology in Gramsci, in: Mouffe, C. (Ed.) *Gramsci Marxist Theory*, pp. 168–204 (London: Routledge and Kegan Paul).

Pashukanis, E. (1978) *Law and Marxism: A General Theory*, trans. B. Einhorn, ed. & intro. C. Arthur (London: Ink Links).

Picciotto, S. & Mayne, R. (Eds) (1999) *Regulating International Business: Beyond Liberalisation* (New York: St Martin's Press).

van der Pijl, K. (1998) *Transnational Classes and International Relations* (London: Routledge).

Poulantzas, N. (1978) *State, Power, Socialism*, trans. P. Camiller (London: Verso).

Robinson, W. (2004) *A Theory of Global Capitalism: Production, Class, and State in a Transnational World* (Baltimore, MD: The Johns Hopkins University Press).

Rupert, M. (2000) *Ideologies of Globalisation: Contending Visions of World Order* (London: Routledge).

Santos, B. (1995) *Towards a New Common Sense: Law, Science and Politics in the Paradigmatic Transition* (London: Routledge).

Santos, B. (1987) Law: a map of misreading. Toward a postmodern conception of law, *Journal of Law and Society*, 14(3), pp. 297–300.

Sassoon, A.S. (2001) Globalisation, hegemony, and passive revolution, *New Political Economy*, 6(1), pp. 5–17.

Spitzer, S. (1983) Marxist perspectives in the sociology of law, *Annual Review of Sociology*, 9, pp. 103–124.

Sugarman, D. (Ed.) (1983) *Legality, Ideology, and the State* (London: Academic Press).

Thompson, E.P. (1975) *Whigs and Hunters: The Origin of the Black Act* (London: Allen Lane).

Trubeck, D., Dezalay, Y., Buchanan, S. & Davis, J. (1994) Global restructuring and the law: studies in the internationalisation of the legal fields and transnational arenas, *Case Western Law Review*, 44, pp. 407–498.

Tucker, R. (Ed.) (1972) *The Marx–Engels Reader* (New York: Norton).

Wood, E.M. (1995) *Democracy Against Capitalism: Renewing Historical Materialism* (Cambridge: Cambridge University Press).

Islam, 'Soft' Orientalism and Hegemony: A Gramscian Rereading

MUSTAPHA KAMAL PASHA

The neo-Gramscian turn has offered a major theoretical and methodological challenge to the conventional wisdom surrounding issues of power and world order (Cox 1987), structure and agency (Bieler & Morton 2001b), and global transformations (Gill 1993), displacing understandings that once appeared firmly established and canonised in the field of International Relations (IR). Developed principally by Robert Cox (1981, 1983, 1987), with significant contributions by scholars on both sides of the Atlantic (Gill & Law 1988; Gill 1990, 1993; Augelli & Murphy 1988; Murphy 1994; Van der Pijl 1998; Rupert 1995; Robinson 1996; among others), the neo-Gramscian framework represents one of the more innovative contributions to a discipline long embedded in the self-same verities of behaviouralism, positivism and neo-realism (Morton 2003a,b), exploring the materialist underpinnings of state structures (Bieler & Morton 2001a; Germain & Kenny 1998), recognising variations in state-civil society complexes (Cox 1987), and showing possibilities of newer forms of political agency (Gill 2000).

Neo-Gramscian scholarship in IR is varied (Bieler & Morton 2001a; Germain & Kenny 1998). A distinction can be made between those who elect to separate Gramsci's metatheoretical commitments from his conceptual and methodological uses (Augelli & Murphy 1988; Murphy 1998) and others who seem to avoid such separation (Rupert 1995). However, they all share skepticism of problem solving or the discovery of scientific laws as the hallmark of theoretical practice (Cox 1983).

Drawn from the richer terrain of Italian political thought exemplified in the works of Machiavelli, Vico, Croce and above all Antonio Gramsci (Cox 1983; for background see Bellamy 1990; Bellamy & Schecter 1993; Fontana 1993; Femia 1981; Finocchiaro 1988; Adamson 1980), the neo-Gramscian variant of realism recognises the changeability of social forms, tempered by historicism (Falk 1997) and an awareness of 'the concrete and the conjunctural' (Kalyvas 1998: 344; see also Buttigieg 1986b). Neo-Gramscians reject formulaic soundings on national compulsions and interests pervasive in the core hermeneutic circles of the IR community in favour of a differentiated character of historical blocs and changing configurations of power. On this view, the fixity of the social and political worlds dissolves (Cox 1987; Gill 1993; Morton 1999; Bieler & Morton 2003).

Antinomies and Silence

Despite producing a self-subsistent alternative mapping of the social and political worlds, however, the neo-Gramscians have not been entirely successful in avoiding the constrictions of *Western* IR, especially with regard to the uneasy presence/ absence of cultural otherness in IR theory (Inayatullah & Blaney 2004; Jahn 2000). Furthermore, as with conventional wisdom, neo-Gramscians reproduce, perhaps inadvertently, either assumptions of *liberal neutrality* or *cultural thickness* in relation to the 'peripheral' zones of the global political economy. Together, these tendencies produce a variant that can be likened to 'soft Orientalism'. In the first instance, cultural difference is not much of an impediment to the establishment of (West-centred) global hegemony. In the second instance, otherness becomes the principal source of counter-hegemonic movements or resistance to a globalising economy and its homogenising cultural accoutrements (Robinson 1998; Rupert 2000, 2003). These contradictory uses of culture are also noticeable in claims about the 'clash of globalisations' (Gill 2002).

This article links the neo-Gramscian treatment of culture to the limits of *Western* IR in general. To illustrate the problem, the discussion takes as its point of departure the apparent consolidation of a natural attitude (Benhabib 2002) toward Islam in the wake of dramatic recent events (Pasha 2003). On this view, established narratives rooted in the Manichean idiom of civiliser-backward have returned to endorse pervasive popular opinion (Euben 2002). Political power has helped unify fragmented popular consciousness, deploying it for its own ends. The cultural boundaries of an increasingly porous West are being fortified, a form of 'enclavisation'

(Shapiro 1999), sealing off the 'body politic' from assumed menacing threats of radical Islam to liberal Western polities. This cultural mood embodies deep historical prejudices that now circulate as common sense (Gramsci 1971, 1992, 1994, 1996). One source of this common sense is the enduring legacy of entangled relations between the worlds of Islam and the West, at once mutually constitutive and conflictual (Daniel 1962), but also overburdened by changing configurations of power (Said 1978; Asad 1993; Arjomand 2004).

The appropriation of Islam in IR reveals the general problem of difference and Islam's assumed resistance to an easy assimilation into a universalised modernity (Davutoglu 1994). The familiar strategy to subsume historical and living forms of otherness as the pre-history of modernity (Fabian 1983) is readily subverted in the face of Islam's nagging presence, neither inside nor outside modernity. The alternative strategy to annihilate the radical otherness of Islam has only produced a vicious cycle (Benhabib 2002). It reproduces the conditions for Islam's insistence for difference, and especially on an Occidental reading, an incommensurable difference (Euben 1999). The quest for reconciliation of one/many worlds, or universality/particularity (Walker 1988) seems increasingly feeble. Neither assimilation nor annihilation promises a resolution.

Thomas Butko (2004) proposes a 'Gramscian' analysis of 'political Islam' to avoid these avenues of resolution. Through an exegetical comparison of Gramsci with key 'modern' Islamic intellectuals (Syed Qutb, Abu al-'Ala Mawdudi and Ayatollah Khomeini), he sees Islamic movements as a genuine 'counter-hegemonic' force. Despite some curious parallels between the Marxian thinker and the organic intellectuals of political Islam, Butko's analysis ends up conflating dominance with hegemony. To be certain, the Muslim Middle East is characterised by an absence, *not* presence, of hegemony, which may be the core basis of movements seeking an Islamic alternative. In Butko's own reading of the Muslim Middle East, the masses do not 'accept the morality, the customs, and the institutionalised rules of behaviour disseminated throughout society as absolute truths that cannot or should not be questioned' (2004: 43), a central dimension of hegemony. Butko also fails to distinguish between shades of movements in, what can be called Islamic Cultural Zones (ICZs), as well as the different strategies of 'war of position with 'war of manoeuvre'. His repeated use of 'hegemon' mischaracterises the dense nature of a conception of hegemony.

In the IR field, neo-Gramscians do not make the question of otherness their principal object of analysis. In some cases (Augelli & Murphy 1988, 1993), they help decipher subaltern claims on a hegemonic system 'crusading against alternatives' (Augelli & Murphy 1988: 138), reading the limits of Third-World political action from the empathetic perspective of the Third World itself. In other cases, they examine the effects of Western (mainly American) hegemony on the Third World (Robinson 1996). Any form of demonisation of others would escape the neo-Gramscian critical project. Yet to the degree that neo-Gramscians share the cultural space of *Western* IR, they unconsciously reproduce binary constructions, mostly congealed in a rather neutral and opaque centre-periphery model with its own cultural baggage of notions of development reflected in differential (core or peripheral) economic capacity.

Culture or Cultures?

The real problem emerges in the neo-Gramscian understanding of transnational hegemony, culture and resistance. First, the tendency amongst neo-Gramscians to over-emphasise the *consensual* aspects of hegemony, and (perhaps inadvertently) to downplay the *coercive* foundations of contemporary IR practice, becomes apparent. This tendency rests upon the mixed appropriation of culture. Initially, 'culture' is seen in rather *thin* terms despite a *diffusionist* core-periphery model of cultural transmission, which subsequently exposes that model's latent economism.

Hegemony, to modify Ortner, 'is often treated as something that arrives, like a ship, from outside the society in question' (Ortner in Crehan 2002: 50). Although, neo-Gramscians eschew a tradition/modernity duality, the transnationalist neo-Gramscians (Robinson 1998), with the notable exception of Davies (1999) and Morton (2003c), do not theorise cultural reception. How do peripheral societies *actively* transform hegemonic effects? In the neo-Gramscian formulation, passivity rules the cultural worlds of the subalterns as they readily succumb to global hegemony. Only in 'resistance', informed by an essentialist culture, can agency materialise.

Second, neo-Gramscians tend to overlook the salience of *otherness* in the constitution of (domestic) hegemony. Although, domestic hegemony has been secured by 'anti-communism and the politics of productivity' (Augelli & Murphy 1988: 140), this is not an extended historical perspective on the constitution of (Western) hegemony, a project implicating cultural practices, distinctions and demarcations over a considerably longer phase in human history (Wolf 1982). Hegemony is seen as a projection of domestic hegemony on a transnational scale. The recognition of the distinction between friend and enemy á la Carl Schmitt (1996), or how otherness *outside* shapes hegemony *inside*, does not interest the neo-Gramscians. On a Schmittian view, an inversion of the relationship between domestic and transnational hegemony can be an important corrective to the diffusionist assumptions underpinning the neo-Gramscian worldview.

The indispensability of the periphery's *difference* in the consolidation of the core's (cultural) *identity* can help bring to the surface the pivotal role of antagonisms in international relations (Mouffe 1999). This is not to essentialise either difference or antagonism (Huntington 1993), but to acknowledge the banality of a conception of politics without a meaningful notion of otherness (Tully 1995). The distinction between friend and enemy 'is a reminder of the inexorable and ineradicable nature of conflicts, which no overall, comprehensive ideological worldview will ever succeed in removing from social relations. The political will never be hegemonic' (Kalyvas 1998: 368). To assume otherwise, is to lend authenticity to claims of sameness and conformity (Tully 1995) and to misperceive the bestial nature of power (Buci-Glucksmann 1980; Showstack 1987). Coercion remains a constitutive basis of consent, though it cannot sustain effective rule without adorning a more benign form. The neo-Gramscian privileging of consent disguises the nature of coercion, manipulation, chicanery, disguise and concealment, which never escaped Gramsci's field of vision.

Third, an unstated assumption underpinning the neo-Gramscian framework is the idea of homogenised cultural space (Chatterjee 1988) on a global scale, drawn from the domestic analogy. This assumption allows neo-Gramscians to erase non-Western cultural regions to a large extent, while sketching out the spatial terrain of hegemony. Hegemony moves vertically and horizontally from the North to the South.

Transnational Hegemony or Diffusion?

The neo-Gramscian historical trajectory for the emergence and consolidation of hegemony follows a familiar Anglo-American path inscribed in the IR canon: the origination of the modern world order with Westphalia and subsequent consolidation of two liberal-imperial hegemonies (Pax Britannica and Pax Americana), punctuated by balance of power, mercantilism, the crisis of liberalism and the constitution of 'hyper-liberalism' after the Second World War (Cox 1987; Gill & Law 1988; Gill 1993; Arrighi 1993), superceded by globalisation (Robinson 1998). This trajectory situates Anglo-American hegemony at the centre of analysis. There is nothing parochial about a renewed subscription to this late post-Westphalian temporal mapping. What remains uncertain, though, is the importance of non-Western regions to the historical *formation* of capitalist hegemony. These regions are not merely peripheral and subordinate to the constitution of hegemony in an historical sense, but appear marginal and external to the theory itself. Paradoxically, the initial neo-Gramscian silence over the integral role of the non-West in the consolidation of hegemony is subsequently broken. These regions are smuggled back into analysis as the principal site of counter-hegemonic struggles in the era of globalisation (Robinson 1996; Augelli & Murphy 1993; Rupert 2000; Gill 2002; Rupert 2003). Their challenge, though, is to an order *already constituted*.

This temporal mapping reveals a *presentist* bias, with an inherent proclivity to deny the *dynamic* and *interactive* aspects of hegemonic consolidation. Without invoking the untidy legacy of primitive accumulation on a world-scale, the neo-Gramscian theorisation of hegemony does not fully integrate *chains of elective affinities* between historical processes in core and peripheral regions either before or during periods of hegemonic consolidation. The initial conditions for the establishment of hegemony are seen as patently *internal* to the core. Hegemony then becomes a process of *diffusion* from North to South.

Another source of paradox is the neo-Gramscian aim to escape the domestic analogy by simultaneously relaxing 'national' categories as they appear beyond the state and to depend upon 'national' processes to concretise hegemonic consolidation. Hegemony is not strictly the product of *national* state-civil society complexes, but the congealment of material practices, ideas, and institutions in *transnational* space, autonomous and bearing no isomorphic relation to those complexes (Robinson 1998; also see Robinson's contribution in this volume). Yet, national processes are indispensable to hegemony's global march. Without securing the spatial confines of national space, transnational or 'global' hegemony is unimaginable. 'A world hegemonic order can be founded only by a country in which social harmony has been or is being achieved', Cox explicitly posits. 'The expansive energies released by a social hegemony-in-formation *move outward onto the world scale* at the same time as they consolidate their strengths at home' (Cox 1987: 149, emphasis added).

Ironically, the diffusionist thrust in the neo-Gramscian formulation, unlike cognate diffusionist thinking in modernisation theories of an earlier scholarly generation (Pye 1963), is based on a *thin* understanding of culture, a slightly modified variant of the idea of culture of the economic determinists despite compulsory references to Gramsci and deployment of the notion of intersubjectivity in social theory (Taylor 1976). Gramsci's sustained battle with economic determinism continues to serve as a preamble for the neo-Gramscians, but the import of his analysis is bid farewell as soon as culture reaches the analytical shores of the international. Inside the nation-state, culture enjoys thickness; outside it gets diluted. One illustration of this dual performativity is the relative ease with which hegemonic transmission across 'national' boundaries is made possible by a fungible and exportable global culture (Robinson 1998). This is not the culture of meanings and interpretations, but an empty container of shallow signifiers, instantly recognisable without attachment to indigenous structures of feeling (Williams 1977). What is the *cultural* content of transnational hegemony? Culture appears principally as ideology. If, indeed, there is a *thick* conception of culture, it only materialises as counter-hegemonic resistance, native, local and particularistic. Thick culture returns but only to record a protest. The unencumbered culture of soft Orientalism confronts the encumbered culture of hard Orientalism.

Unlike Gramsci's understanding of culture as a complex ensemble of materialist, symbolic, and interpretative practices—as common sense and good sense, aesthetics and literature, theatre and poetry, high and low brow (Gramsci 1992, 1996) – neo-Gramscians offer a nominalist and formal view of culture: culture as intersubjectivity but intersubjectivity restricted to the domain of dominant ideology (Cox 1987). Though neo-Gramscians self-consciously repudiate the equation of hegemony with ideological practices, trying to preserve, as in Cox's case, Gramsci's Crocean and neo-Hegelian intellectual lineages, transnational hegemony assumes easily the form of *dominant ideological practices* of core ruling classes on a transnational scale, imbued with the accoutrements of a commoditised global culture. The richness of differentiation collapses into the parsimony of homogenisation.

Hegemony or Dominance?

Cox's observation that hegemony 'means dominance of a particular kind where the dominant state creates an order based ideologically on a broad measure of consent' initially opens up an alternative avenue of investigation. Yet *ideology* continues to maintain its grip on the Coxian formulation. Translated in transnational space, hegemony rarely engages with culture or *cultures* either as singular or heterodox materialisation in a meaningful sense, limited to the domain of 'mutual interests' and 'ideological perspectives' (Cox 1987: 7).

'Later' Cox (2002) eschews the productionist bias and moves to an entirely new discursive field overriding neo-Gramscian understandings of transnational hegemony, all but abandoning the parsimony of his earlier historical materialist leanings in favour of an open-ended engagement with civilisational concerns. This is a major (and welcome) adjustment to his earlier commitments. Yet, how other worlds enter and reframe Cox's fundamental understanding of global hegemony in 'later' Cox still remains an open question. Recognition of a 'plural world' and its multiple intersubjectivities does not resolve the analytical conundrums of neo-Gramscian thinking on 'transnational hegemony'. Without fully appreciating the coercive nature of power in the so-called 'periphery', and the mutually constitutive nature of inside/outside, appreciation of a plural world appears more nominal than real.

Rupert tries to resolve the problem partially by stressing the need to understand the 'mutually constitutive relations of governance/resistance' in the making of global politics (2003: 181), but he fails to identify the processes that allow 'resistance' to reshape hegemony beyond its obvious oppositional instantiation, as for example in Zapatista claims for cultural autonomy (Rupert 2003: 194–195; but see Morton 2002). In part, Rupert is unable to overcome the paradox inherent with the neo-Gramscian enterprise of theorising global capitalism, simultaneously as a reified totality in the core and as a non-reified particularity in the Third World. Without resolving this problem, the formation of a 'counter-hegemonic bloc' (Rupert 2000, 2003) faces an insurmountable theoretical hurdle in addition to the lived (cultural) diversity of its constituents.

In the strictly neo-Gramscian mode in his magnum opus, *Production, Power and World Order*, however, Cox essentially tells a *Western* story of late modernity. The non-West remains a silent spectator, marginal both historically, but also analytically. To the point, the mutual interactions between the West and the Rest (including especially the Islamic world) are largely absent from an account devoted to what is essentially a more subtle reading of imperialism, its genesis, and evolution. The question is not merely of silencing the effects of the periphery on the core, but recognition of the *indivisibility, not juxtaposition*, of the core and periphery. The trajectory of societal development in Europe is largely insulated from other worlds. Although Cox recognises that 'the liberal state and the liberal world order emerged together, taking shape through the establishment of bourgeois hegemony in Britain and of British hegemony in the world economy' (Cox 1987: 123), he avoids the historical burden of exploring the mutual constitution of core and periphery. That burden is restricted to an investigation of development in the core. The postcolonial unease regarding comparative, not 'connected histories' (Subramahmanyam 1997) or what Said calls 'intertwined histories' (Said 1993), is a spectre that would haunt the neo-Gramscians. The notion of connected histories renders the two-stage model of hegemony (first 'national' then 'transnational', first European or American, then the non-Western world), highly problematic. Conversely, a largely Anglo-American historical lens enfeebles the notion of 'transnational' or 'global' hegemony if that notion empties out the 'transnational' and 'global' of much of the spatial world outside of the West. Why call it hegemony?

Cox provides a densely structured account of class struggles that produced the hegemonic order in Britain, especially regarding the diffusion of conflict (1987: 138). However, a similar commitment to dynamic processes is missing when the international appears, how peripheral struggles reframe hegemony or annul it, how culture complicates things. At most, a theory of compliance is summoned (Cox 1987: 146). Cox's cartography of the spatial terrain of hegemony helps fully explain the theoretical dilemma: 'Hegemony, though firmly established at the center of the world order, wears thin at its peripheries' (Cox 1987: 150).

Then, what are the transnational *political* processes that shape hegemony? On a Gramscian interrogation, what are the transnational *cultural* processes that produce hegemony? On one hand, the 'transnational' in the neo-Gramscian formulation is an amalgam of distinct national fragments. On the other hand, the 'transnational' stands above the interstate system, but in political and cultural terms, it embodies a very thin layer. Hegemony works primarily through states, although their form may be quite diverse (Cox 1987: 218).

States remain pivotal to transnational hegemony. Transformations of historical structures of world order must rely on changing configurations of the dominant states accompanied by 'uneven development of productive forces leading to a new distribution of productive powers among social formations', the rise of new historical blocs in social formations as well as new production structures of accumulation (Cox 1987: 209). Recognising the separation of politics from economics, the hegemonic order circumscribes state form and is hospitable only to structures that agree with the hegemonic order. The centrality of states to hegemony complicates the relative autonomy of the transnational sphere. To the point, the character of the state in the Third World, in Cox's own reading (1987: 230–244), affirms its non-hegemonic character, a case of dominance without hegemony (Guha 1997).

To recapitulate, the absence of hegemony in those vast zones of the world makes transnational or global hegemony problematic. There are two principal ways to overcome the problem. First, transnational hegemony can be seen as a mixture of hegemony *and* dominance: hegemony in the core, dominance in the peripheral zones of the global political economy. Clearly, this is the neo-Gramscian intent, which is subverted by more ambitious claims of the coming of a 'global culture' (Robinson 1998). The other option is to reframe global hegemony as an inter-state project in which dominant classes collaborate. However, this formulation, which is closer to the textual utterances of the neo-Gramscians, contradicts statements on the *transnational* character of hegemony. In actuality, the analysis suggests the absence of transnational hegemony given basic cleavages between subordinate groups in core and peripheral zones.

The *inter-state* nature of transnational hegemony is borne out by Cox's examination of the internationalisation of the state, which is characterised by 'a process of interstate consensus formation regarding the needs or requirements of the world economy that takes place within a common ideological framework (i.e., common criteria of interpretation of economic events and goals anchored in the idea of an open economy)' (Cox 1987: 254).

However, Cox recognises the contrast between the core and the periphery in that 'a stricter regime than that applying to advanced capitalist countries has been enforced on Third World countries ... Third World elites do not participate with the same effective status as top-level elites in the formation of the consensus' (Cox 1987: 260). Cox is also quite aware of the incidence of violence as a stubborn feature of parts of the world system:

> Militarism is a symptom of the regression of global economy on which the world economic order has rested. The more that military force has to be increased and the more it is actually employed, the less the world order rests on consent and the less it is hegemonic. *Economic benefits appear to flow less from the operation of universal laws of the market that is the basic article of faith of liberalism and more from power positions backed by force.* (Cox 1987: 289, emphasis added)

The difficulty of producing transnational hegemony is also borne out by Cox's recognition of resistance in the periphery. 'The internationalising of the Third World state is more openly induced by external pressures than the internationalising of the advanced capitalist state is and thus provokes more awareness and resentment' (Cox 1987: 265). Why the need for external pressures? Cox's answer sums up the nature of the problem and the latent Orientalism in neo-Gramscian international cultural cartography:

> Hegemony was more secure at the center of the world system, less secure in its peripheries ... While caesarism secured the passive acquiescence of Third World societies in a global hegemony centred in the advanced capitalist countries, counter-hegemonic movements in other Third World countries constituted open and active challenges to global hegemony. Corresponding to this differentiation in hegemonic intensity between core and periphery of the world system, class struggles were muted by corporatist structures in the core but more open and self-conscious in peripheral areas. (Cox 1987: 266–227)

Robinson's discussion of transnational hegemony demonstrates even more intensely the analytical conundrum. His bold plea 'to study transnational social structure' (1998: 562) in place of 'national' social structures, assumes the redundancy of the 'nation-state' system. Yet, the emergent transnational networks 'operate both "over" and "under" the nation-state system and undermine its institutional logic and any rationality in conceiving of social structure in national terms' (Robinson 1998: 567; also see Robinson this volume). The demand for a new vision for Robinson is necessitated by globalisation, which 'denotes a transition from the linkage of national societies predicated on a *world economy* to an emergent transnational or *global society* predicated on a global economy' (Robinson 1998: 563). The introduction of 'global society' is not gratuitous, but an important plank of Robinson's theory of transnational hegemony. Although he fully recognises the non-economic aspects of globalisation, he remains wedded to an unyielding economic determinism. In the first and last instance, economic forces are in the driver's seat:

> Economic globalisation brings with it the material basis for the emergence of a singular global society, marked by the transnationalisation of civil society and political processes, the global integration of social life, and a 'global culture'. In this view, nations are no longer linked externally to a broader system but internally to a singular global social formation. (Robinson 1998: 563–564)

Robinson is fully cognisant of 'mutually reinforcing economic, political, and cultural forms' of a 'new global social structure of accumulation', but culture consists mainly of consumerism and individualism, 'diffused globally through mass communications and advertising' (Robinson 1998: 588). Under globalisation – 'the central dynamic of our epoch' – 'developed and underdeveloped populations (have) no nationally defined geographic identity' (Robinson 1998: 581, 578). Transnational capital 'brings with it the transnationalisation of classes in general' (Robinson 1998: 581). This formulation of globalisation cannot escape the legacy of economic determinism:

> A full capitalist global society would mean the integration of all national markets into a single market and the division of labour and the disappearance of all national affiliations of capital. These economic tendencies are already underway. *What is* [sic] *lagging behind are the political and institutional concomitants – the globalisation of the entire superstructure of legal, political, and other national institutions, and the transnationalisation of social consciousness and cultural patterns.* (Robinson 1998: 581, emphasis added)

Robinson's lag theory of social movement is fully evidenced in the transnationalisation of the state which is 'lagging behind the globalisation of production' (Robinson 1998: 585). Supranational economic institutions are considerably more developed than their political and cultural counterparts (Robinson 1998: 586). To the extent that a base-superstructure model is awkwardly placed to recognise the richness and autonomy of difference, it should come as no surprise that the neo-Gramscian formulation of transnational hegemony necessitates and employs a *thin* notion of culture. The irony is the competing requirement for a notion of *thick* culture to bestow counter-hegemonic substance and political meaning.

Neo-Gramscians fail to recognise the autonomy of the political, which is *the* instantiation of the cultural. Unlike Gramsci, who saw the political 'as a distinct realm of human experience and as an independent domain of investigation with its own internal laws (Kalyvas 1998: 344; also see Laclau & Mouffe 1985), neo-Gramscians tend to subsume the political with the economic. The political appears as an append-age to transnational processes of the workings of capitalism on a world scale. In developing their theory of transnational hegemony, 'questions about the constitution of legitimate authority especially have been sidelined in favour of worries about other things' (Walker 2002: 7). Efforts to analyse the new global constitutionalism (Gill 2002) have injected an important corrective to the prevailing, albeit, diluted economic determinism, but it clings to a notion of politics not fully recognising its self-subsistent character. Invariably, the political remains trapped in a logic not of its own making.

Davies (1999), Morton (2003c) and Bieler and Morton (2001a) offer solid disclaimers to a self-subsistent transnational logic divorced from local context and texture. Proposing a non-deterministic understanding of culture, they all recognise the particularity of culture and its relative autonomy, as well as the contradictory nature of intellectuals as 'critical substitutes of civil society' and/or perpetuators of the social order (Morton 2003c: 28). Morton uses a Gramscian framework to analyse the tensions between national and cosmopolitan cultural impulses in Mexico, but also shows the complex nexus between the realms of 'pure art' and 'pure politics'. Davies recognises both the political agency of (Chilean) intellectuals and the international context of programmes of social transformation without reduc-ing one to the other. By analysing various forces conditioning national politics and intellectuals operating transnationally, or with both national and transnational resources at their disposal, the national-transnational divide is obviated. The focus on communication theory and its creative reception, furthermore, injects agency into the notion of transnational hegemony (Davies 1999). Similarly, Bieler and Morton (2003) address the relative autonomy of the state, showing sensitivity to the autonomous realm of the political, not reducing it to the economic, nor trading the transnational for the national.

Gramsci, Culture and IR

The neo-Gramscian appropriation of culture generally fails to match Gramsci's acute awareness of culture's relative autonomy from material production, peripherality and its real and symbolic materialisation, and the limits of proletarian hegemony (or its neo-Gramscian counterpart, counter-hegemony). Neither Gramsci's critique of economic determinism nor his astute understanding of the role of intellectuals affords a greater analytical resource for IR than his sensitivity to the *relation between subor-dination and forms of political life*. Ironically, the theoretical marginalisation of the periphery in the neo-Gramscian framework ends up peripheralising the question of uneven development, strategies to foment a new (integrated) order under those condi-tions and the difficulty to overcome the historical legacy of structural deprivation. Gramsci's location within the West's economic and political periphery sensitised him to Italy's cultural division between 'particularly the developing north and the underdeveloped south, and the educated classes and the unschooled masses' (Bellamy in Gramsci 1994: x, xi). On a Gramscian reading, global tensions between a West-centred liberal order and its assumed antithesis in much of the Third World (particularly the Islamic World), becomes explicable not simply in material terms, nor as a cultural clash, but as the cumulative effect of a culturally partitioned world of privilege and unity, want and fragmentation.

The neo-Gramscian preoccupation with global hegemonic consolidation, which is primarily a process of extending hegemony from the core to the periphery, expunges the cultural question raised by the nagging presence of conflicting intersubjectivities of dominant and subaltern social forces on a world scale. Yet, neo-Gramscians are quick to embrace the cultural question as it clings to notions of resistance. Gramsci's recognition of the mixed heritage of native culture (Gramsci 1994; Buttigieg 1986a), its cultural richness and docility, tradition and the fetters it places on collective societal action, or embeddedness and its concomitant denial of certain forms of agency, contradicts the celebratory tone and content of many self-avowed neo-Gramscian accounts of counter-hegemonic struggles in the Third World. Neo-Gramscians do not fully appreciate the Gramscian necessity of the acquisition of 'self-knowledge and with it self-mastery' (Bellamy in Gramsci 1994: 9–10) to lend proletarian (counter) hegemony the (alternative) character of transcendence. The lure of resistance against global capitalism or globalisation, without the additional burden of seeking 'the attainment of a higher awareness, through which we can come to understand our value and place in history, our proper function in life, our rights and duties (Bellamy in Gramsci 1994: xvi), merely endorses a 'soft' Orientalism.

On a Gramscian reading, the incorporation of many non-Western zones into the global political economy has subordinated them politically, economically, and culturally. As Gramsci recognised, structures of 'patronage and compromise between elites and clienteles' (Bellamy in Gramsci 1994: xii) can produce both insurmountable obstacles to social reform and unorthodox forms of political expression. The virtual disenfranchisement of many cultural zones in global politics is not coincidentally linked to political nihilism on the global plane. In this reading, the exacerbation of culturally and religiously coded conflict becomes less opaque. Equally pertinent in this context are Gramsci's analysis of fascism and his acute recognition of the dual face of power (Gramsci 1971; Fontana 1993). Centaur's beastly side is not simply a theoretical, but a real possibility in a world increasingly drawn towards a Manichean logic in the centres of global power. The difficulty of acknowledging the persistent and significant presence of violence as the political grammar of capitalist modernity, especially in the peripheral zones, gives the neo-Gramscian theory of transnational hegemony the character of a benign, mostly apolitical, project. Gramsci's constant disquiet over the Southern question (Bellamy & Schecter 1993; Brennan 1988–89) provides an effective riposte to the diffusionist proclivities of the neo-Gramscians.

An important implication of the dual deployment of culture in the neo-Gramscian framework is to circumscribe the theoretical possibility to fully recognise the nature of hegemonic and peripheral fractures in the ICZs (Pasha 2003). Either the homogenising force of West-centred globalisation brooks no resistance or an essentialised (unchanging and monolithic) Islam stands firm against assimilation. In the first instance, the culturally textured world of Islam appears simply as an atavistic residue of an unfinished modernity. In the second instance, an undifferentiated faith successfully launches counter-hegemonic struggles. Absent in this framework is the *transformed* and *transformative* nature of both hegemony and the ICZs. The one-dimensional picture of homogenisation is readily compromised. Politics refracts culture in fundamental ways. The insistence on relative cultural fixity to authenticate counter-hegemony faces the burden of differentiation and fissure. To recognise sites of resistance, therefore, entails a bit more than recognising difference. It rests on an appreciation of the possibility of tensions within otherness and attempted resolutions that can no longer remain insulated from the wider worlds inhabiting that otherness.

Acknowledgements

The constructive comments and suggestions of the editors and two anonymous referees for this journal were gratefully received.

References

Adamson, W.L. (1980) *Hegemony and Revolution: A Study of Antonio Gramsci's Political and Cultural Theory* (Berkeley, CA: California University Press).

Arjomand, S.A. (2004) Islam, political change and globalisation, *Thesis Eleven*, 76(February), pp. 9–28.

Arrighi, G. (1993) The three histories of historical materialism, in: Gill, S. (Ed.), *Gramsci, Historical Materialism and International Relations*, pp. 148–185 (Cambridge: Cambridge University Press).

Asad, T. (1993) *Genealogies of Religion: Discipline and Reason of Power in Christianity and Islam* (Baltimore, MD: John Hopkins University Press).

Augelli, E. & Murphy, C.N. (1988) *America's Quest for Supremacy and the Third World: A Gramscian Analysis* (London: Pinter).

Augelli, E. & Murphy, C.N. (1993) Gramsci and International Relations: a general perspective with examples from recent US policy toward the third world, in: Gill, S. (Ed.), *Gramsci, Historical Materialism and International Relations*, pp. 127–147 (Cambridge: Cambridge University Press).

Bellamy, R. (1990) Gramsci, Croce and the Italian tradition, *History of Political Thought*, 11(2), pp. 313–337.

Bellamy, R. & Schecter, D. (1993) *Gramsci and the Italian State* (Manchester: Manchester University Press).

Benhabib, S. (2002) Unholy wars, *Constellations*, 9(1), pp. 34–45.

Bieler, A. & Morton, A.D. (Eds) (2001a) *Social Forces in the Making of the New Europe: The Restructuring of European Social Relations in the Global Political Economy* (London: Palgrave).

Bieler, A. & Morton, A.D. (2001b) The Gordian knot of agency-structure in international relations: a neo-Gramscian perspective, *European Journal of International Relations*, 7(1), pp. 5–35.

Bieler, A. & Morton, A.D. (2003) Globalisation, the state and class struggle: a "critical economy" engagement with open Marxism, *British Journal of Politics and International Relations*, 5(4), pp. 467–499.

Brennan, T. (1988–89) Literary criticism and the southern question, *Cultural Critique*, 11, pp. 87–114.

Buci-Glucksmann, C. (1980) *Gramsci and the State*, trans. David Fernbach (London: Lawrence and Wishart).

Butko, T.J. (2004) Revelation or revolution: a Gramscian approach to the rise of political Islam, *British Journal of Middle Eastern Studies*, 31(1), pp. 41–62.

Buttigieg, J.A. (1986a) The legacy of Antonio Gramsci, *Boundary 2*, 14(3), pp. 1–17.

1986b)Gramsci's Method'. *Boundary 2*, 17/2, 60–81.

Chatterjee, P. (1988) On Gramsci's 'fundamental mistake', *Economic and Political Weekly*, 23(5), PE, pp. 24–26.

Connerton, P. (Ed.) (1976) *Critical Sociology* (Harmondsworth: Penguin).

Cox, R.W. (1981) Social forces, states and world orders: beyond International Relations theory, *Millennium: Journal of International Studies*, 10(2), pp. 126–155.

Cox R.W. (1983) Gramsci, hegemony and international relations: an essay in method, *Millennium: Journal of International Studies*, 12(2), pp. 162–175.

Cox R.W. (1987) *Production, Power and World Order: Social Forces in the Making of History* (New York: Columbia University Press).

Cox, R.W. & Schecter, M.G. (2002) *The Political Economy of a Plural World: Critical Reflections on Power, Morals and Civilisation* (London: Routledge).

Crehan, K. (2002) *Gramsci, Culture and Anthropology* (London: Pluto Press).

Daniel. N. (1962) *Islam and the West: The Making of an Image* (Edinburgh: University Press).

Davies, M. (1999) *International Political Economy and Mass Communication in Chile: National Intellectuals and Transnational Hegemony* (London: Macmillan).

Davutoglu, A. (1994) *Alternative Paradigms: The Impact of Islamic and Western Weltanschauungs on Political Theory* (New York and London: University Press of America).

Derlugiuan, G & Greer, S.L. (Eds) (2000) *Questioning Geopolitics: Political Projects in a Changing World-System* (Westport, CT: Praeger).

Euben, R.L. (1999) *Enemy in the Mirror: Islamic Fundamentalism and the Limits of Modern Rationalism* (Princeton, NJ: Princeton University Press).

Euben, R.L. (2002) The new Manicheans, *Theory and Event*, 5(4), ⟨http://muse.jhu.edu/journals/tae/⟩.

Fabian, J. (1983) *Time and the Other: How Anthropology Makes its Object* (New York: Columbia University Press).

Falk. R. (1997) The critical realist tradition and the demystification of interstate power: E.H. Carr, Hedley Bull, and Robert Cox, in: Gill, S. & Mittelman, J.H. (Eds), *Innovation and Transformation in International Studies*, pp. 39–55 (Cambridge: Cambridge University Press).

Falk. R. *et al.* (2002) *Reframing the International: Law, Culture, Politics* (London: Routledge).

Femia, J.V. (1981) *Gramsci's Political Thought: Hegemony, Consciousness and the Revolutionary Process* (Oxford: Clarendon Press).

Finocchiaro, M.A. (1988) *Gramsci and the History of Dialectical Thought* (Cambridge: Cambridge University Press).

Fontana, B. (1993) *Hegemony and Power: On the Relation between Gramsci and Machiavelli* (Minneapolis, MN: University of Minnesota Press).

Germain, R.D. & Kenny, M. (1998) Engaging Gramsci: international relations and the new Gramscians, *Review of International Studies*, 5(2), pp. 252–283.

Gill, S. (1990) *American Hegemony and the Trilateral Commission* (Cambridge: Cambridge University Press).

Gill, S. (Ed.) (1993) *Gramsci, Historical Materialism and International Relations* (Cambridge: Cambridge University Press).

Gill, S. (2000) Globalising capital and political agency in the twenty-first century, in: Derlugiuan, G & Greer, S.L. (Eds) (2000) *Questioning Geopolitics: Political Projects in a Changing World-System*, pp. 15–32 (Westport, CT: Praeger).

Gill, S. (2002)Constitutionalising inequality and the clash of globalisations, in: Pasha, M.K. & Murphy, C.N. (Eds) (2002) *International Relations and the New Inequality*, pp. 47–65 (Oxford: Blackwell).

Gill, S. & Law, D. (1988) *The Global Political Economy: Perspectives, Problems and Policies* (Baltimore, MD: John Hopkins University Press).

Gill, S. & Mittelman, J.H. (Eds) (1997) *Innovation and Transformation in International Studies* (Cambridge: Cambridge University Press).

Gramsci, A. (1971) *Selections from the Prison Notebooks*, ed. & trans. Q. Hoare & G. Nowell-Smith (London: Lawrence and Wishart).

Gramsci, A. (1992) *Prison Notebooks*, vol. 1, ed. J.A. Buttigieg, trans. J.A. Buttigieg & A. Callari (New York: Columbia University Press).

Gramsci, A. (1994) *Pre-Prison Writings*, ed. R. Bellamy, trans. V. Cox (Cambridge: Cambridge University Press).

Gramsci, A. (1996) *Prison Notebooks*, vol. 2, ed. & trans. J.A. Buttigieg (New York: Columbia University Press).

Guha, R. (1997) *Dominance without Hegemony: History and Power in Colonial India* Cambridge, MA: Harvard University Press).

Huntington, S.P. (1993) The clash of civilisations?, *Foreign Affairs*, 72(3), pp. 22–49.

Inayatullah, N. & Blaney, D.L. (2004) *International Relations and the Problem of Difference* (London: Routledge).

Jahn, B. (2000) *The Cultural Construction of International Relations: The Invention of the State of Nature* (London: Palgrave).

Kalyvas, A. (1998) Hegemonic sovereignty: Carl Schmitt, Antonio Gramsci and the constituent prince, *Journal of Political Ideologies*, 5(3), pp. 343–376.

Laclau, E. & Mouffe, C. (1985) *Hegemony and Socialist Strategy: Towards a Radical Democratic Politics*, trans. W. Moore & P. Cammack (London: Verso).

Morton, A.D. (1999) On Gramsci, *Politics*, 19(1), pp. 1–8.

Morton, A.D. (2002) 'La Resurrección del Maíz': globalisation, resistance and the Zapatistas, *Millennium: Journal of International Studies*, 31(1), pp. 27–54.

Morton, A.D. (2003a) Social forces in the struggle over hegemony: neo-Gramscian perspectives in international political economy, *Rethinking Marxism*, 15(2), pp. 153–179.

Morton, A.D. (2003b) Historicising Gramsci: situating ideas in and beyond their context, *Review of International Political Economy*, 10(1), pp. 118–146.

Morton, A.D. (2003c)The social function of Carlos Fuentes: a critical intellectual or in the 'shadow of the state'?, *Bulletin of Latin American Research*, 22(1), pp. 27–51.

Mouffe, C., (Ed.) (1999) *The Challenge of Carl Schmitt* (London: Verso).

Murphy, C.N. (1994) *International Organisation and Industrial Change: Global Governance since 1850* (New York: Oxford University Press).

Murphy, C.N. (1998)Understanding IR: understanding Gramsci, *Review of International Studies*, 24(3), pp. 417–425.

Ortner, S. (1984)Theory in anthropology since the sixties, *Comparative Studies in Society and History*, 26(1), pp. 142–166.

Pasha, M.K. & Murphy, C.N. (Eds) (2002) *International Relations and the New Inequality* (Oxford: Blackwell).

Pasha, M.K. (2003) Fractured worlds: Islam, identity and international relations, *Global Society*, 17(2), pp. 111–120.

van der Pijl, K. (1998) *Transnational Classes and International Relations* (London: Routledge).

Pye, L. (1963) *Aspects of Political Development: An Analytic Study* (Princeton, NJ: Princeton University Press).

Robinson, W.I. (1996) *Promoting Polyarchy: Globalisation, US Intervention and Hegemony* (Cambridge: Cambridge University Press).

Robinson, W.I. (1998) Beyond nation-state paradigms: globalisation, sociology and the challenge of transnational studies, *Sociological Forum*, 13(4), pp. 561–594.

Rupert, M. (1995) *Producing Hegemony: The Politics of Mass Production and American Global Power* (Cambridge: Cambridge University Press).

Rupert, M. (2000) *Ideologies of Globalisation: Contending Visions of a New World Order* (London: Routledge).

Rupert, M. (2003)Globalising common sense: a Marxian–Gramscian (re-)vision of the politics of governance/resistance, *Review of International Studies*, 29(Special Issue), pp. 181–198.

Said, E. (1978) *Orientalism* (New York: Vintage).

Said, E. (1993) *Culture and Imperialism* (New York: Vintage).

Schmitt, C. (1996 [1932]) *The Concept of the Political*, trans. & intro. G. Schwab (Chicago, IL: The University of Chicago Press).

Shapiro, M.J. (1999) Samuel Huntington's moral geography, *Theory and Event*, 2(4), ⟨http://muse.jhu.edu/journals/tae/⟩.

Showstack, A.S. (1987) *Gramsci's Politics*, 2nd ed. (Minneapolis, MN: University of Minnesota Press).

Subrahmanyam, S. (1997) Connected histories: notes towards a reconfiguration of Eurasia, *Modern Asian Studies*, 31(3), p. 735.

Taylor, C. (1976) Hermeneutics and politics, in: Connerton, P. (Ed.), *Critical Sociology*, pp. 153–193 (Harmondsworth: Penguin).

Tully, J. (1995) *Strange Multiplicity: Constitutionalism in an Age of Diversity* (Cambridge: Cambridge University Press).

Walker, R.B.J. (1988) *One Worlds/Many Worlds: Struggles for a Just Peace* (Boulder, CO: Lynne Rienner).

Walker, R.B.J. (2002) After the future: enclosures, connections, politics, in: Falk, R. *et al.*, *Reframing the International: Law, Culture, Politics*, pp. 3–25 (London: Routledge).

Williams, R. (1977) *Marxism and Literature* (Oxford: Oxford University Press).

Wolf, E. (1982) *Europe and the People without History* (Berkeley, CA: University of California Press).

Gramsci and Globalisation: From Nation-State to Transnational Hegemony

WILLIAM I. ROBINSON

Globalisation and hegemony are concepts that occupy an increasingly important place in social science research and are central to out understanding of twenty-first-century world society. My objective in the present essay is to examine the matter of hegemony in the global system from the standpoint of global capitalism theory, in contrast to extant approaches that analyse this phenomenon from the standpoint of the nation-state and the inter-state system. Hegemony may be firmly situated in our social science lexicon, yet it means different things to different speakers. There are at least four interwoven conceptions in the literature on the international order and the world capitalist system:

(1) *Hegemony as international domination.* Hegemony in the Realist tradition in International Relations (IR), world politics, and some International Political Economy, understood as dominance backed up by active domination, or 'hegemonism'. Thus the former Soviet Union exercised hegemony over Eastern

Europe and the United States exercised hegemony over the capitalist world during the Cold War.

(2) *Hegemony as state hegemony.* Hegemony in the loose sense as evoked in much world-systems and IR literature, in reference to a dominant nation-state within the core that serves to anchor the world capitalist system or to impose the rules and enforcement that allows the inter-state system to function over time. Thus, there has been a succession of hegemonic powers in the history of world capitalism, e.g., from Dutch, to British and then to US hegemony, and a particular power is a 'hegemon'.

(3) *Hegemony as consensual domination* or *ideological hegemony.* Hegemony in the more generic sense meant by Antonio Gramsci as the way in which a ruling group establishes and maintains its rule. Hegemony is rule by consent, or the cultural and intellectual leadership achieved by a particular class, class fraction, stratum or social group, as part of a larger project of class rule or domination. Thus, in modern capitalist societies the bourgeoisie has managed to achieve its hegemony during periods of stable rule, although that hegemony has broken down during periods of crisis, such as in the twentieth-century period of world wars and authoritarian rule in a number of countries.

(4) *Hegemony as the exercise of leadership within historical blocs within a particular world order.* A view of hegemony that combines the loose sense of some preeminent state power in the world system with the more specific sense of the construction of consent or ideological leadership around a particular historic project. Thus the United States was able to achieve an international hegemony in the post-Second World War period as a result, not so much of its economic dominance in the global political economy and military might to back it up, than due to the development of a Fordist-Keynesian social structure of accumulation that became internationalised under the leadership of the US capitalist class.

The above is, of course, a simplification and these four approaches are not mutually exclusive. But for argument's sake the first approach is epitomised by such realist paradigms as the theory of hegemonic stability, as developed by Kenneth Waltz (1979) and Robert Keohane (1984), among others. We could characterise Wallerstein's well-known essay, 'The Three Instances of Hegemony in the History of the Capitalist World-Economy' (1984), as archetypical of the second approach, while Arrighi's 1994 study, *The Long Twentieth Century*, may be its most elegant expression in the world-systems tradition. Gramsci's own writings (1971) epitomise the third approach. The Frankfurt school writings, and perhaps more recently, some of the theoretical work of Habermas and of Bordeau, may draw on or develop out of this approach. The fourth is closely associated with the work of Cox (see, *inter alia*, 1987) and neo-Gramscian perspectives in IR, and may be best illustrated by Rupert's study, *Producing Hegemony* (1995).

All four conceptions of hegemony may be of value insofar as they have contributed to understanding the evolving historical structures of the world capitalist system. But here I want to call for expunging *nation-state centrism* from the discussion of hegemony. This would allow us to see *transnational social forces* not necessarily tied to any one nation-state behind contests over hegemony and other global political dynamics. We need to move away altogether from a statist conception of hegemony – from *statism* - and revert to a more 'pure' Gramscian view of hegemony as a form of social domination exercised not by states but by social groups and classes operating through states and other institutions. My aim is to apply a global capitalism approach to the current global order by explicitly linking the process of globalisation to the construction of hegemonies and counter-hegemonies in the twenty-first century. While I draw on the neo-Gramscian and related schools of critical global political economy, I want to move beyond what I see as excessive state-centric emphasis in much of this literature, or what I have critiqued as a 'nation-state framework of analysis' (Robinson 1998, 2002). A national/international approach focuses on the pre-existing system of nation-states as an immutable structural feature of the larger world or inter-state system, whereas by contrast *trans*national or global approaches focus on how the system of nation-states and national economies, etc., are becoming transcended by transnational social forces and institutions grounded in the global system rather than the interstate system. I want to challenge the assumption – so ingrained that it is often only implicit and taken-for-granted – that by fiat we are speaking of the hegemony of a particular nation-state or coalition of states when we discuss hegemony in the global system.

Indeed, of the four conceptions of hegemony mentioned above, (1), (2), and (4) all place a particular (nation-) state, coalition or bloc of states, or region, at the center of the analysis of hegemony in global society. World-system and much Marxist and realist approaches to hegemony focus on successive *state hegemons.* Looking backward, the baton was passed from the Italian city states to Holland, Great Britain and then the United States. The predominant view now seems to be the rise of an East Asian hegemony (Arrighi & Silver 1999; Frank 1998). For their part, neo-Gramscian perspectives focus on a succession of *hegemonic projects*, from the liberal international economy (1789-1873) under British leadership, to an era of rival imperialisms (1873-1945), and then to the post-Second World War era of *pax Americana*, under US leadership (Cox 1987: 109) – each with a hegemonic *state* or *state* contender. The neo-Gramscians acknowledge profound changes to world order but many, although not all, retain the framework of the nation-state and the inter-state system in their concrete analyses of hegemony, *despite* the concomitant focus on transnational processes and forces.

The neo-Gramscian approach takes us beyond the limitations of realism in IR by utilising Gramscian insights and concepts to conceive of an integrated civil society and the state in international relations – this was Cox's groundbreaking contribution (for a sympathetic overview of the neo-Gramscian literature, and criticism of it, see Morton 2003). But I do not agree with Henk Overbeek that this approach has achieved a break with state-centrism in analysing world order (2000: 68-69). Such leading neo-Gramscians as Augelli and Murphy (1988), Gill (1990, 2003), and Gill and Law (1988) have argued that US supremacy (whether based more on direct domination or on consent) has been transformed and renewed in recent years in the face of transnational processes. For Gill, the 'crisis of hegemony' of the 1970s represented by the breakdown of the old Fordist-Keynesian model of nation-state capitalism 'facilitated the material and ideological refurbishing of U.S. hegemony' (2003: 89) in the 1980s and on. Gill and Law posit a transnational hegemony in nation-state centric terms. 'Using a Gramscian approach, some writers have argued that a "transnational" hegemony may be emerging in which a transnational capitalist class predominates, leading a hegemonic bloc of mainly transnational capital and 'incorporated' labour', they note. 'We would suggest that at the geographical centre of such a potential "transnational" hegemony would be a group of capitalist countries led by the United States' and based on the 'organic' blocs that develop among nations (Gill & Law 1988: 355). The problematic remains state-centric; hegemony is seen as being organised or exercised by states in an international arena and as involving the leadership or supremacy of nation-states.

IR, of course, does what it is supposed to do: study relations among nations. I am trying, in contrast, to get away from the whole notion of hegemony in *international relations* and towards a distinct conception of hegemony in *global society*. I want to draw us away from the imagery of social forces moving 'up' to the national state and then 'out' to the international arena. This imagery is quintessential to Cox's construct, in which the (national) state is the point of backward linkage to society and forward linkage to the international order. Classes and social forces are integrated vertically into these (national) states that then develop inter-national relations horizontally. 'A world hegemony is thus in its beginnings an outward expansion of the internal (national) hegemony established by a ... social class', according to Cox (1983: 171), while Morton, interpreting Cox, adds that 'once hegemony has been consolidated domestically, it may expand beyond a particular social order to move outward on a world scale and insert itself through the world order' (2003: 160).[1] In contrast, I want to focus on the horizontal integration of classes and social forces that then operate through webs of national and transnational institutions. In this imagery, transnational capitalists and allied dominant strata integrate horizontally and in the process move 'up' cross-nationally, penetrating and utilising numerous national and transnational state apparatuses to forge their rule, as I discuss below.

In his writings on 'State and Civil Society', Gramsci critiques as 'statolatry' the conception of the state developed by ideologues of capitalist society as derived from the separation of politics and economics and 'conceived of as something in itself, as a rational absolute' (1971: 117, Q10II§61; 268-269, Q8§130).[2] Instead, the state is 'the entire complex of practical and theoretical activities with which the ruling class not only justifies and maintains its dominance, but manages to win the active consent of those over whom it rules' (Gramsci 1971: 244, Q15§10). Here the state becomes the 'integral' or 'extended' state, in Gramsci's formula, encompassing political plus civil society, a conception aimed at overcoming the illusory dualism of the political and the economic. Somewhere along the way between the early twentieth century of Gramsci's time and the post-Second World War period – I won't attempt here to retrace the genealogy – Gramsci's concept of the hegemony of ruling groups and the historical blocs of social forces they construct became transformed into the notion of the hegemony of a state in the inter-state system. Was this justified? Is it still? I will return to these queries momentarily. The remainder of this article, limited as it is by space constraints, is a synthesis of my earlier work on global capitalism conjoined with the critique of the statist conception of hegemony and some propositions on transnational hegemony, to be explored at more length in future research.

Global Capitalism and Transnational Class Formation

My approach to globalisation can be broadly identified with the 'global capitalism' thesis (see, *inter alia*, McMichael 2000; Went 2002; Sklair 2001, 2002; Robinson 1996, 2003, 2004) that sees globalisation as representing a new stage in the history of world capitalism involving the integration of national and regional economies into a new global production and financial system and such related processes as transnational class formation. Recent claims by Sklair (2001), Robinson and Harris (2000), and Robinson (2001, 2004) on the rise of a transnational capitalist class, or TCC, as a group increasingly detached from specific nation-states, build on more general theories of global class formation (see, *inter alia*, van der Pijl 1984; 1998; Cox 1987; Gill 1990, 2003; Embong 2001; Sunkel 1993). Here, I want to suggest that the transnationalisation of classes allows us to imagine a transnationalisation of hegemony.

Under globalisation, a new class fractionation, or axis, has been occurring between national and transnational fractions of classes. In the main, states have been captured by transnationally oriented dominant groups who use them to integrate their countries into emergent global capitalist structures. The globalisation of production and the extensive and intensive enlargement of capitalism in recent decades constitute the material basis for the process of transnational class formation. What most accounts of global class formation share is a nation-state centered concept of class that postulates *national* capitalist classes that converge externally with other national classes at the level of the international system through the internationalisation of capital and concomitantly of civil society. World ruling class formation in the age of globalisation is seen as the international collusion of these national bourgeoisies and their resultant international coalitions. Many aspects of international relations and world development over the past five centuries can be explained by the dynamics of national capitalist competition and consequent inter-state rivalries. The problem begins when we fail to acknowledge the historic specificity of these phenomena and instead extrapolate a transhistoric conclusion regarding the dynamics of world class formation from a certain historic period in the development of capitalism.

As national productive structures become transnationally integrated through the globalisation process, world classes whose organic development took place through the nation-state are experiencing supra-national integration with 'national' classes of other countries. Globalisation creates new forms of transnational class relations across borders and new forms of class cleavages globally and within countries, regions, cities and local communities, in ways quite distinct from the old national class structures and international class conflicts and alliances. It is not possible to explore here the growing body of empirical research on TCC formation (but see, *inter alia*, Robinson & Harris 2000; Sklair 2001; Carroll & Fennema 2002; Carroll & Carson 2003; Robinson 2004). Suffice it to note here that what distinguishes the TCC from national or local capitalists is that it is involved in globalised production, marketing and finance and manages globalised circuits of accumulation that give it an objective class existence and identity spatially and politically in the global system above any local territories and polities.

Neo-Gramscian perspectives, following Cox (1987), have focused on the reciprocal relationship between production and power; on how distinct modes of social relations of production may give rise to certain social forces, how these forces may become the bases of power within and across states, and how these configurations may shape world order. I want here to push the formulation a bit further, moving beyond a conception that rests on (nation-) state power and state hegemony, and drawing on Gramsci's concept of historical blocs as hegemonic projects. In modern conditions, argues Gramsci, a class maintains its dominance not simply through a special organisation of force, but because it is able to go beyond its narrow, corporative interests, exert a moral and intellectual leadership, and make compromises, within certain limits, with a variety of allies who are unified in a social bloc of forces which Gramsci calls the historical bloc (Gramsci 1971: 168, Q13§23; 366, Q10II§12; 418, Q15§61). The bloc represents the basis of consent for a certain social order, in which the hegemony of a dominant class is created and re-created in a web of institutions, social relations, and ideas. If we return to Gramsci's original notion of hegemony as a form of social domination and apply it to twenty-first-century global society, the key question becomes, *who is the ruling class?* Is the ruling group a class or class fraction from a particular nation-state? Are there still distinct national ruling classes?

I want to argue that, stated simply, we *cannot speak of the hegemony of a state. Hegemony is exercised by social groups*, by classes or class fractions, by a particular social configuration of these fractions and groups. When we speak of 'British' hegemony or 'US' hegemony we do not really mean 'British' or 'US' as in the country. This is merely shorthand for saying the hegemony of British capitalist groups and allied strata, such as British state managers and middle-class sectors, in the context of world capitalism. But problems arise when we forget that this is just shorthand. If classes and groups *are* nationally organised then this shorthand is justified. In an earlier moment in the history of world capitalism classes were organised around national markets and national circuits of accumulation, even as these national markets and capital circuits were in turn linked to a more encompassing world market and processes of accumulation on a world scale. The process of economic globalisation is creating the conditions for a shift in the locus of class and social group formation from the nation-state to the global system. The problem of state-centric and nation-state-centric analysis is that it does not allow us to conceive of an emergent or potential global hegemony in terms of transnational classes and groups not centred in any one state or in specific geographies. Can we perceive a hegemony in twenty-first-century global society not exercised by a nation-state – which in any event is shorthand for saying it will not be exercised by dominant groups from any particular nation-state or region – but by an emergent global capitalist historical bloc led by a TCC? Such a transnational hegemony should be seen as a project that is incomplete, contested, and – we shall see – in crisis, constructed on the shaky basis of a disjuncture between the development of transnational class and social forces, and the very incipient and partial development of what I have termed transnational state (TNS) structures (Robinson 2001, 2004).

The TCC has been attempting to position itself as a new ruling class group worldwide and to bring some coherence and stability to its rule through an emergent TNS apparatus. What would a potentially hegemonic bloc – henceforth referred to as a globalist bloc – under the leadership of the TCC look like? It would clearly consist of various economic and political forces whose politics and policies are conditioned by the new global structure of accumulation. At the center of the globalist bloc would be the TCC, comprised of the owners and managers of the transnational corporations and private financial institutions and other capitalists around the world who manage transnational capital. The bloc would also include the cadre, bureaucratic managers and technicians who administer the agencies of the TNS, such as the IMF, the World Bank and the WTO, other transnational forums, and the states of the North and the South. Also brought into the bloc would be an array of politicians and charismatic public figures, along with select organic intellectuals, who provide ideological legitimacy and technical solutions. Below this transnational elite would be a small layer, shrinking in some locales (such as the United States) and expanding in others (such as in India and China), of old and new middle classes, highly paid workers, and cosmopolitan professionals who exercise very little real power but who – pacified with mass consumption – form a fragile buffer between the transnational elite and the world's poor majority.

It is in this way that we can speak of a historical bloc in the Gramscian sense as a social ensemble involving dominant strata and a social base beyond the ruling group, and in which one group exercises leadership (the TCC) and imposes its project through the consent of those drawn into the bloc. Those from the poor majority not drawn into the hegemonic project, either through material mechanisms or ideologically, are contained or repressed. '[It is necessary] to change the political direction of certain forces which have to be absorbed if a new, homogenous politico-economic historical bloc, without internal contradictions, is to be successfully formed', writes Gramsci. 'And since two "similar" forces can only be welded into a new organism either through a series of compromise or by force of arms, either by binding them to each other as allies or by forcibly subordinating one to the other, the question is whether one has the necessary force, and whether it is "productive" to use it' (1971: 168, Q13§23). All social orders in class society, and all historical blocs, involve in their genesis and reproduction an ongoing combination of consent and coercion. To what extent (and degree) an historical bloc must rely on more direct domination or coercion as opposed to consent in securing its rule is open to debate and is more a problem of concrete historical and conjunctural analysis than of theoretical determination. There has been a debate as to whether an historical bloc can emerge without first securing its hegemony, that is, the prevalence of consensual over coercive domination, and as to whether supremacy prevails in the absence of such hegemony (see Morton, 2003: 163-165). One cannot rely on Gramsci for the final word in this debate, as he has insisted on 'the moment of hegemony and consent as the necessary form of the concrete historical bloc' (1995: 332, Q10I§Summary; 357, Q10I§12) *and* that 'the supremacy of a social group manifests itself in two ways, as "domination" and as "intellectual and moral leadership"' (1971: 57, Q19§24). For our purposes it is clear that the globalist bloc achieved in the 1980s and 1990s – at best – a certain 'restricted' as opposed to 'expansive' hegemony in global society, less through the internalisation by popular classes worldwide of the neoliberal worldview than through the disorganisation of these classes in the wake of the juggernaut of capitalist globalisation. Since the late 1990s, as I will elaborate below, it has been unable to reproduce even this 'restricted' hegemony and has had to resort to increasing worldwide use of direct coercion in order to maintain its supremacy.

The Debate on US Hegemony and Hegemonic Transitions

My propositions on transnational hegemony have met stiff resistance from social scientists from a variety of traditions who advance such scenarios as revived Great Power rivalry, competing geopolitical regions, and a renewed US drive for world hegemony (see, e.g., Arrighi & Silver 1999; Gowan 1999; Frank 1998; Goldfrank 2001; Freeman 2004; Gibbs 2001). The claim that Great Power rivalry is again on the increase was popular in the early 1990s and enjoyed a comeback after the 2003 US invasion of Iraq in the face of French, German and Russian opposition. A more nuanced approach saw struggle among competing core power blocs for hegemonic succession in the wake of US decline. In this 'three competing blocs' (or 'regionalisation') scenario, EU, US, and East Asian blocs were seen as non-global regional formations (see, e.g., Hirsch & Thompson 1996; Held et al., 1999: 5). Each core grouping was said to be integrating its periphery into a regional formation in competition with rival regional blocs and a number of scholars predicted the rise of an East Asia hegemon. But global investment patterns by TNCs suggest each bloc is interpenetrated by the other two and form an increasingly integrated global 'triad' based on the expanding interpenetration of capital among the world's top TNCs. As these capitalists integrate they draw in local networks and production chains into complex cross-national webs, making it difficult to box political relations among states and competition among economic groups into the old nation-state geopolitical framework.

'Asian' economic success is said by some (see, e.g., Arrighi & Silver 1999) to constitute a competitive threat to 'US' interests and a sign of geopolitical competition.

But we could only reach such a conclusion by ignoring the fact that East Asian dynamism is inseparable from the massive entrance of transnational capital and that local elites have sought not a regional circuit of accumulation in rivalry with circuits elsewhere but a more complete *integration* into globalised circuits. Given an open global economy and capital's global mobility, superior economic performance in a particular region clearly benefits all investor groups in that region. Even if the argument could be made that leading national states protect the interests of investors within determined national borders – that is, even if there still exists a territorial dimension to capital and a geopolitical content to world politics – the fact remains that those investors originate from many countries. A more satisfying explanation than geopolitical competition, I suggest, is that regional accumulation patterns reflect certain spatial distinctions complementary to an increasingly integrated global capitalist configuration. We do not see so much a *recentring* of the global economy in East Asia, as Arrighi and Silver (1999: 219) claim, as much as a *decentring* of the global economy; its fragmentation and the rise of several zones of intense global accumulation. These may not be territorially-bounded rivals for hegemony as much as sites of intensive accumulation within a global economy that bring together transnational capitalists and elites in diverse locations around the world, precisely what we would expect from a supranational and decentred transnational configuration.

The rise of a TCC and a TNS does not imply the absence of conflict among distinct capitalist groups and state elites. Conflict is prone to occur at multiple levels: between transnationally oriented elites and those with a more local, national or regional orientation; between agents of global capitalism and popular forces; among competing groups within the globalist bloc who may foment inter-state conflicts in pursuit of their particular interests; and so on. The picture is further complicated by the instability wrought by the breakdown of social order and the collapse of national state authority in many regions. However, the key point is this: conflict and competition must take place through institutions that either already exist or that groups in conflict create. National states may be utilised by a multiplicity of capitals, none of which are necessarily 'national' capitals to the extent that national networks of capital have become overlapping and interpenetrating. As Went has observed, concurrent with my analysis, 'capital's home government need not necessarily undertake [these functions]. The domestic state where capital originates from may do so, but there are alternatives, such as, e.g., foreign state structures, capital itself either singly or in conjunction with other capitals, or state bodies in cooperation with each other' (Went 2002: 108). The TNS does not yet (and may never!) constitute a centralised global state and *formal* political authority remains to a considerable extent fragmented, and fragmented unevenly, among weaker and stronger national states. This peculiar institutional structure, an historic contradiction of the global capitalist system, presents transnational elites with the possibility, and the need, to influence a multitude of national states.

What about challenges to the global capitalist bloc from forces opposed to its transnational agenda? Challenges of this sort are likely to come from two sources. The first is from subordinate groups in transnational civil society or from specific nation-states when these states are captured by subordinate groups. The second is from dominant groups who are less integrated into (or even opposed to) global capitalism, such as, for example, the Baath Party/Iraq state elite prior to the 2003 US invasion, sectors among the Russian oligarchy, or Chinese economic and political elites. This uneven development of the transnationalisation process is an important source of conflict. The emerging global order, we should bear in mind, is *unevenly* hegemonic. Hegemonic power does not operate in a uniform manner across the globe.

How do we understand such 'evident' realities of trade wars, often acrimonious differences among core power governments, and above all, the preponderant role of the United States in world affairs, its seeming 'hegemony,' and its often unilateral military intervention abroad? According to extant paradigms US state behavior in the global arena are undertaken in defense of 'U.S. interests' (e.g., Gibbs 2001; Gowan 1999). Most scholars and analysts see TNS institutions as instruments of US hegemony (Bello 2002: 39). But when the IMF or the World Bank opens up a country through liberalisation measures it is opened not exclusively to 'US' capital but to capitalists from anywhere in the world. TNS institutions have acted less to enforce 'US' policies than to force nationally oriented policies in general into transnational alignment. The TCC and its globalist bloc to advance its interests has relied on existing national state apparatuses and also increasingly on the emergent apparatus of a TNS, and in doing so it has found the US national state, for evident historic reasons, to be the most powerful of these apparatuses. This is the particular form through which the old geopolitics of the nation-state are simultaneously being played out and winding down.

Scholars such as Brenner (2002) insist that national 'trade wars' and 'national competition' drive world political dynamics in the twenty-first century. Trade tensions may well break out between individual sectors (such as bananas or steel) that turn to specific national states for support. But the evidence suggests a process of mutual competition and integration across borders rather than 'US' hegemony. Capitalist groups that in earlier epochs produced nationally and then exported to the world market have largely replaced this strategy with 'in-country production'. In 1997, global figures for sales by TNC in-country affiliates reached $9.7 trillion, compared to cross-border trade that totaled $5.3 trillion (USITC 2001: 1-3). According to the US International Trade Commission, in 1997 sales by US-owned foreign affiliates abroad totaled $2.4 trillion compared to $928 billion in US exports. Sales by foreign affiliates inside the US reached $1.7 trillion while their imports amounted to $1 trillion (USITC 2001: 2-6). Under these circumstances 'trade wars' begin to lose all meaning if analysed in conventional terms of rival national capitalist groups and their respective states. This does *not* mean that trade conflicts are illusory. Fierce competition in the globalisation epoch takes place among dense networks of transnational corporate alliances and through struggles within every country and within transnational institutions. Given their global interests and the extent of their transnational interpenetration, TNCs must take an active political and economic interest in each country and region in which they operate. They may turn to any national state to gain competitive advantage as part of their corporate strategy. Globalisation is not a 'national' project but a class project without a national strategy, or rather, with a strategy that seeks to utilise the existing political infrastructure of the nation-state system and simultaneously to craft TNS structures.

We have not seen a resurgence of the old imperialism or an intensification of inter-imperialist rivalry. The classical theories of imperialism emphasised core national state control over peripheral regions in order to open these regions to capital export from the particular imperialist country and to exclude capital from other countries (Hilferding 1910; Lenin 1917). The competition among these competing national capitals, according to the theory, led to inter-state competition and military rivalry among the main capitalist countries. The structural changes that have led to the transnationalisation of national capitals, finances, and markets, and the actual outcomes of recent US-led political and military campaigns, suggest new forms of global capitalist domination, whereby intervention creates conditions favourable to the penetration of transnational capital and the renewed integration of the intervened region into the global system. US intervention facilitates a shift in power from locally and regionally-oriented elites to new groups more favourable to the transnational project (Robinson 1996). The result of US military conquest is not the creation of exclusive zones for 'US' exploitation, as was the result of the Spanish conquest of Latin America, the British of South Africa and India, the Dutch of Indonesia, and so forth, in earlier moments of the world capitalist system. Rather, the beneficiaries of US military action are transnational capitalist groups and the US state has, in the main, advanced transnational capitalist interests. Shortly after taking control of Iraq in 2003, for instance, the US occupation force unveiled 'Order 39', which provided unrestricted access to Iraq for investors from anywhere in the world (Docena 2004).

The US state is the *point of condensation* for pressures from dominant groups to resolve problems of global capitalism and for pressures to secure the legitimacy of the system overall. This subjects it to great strain. Moreover, although US state managers face institutional constraints and structural imperatives to bolster global accumulation processes they also face direct instrumental pressures of groups seeking their particular interests. It was notorious, for instance, that oil and military-industrial concerns brazenly utilised the administration of George W. Bush to pursue narrow corporate gains in a way that appeared to have contravened the more long-term interests of the transnational project. But *narrow* corporate interests do *not* mean *US* corporate interests. We see *not* a re-enactment of this old imperialism but the colonisation and recolonisation of the vanquished for the new global capitalism and its agents. The underlying class relation between the TCC and the US national state needs to be understood in these terms. *The empire of capital is headquartered in Washington.*

The Problematic Nature of Transnational Hegemony and Prospects of Counter-hegemonies

The globalist bloc may have appeared insurgent and triumphalist in the 1990s but it has run up against one crisis after another in its effort to secure its leadership and reproduce its hegemony. A necessary condition for the attainment of hegemony by a class or class fraction is the supercession of narrow economic interests by a more universal social vision or ideology, and the concrete coordination of the interests of other groups with those of the leading class or fraction in the process of securing their participation in this social vision. Here, the narrow interests of transnational finance capital (currency speculators, bankers, portfolio investors, etc.) seemed to hold out the prospects of frustrating a hegemonic project. As well, a unified social vision has been difficult to secure because distinct elites seek different and even conflicting solutions to the problems of global capitalism based in the historic experiences of their regional systems. The system of global capitalism entered into a deep crisis in the late 1990s. There were twin dimensions to this crisis.

The first was a *structural crisis of overaccumulation and of social polarisation.* By undermining the state redistribution and other mechanisms that acted in earlier epochs to offset the inherent tendency within capitalism towards polarisation, globalisation has resulted in a process of rapid global social polarisation and a crisis of social reproduction, as has been amply documented (see, *inter alia*, Freeman 2004; Korzeniewicz & Moran 1997). This has restricted the capacity of the world market to absorb world output and constricted the ability of the system to expand. This is the structural underpinning to the series of crises that began in Mexico in 1995 and then intensified with the Asian financial meltdown of 1997-98, and the world recession that began in 2001. Overaccumulation pressures make state-driven military spending and the growth of a military-industrial complex an outlet for surplus and give the current global order a frightening built-in war drive.

The second dimension is a *crisis of legitimacy and authority.* The legitimacy of the system has increasingly been called into question by millions, perhaps even billions, of people around the world. Global elites have clamoured for reform from the top down, reflecting a breakdown of confidence and a willingness among the more politically astute transnational elites to seek reform – a so-called 'globalisation with a human face' – in the interests of saving the system itself (Rupert 2000). No emergent ruling class can construct an historical bloc without developing diverse mechanisms of legitimation and securing a social base – a combination of the consensual integration through material reward for some, and the coercive exclusion of others that the system is unwilling or unable to co-opt. The ruling group has had to increasingly forsake hegemony and resort to direct coercion to maintain its supremacy, although achieving *either* consensual integration or effective coercive exclusion has been increasingly difficult, given the extent of social polarisation and of resistance worldwide, which seems to have contributed to a new 'politics of exclusion' in which the problem of social control becomes paramount and coercion plays an increasingly salient role over consent.

Whether a transnational capitalist hegemony can become stabilised and what institutional configuration could achieve its maintenance and reproduction remains to be seen. Faced with the increasingly dim prospects of constructing a viable transnational hegemony in the Gramscian sense of a stable system of consensual domination, transnational elites have mustered up fragmented and incoherent responses involving heightened military coercion, the search for a post-Washington consensus, and acrimonious internal disputes around parochial interests, strategic and tactical differences. In the post-11 September period the military dimension appears to exercise an overdetermining influence in the reconfiguration of global politics. Militarised globalisation represents a contradictory political response to the explosive crisis of global capitalism – to economic stagnation, legitimation problems and the rise of counter-hegemonic forces.

What, then, are the prospects of counter-hegemonic resistance to the globalist bloc? Challenges to its hegemony have come from several quarters:

1. The anti-globalist Far Right. This Far Right has been able to capitalise in numerous countries on the insecurities of working and middle classes in the face of rapidly changing circumstances to mobilise a reactionary bloc. The Far Right draws in particular on the insecurities of those sectors formerly privileged within national social structures of accumulation, such as white workers, family farm sectors, middle and professional strata facing deskilling and downward mobility, and national fractions of capital threatened by globalisation. Pat Buchanan in the United States (and possibly, the G.W. Bush clique), Jörg Haider and the Freedom Party in Austria, the One Nation party in Australia, Le Pen's National Front in France, Russia's Vladimir Zhirinovsky, and so on, epitomise the rise of this reactionary bloc. It is possible that some reactionary forces become drawn into the globalist bloc and in some cases its program may even generate conditions more favorable to the transnational elite agenda.
2. Progressive elites and nationalist groups in Third World countries, such as Hugo Chávez in Venezuela. These elites may well draw on insecurities of vulnerable sectors but articulate a progressive vision as distinct from the far right. In this category are also elites from certain countries and regions that have not been fully drawn into the global economy, or are being integrated into it in a way that is structurally distinct from that of national contingents of the TCC in most countries and regions. Here China and Russia, and perhaps India, stand out. Political projects that emerge could well be one of cooptation or accommodation with the globalist bloc or heightened conflict with it.
3. Popular sectors worldwide, as expressed in the rise of a global justice movement. In the closing years of the twentieth-century popular resistance movements and forces began to coalesce around an anti-neoliberal agenda for social justice, epitomised in the Seattle protest of late 1999 and the Porto Alegre encounters of 2001-2004 (e.g., see Rupert in this volume).

A counter-hegemonic impulse could come from any of these sectors, or from a combination of these forces, in ways that cannot be anticipated. Clearly the counter-hegemonic discourse of the global justice movement was in ascendance in the late twentieth century and popular forces had begun to conjoin with progressive elites, as exhibited, for instance, in South American politics. It is impossible to predict the outcome of the crisis of global capitalism. No doubt world capitalism has tremendous reserves upon which to draw. We may see a reassertion of productive over financial capital in the global economy and a global redistributive project just as we may see a global fascism founded on military spending and wars to contain the downtrodden and the irrepented. Perhaps the more reformist (as opposed to radical) wing of the global justice movement will ally with the more reformist (as opposed to conservative) wing of the TCC to push a reformist or global redistributive project, along the lines of what Gramsci (borrowing from Croce) called *trasformismo* (Gramsci, 1971: 58-59, Q19§24), whereby actual and potential leaders and sectors from the subordinate groups are incorporated into the dominant project in an effort to prevent the formation of counter-hegemony.

Fundamental change in a social order becomes possible when an organic crisis occurs. An organic crisis is one in which the system faces a structural (objective) crisis and *also* a crisis of legitimacy or hegemony (subjective). At times of great social crisis, such as the one we appear to face in early twenty-first century global society, sound theoretical understandings are crucial if we hope to intervene effectively in the resolution of such crises. The task is certainly daunting, given such a vast and complex theoretical object as emergent global society, and the character of the current situation as transitionary and not accomplished. As we work towards gaining a more nuanced theoretical understanding of emergent global social structures it is useful to recall that the power of collective agencies to influence history is enhanced at such times of crisis rather than during periods of stability and equilibrium.

Acknowledgements

The constructive comments and suggestions of the editors and two anonymous referees for this journal were gratefully received.

Notes

1. I do not agree with Cox's assertion, following Gramsci, that 'the national context remains the only place where an historical bloc can be founded' (1983: 174). I cannot take up this debate here. However, my broader concern is the danger of a canonical or theological Gramscianism, in which such concepts that Gramsci introduced as historical blocs can only be legitimately employed if the prior conditions (e.g. a world of national capitalisms), upon which Gramsci first abstracted these concepts, are projected into the present (global capitalism). I do not suggest that Cox commits this mistake, but the impulse to dig up competing Gramsci quotes in order to resolve contemporary debates that involve concepts first introduced by Gramsci is symptomatic of the problem.
2. Following the convention established throughout this volume, reference to the Gramsci anthologies is accompanied by a citation of the notebook number (Q) and section (§).

References

Augelli, E. and C. N. Murphy. 1988. *America's Quest for Supremacy and the Third World: A Gramscian Analysis*. London: Pinter.
Arrighi, G. 1994. *The Long Twentieth Century*. London: Verso.

Arrighi, G. and B. J. Silver. 1999. *Chaos and Governance in the Modern World System*. Minneapolis: University of Minnesota Press.

Bello, W. 2002. 'Notes for a New Economy'. *Race and Class*, 43/4, 34–44.

Brenner, R. 2002. *The Boom and the Bubble: The US in the World Economy*. London: Verso.

Carroll, W. K. and M. Fennema. 2002. 'Is There a Transnational Business Community?' *International Sociology*, 17/3, 393–419.

Carroll, W. K. and C. Carson. 2003. 'The Network of Global Corporations and Elite Policy Groups: A Structure for Transnational Capitalist Class Formation?' *Global Networks*, 3/1, 29–57.

Cox, R. W. 1983. 'Gramsci, Hegemony, and International Relations: An Essay in Method'. *Millennium: Journal of International Studies*, 12/2, 162–175.

Cox, R. W. 1987. *Production, Power, and World Order: Social Forces in the Making of History*. New York: Columbia University Press.

Docena, H. 2004. 'The Other Reconstruction: How Private Contractors are Transforming Iraqi Society'. *Focus on Trade*, 101, July.

Embong, A. R. 2001. 'Globalisation and Transnational Class Relations: Some Problems of Conceptualisation'. Mittelman and Othman 2001: 92–106.

Frank, A. G. 1998. *ReOrient: Global Economy in the Asian Age*. Berkeley: University of California Press.

Freeman, A. 2004. 'The New Political Geography of Poverty'. Freeman and Kagarlitsky 2004: 46–83.

Freeman, A. and B. Kagarlitsky, eds. 2004. *The Politics of Empire: The Crisis of Globalisation*. London: Pluto Press.

Gibbs, D. 2001. 'Washington's New Interventionism: U.S. Hegemony and Inter-Imperialist Rivalries'. *Monthly Review*, 53/4, 15–37.

Gill, S. 1990. *American Hegemony and the Trilateral Commission*. Cambridge: Cambridge University Press.

Gill, S. 2003. *Power and Resistance in the New World Order*. New York: Palgrave MacMillan.

Gill, S. and D. Law. 1988. *The Global Political Economy: Perspectives, Problems and Policies*. Baltimore: Johns Hopkins University Press.

Goldfrank, W. L. 2001. 'Rational Kernels in a Mystical Shell: A Comment on Robinson'. *Theory and Society*, 30/2, 211–14.

Gowan, P. 1999. *The Global Gamble: Washington's Faustian Bid for World Dominance*. London: Verso.

Gramsci, A. 1971. *Selections from the Prison Notebooks*, ed. and trans. Q. Hoare and G. Nowell-Smith. London: Lawrence and Wishart.

Gramsci, A. 1995. *Further Selections from the Prison Notebooks*, ed. and trans. D. Boothman. London: Lawrence and Wishart.

Held, D., A. McGrew, D. Goldblatt and J. Perraton. 1999. *Global Transformations: Politics, Economics and Culture*. Stanford: Stanford University Press.

Hilferding, R. 1981 [1910]. *Finance Capital: A Study of the Latest Phase of Capitalist Development*. London: Routledge.

Keohane, R. O. 1984. *After Hegemony: Cooperation and Discord in the World Political Economy*. Princeton: Princeton University Press.

Korzeniewicz, R. P. and T. P. Moran. 1997. 'World Economic Trends in the Distribution of Income, 1965-1992'. *American Journal of Sociology*, 102/4, 1000–39.

Lenin, V. I. 1917. *Imperialism: The Hightest Stage of Capitalism*. Moscow: International Publishers.

McMichael, P. 2000. *Development and Social Change: A Global Perspective*, 2d ed. Thousand Oaks: Pine Forge.

Mittelman, J. H. and N. Othman, eds. 2001. *Capturing Globalisation*. London: Routledge.

Morton, A. D. 2003. 'Social Forces in the Struggle over Hegemony: Neo-Gramscian Perspectives in International Political Economy'. *Rethinking Marxism*, 15/2, 153–79.

Overbeek, H. 2000. 'Transnational Historical Materialism: Theories of Transnational Class Formation and World Order'. Palan 2000: 168–83.

Palan, R. 2000. *Global Political Economy: Contemporary Theories*. London: Routledge.

Robinson, W. I. 1996. *Promoting Polyarchy: Globalisation, US Intervention and Hegemony.* Cambridge: Cambridge University Press.

Robinson, W. I. 1998.'Beyond Nation-State Paradigms: Globalisation, Sociology, and the Challenge of Transnational Studies'. *Sociological Forum,* 13/4, 561–94.

Robinson, W. I. 2001.'Social Theory and Globalisation: The Rise of a Transnational State'. *Theory and Society,* 30/2, 157–2000.

Robinson, W. I. 2002.'Global Capitalism and Nation-State Centric Thinking: What We Don't See When We Do See Nation-States. Response to Arrighi, Mann, Moore, van der Pijl, and Went'. *Science and Society,* 65/4, 500–08.

Robinson, W. I. 2004. *A Theory of Global Capitalism: Production, Class, and State in a Transnational World.* Baltimore: Johns Hopkins University Press.

Robinson, W. I. and J. Harris. 2000.'Toward a Global Ruling Class?: Globalisation and the Transnational Capitalist Class'. *Science and Society,* 64/1, 11–54.

Rupert, M. 1995. *Producing Hegemony: The Politics of Mass Production and American Global Power.* Cambridge: Cambridge University Press.

Rupert, M. 2000. *Ideologies of Globalisation: Contending Visions of a New World Order.* London: Routledge.

Sklair, L. 2001. *The Transnational Capitalist Class.* Oxford: Blackwell.

Sklair, L. 2002. *Globalisation: Capitalism, and Its Alternatives.* New York: Oxford University Press.

Sunkel, O., ed. 1993. *Development from Within: Toward a Neostructuralist Approach for Latin America.* Boulder: Lynne Rienner.

United States International Trade Commission. 2001. *Examination of U.S. Inbound and Outbound Direct Investment.* Office of Industries. January. Washington: USITC.

Van der Pijl, K. 1984. *The Making of an Atlantic Ruling Class.* London: Verso.

Van der Pijl, K. 1998. *Transnational Classes and International Relations.* London: Routledge.

Wallerstein, I. 1984.'The Three Instances of Hegemony in the History of the Capitalist World-Economy'. *International Journal of Comparative Sociology,* 24/1-2, 100–08.

Waltz, K. N. 1979. *Theory of International Politics.* Reading, Mass: Addison-Wesley.

Went, R. 2002. *The Enigma of Globalisation: A Journey to a New Stage of Capitalism.* London: Routledge.

INDEX

Lightning Source UK Ltd.
Milton Keynes UK
27 January 2011

166508UK00002B/65/A